THE WORLD'S CLASSICS

THE SOUL OF MAN AND PRISON WRITINGS

OSCAR WILDE was born in Dublin in 1854. Self-advertised, he became the most notorious of late nine-teenth century aesthetes, renowned for his conversation and wit. He published early poetry, followed by short stories, fairy-tales, and the sensational novel *The Picture of Dorian Gray*. He achieved public success as a comic playwright, crowned by *The Importance of Being Earnest* in 1895.

But in that year the Marquess of Queensberry, enraged by Wilde's friendship with his son, Lord Alfred Douglas, and the flamboyance of their lifestyle, accused Wilde of being a 'posing Sodomite'. This led to a series of trials, and Wilde's eventual imprisonment for two years' hard labour, for homosexual offences. After his imprisonment he wrote his most famous poem, *The Ballad of Reading Gaol*. He died in Paris in 1900.

ISOBEL MURRAY, Senior Lecturer in English at Aberdeen University, edited *The Picture of Dorian Gray* in the Oxford English Novels series in 1974, and Wilde's *Complete Shorter Fiction* for Oxford University Press in 1979. She edited a large annotated selection of Wilde in the Oxford Authors series, *Writings of Oscar Wilde*, 1989.

THE WORLD'S CLASSICS

OSCAR WILDE

The Soul of Man
and
Prison Writings

Edited with an Introduction by
ISOBEL MURRAY

Oxford   New York
OXFORD UNIVERSITY PRESS

Oxford University Press, Walton Street, Oxford OX2 6DP

Oxford New York

Athens Auckland Bangkok Bogota Bombay
Buenos Aires Calcutta Cape Town Dar es Salaam
Delhi Florence Hong Kong Istanbul Karachi
Kuala Lumpur Madras Madrid Melbourne
Mexico City Nairobi Paris Singapore
Taipei Tokyo Toronto

and associated companies in
Berlin Ibadan

Oxford is a trade mark of Oxford University Press

First published as a World's Classics paperback 1990

British Library Cataloguing in Publication Data
Data available

Library of Congress Cataloging in Publication Data
Wilde, Oscar, 1854-1900.
The soul of man and prison writings / Oscar Wilde;
edited with an introduction by Isobel Murray.
p. cm. --(The World's classics)
1. Prisons—Literary collections.
2. Wilde, Oscar, 1854-1900—Correspondence.
3. Authors, Irish— 19th century Correspondence.
I. Murray, Isobel. II. Title. III. Series.
828'.809—dc20 PR5812.M87 1990 89-22875
ISBN 0-19-281797-3

5 7 9 10 8 6

Printed in Great Britain by
BPC Paperbacks Ltd.
Aylesbury, Bucks

CONTENTS

CONTENTS

INTRODUCTION

THE fall of Oscar Wilde is the most dramatic literary fall of modern times. When he was arrested in 1895, two of his sparkling social comedies were playing to packed houses in London's West End. *An Ideal Husband* was produced at the Haymarket Theatre on 3 January, and *The Importance of Being Earnest* opened on St Valentine's Day, 14 February, at the St James's. Wilde was at the height of his success, and at last making a lot of money. But on 18 February Lord Alfred Douglas's father, the Marquess of Queensberry, left a card for Wilde at the Albemarle Club, inscribed 'To Oscar Wilde posing Somdomite.' On 28 February Wilde called at the Club and received the card, beginning the horrific series of events that was to lead to the Marquess being tried for libel, and to Wilde himself being twice tried for committing homosexual offences. On 25 May Wilde was sentenced to the maximum punishment, two years' hard labour, and after two days in Newgate began his sentence at Pentonville. In three months the fall was complete.

The upward climb had been an infinitely slower process. Wilde had left Oxford in 1878 at the age of 24, and he had to wait a long time for literary success and recognition, filling in the time with a great deal of determined self-publicity, a year-long lecture tour of America, lecturing in Britain, book reviewing, job hunting, and at last undertaking the editorship of a magazine, *The Woman's World*, from 1887 to 1889. His first book, *Poems*, which he published in 1881, was slight and derivative, and soon left behind, but as his work matured he found some discriminating critical recognition. Some of the best judges of the day, men such as Pater, Yeats, and Arthur Symons, began to praise his work, and his literary output began to speed up. But the *annus mirabilis* was 1891. In that one year Wilde published four books. In April the revised and greatly expanded version of his sensational novel, *The Picture of Dorian Gray*, was first published in book form. In May the two critical dialogues *The Decay of Lying* and *The Critic as Artist* were carefully revised and published in book form with two essays, 'Pen, Pencil and Poison' and 'The Truth of Masks', again revised after previous periodical publication. This book, *Intentions*, caused Pater to describe Wilde as the successor to 'the brilliant critical work of Matthew Arnold', and Yeats saw in it 'some of the most subtle literary criticism we are likely to see for many a long day'. A volume of witty modern stories, *Lord Arthur Savile's Crime and Other Stories*, followed in July, and in November came *A House of Pomegranates*, containing four long fairy-tales, 'The Young King', 'The Birthday of the Infanta', 'The Fisherman and his Soul', and 'The Star-Child'. And it was in this year also that he first published an essay in *The Fortnightly Review* called 'The Soul of Man Under Socialism'. This is the essay given here as *The Soul of Man*: Wilde later preferred the shorter title.

Wilde is generally accepted to have started his homosexual life with Robert Ross in 1886, but it was in this fateful year of 1891 that he began his friendship with Lord Alfred Douglas, still an undergraduate at Oxford. Significantly, they became better acquainted when Douglas sought Wilde's help in dealing with blackmail over an indiscreet letter: Douglas was no novice, for all his youth.

Discriminating critical recognition was all very well, and very gratifying, but financial success was urgently required. Wilde had a wife and two young sons, and a home in Chelsea to keep up: Constance's modest competence had already proved inadequate to the style in which they were living. Now Wilde embarked on a much more extravagant lifestyle, very much influenced by the whims of Douglas, as he points out at length in *De Profundis*. But in 1891 he wrote his first successful play, *Lady Windermere's Fan*, which was produced in 1892: it was so successful that he made £7,000 in the first year. So he reached his pinnacle of success, which was to last for just three years.

The dramatic quality of his life, the spectacular nature of both his glittering success and his much publicized disgrace, caught the imagination of the public and holds it still. Few writers can have been the subject of more exercises in biography: indeed, his life has always commanded more attention than his books. There must be ten biographies for every critical book on his contribution to literature. The nature of his offence against society has roused strong feelings, and many of these books were strongly partisan, attacking or defending homosexuality, demonstrating or denying any connection with his art. Although the subject remains one on which people continue to have strong feelings, a great body of facts has now been built up, most notably by Sir Rupert Hart-Davis, editor in turn of the *Letters* in 1962, the *Selected Letters* in 1979, and *More Letters* in 1985. It is Sir Rupert's masterly text of *De Profundis,* Wilde's long letter to Douglas from prison, that follows *The Soul of Man* in this volume, and many of the notes given to that work are his also: these are marked RH-D in each case. These editions of the letters have helped to make possible a new generation of biographies, based on more reliable information: the best of these beyond doubt is *Oscar Wilde* by the late Richard Ellmann (1987), which combines the fruits of a lot of new research with a fine literary sensibility. If this volume makes you want to know more about Wilde, Hart-Davis and Ellmann are the names to look for.

In the meantime, the popularity of Wilde's works with the general reader has been steadily growing, as can be seen, for example, by the number of one-volume Collected Works that have appeared. And now modern commentators have begun to review him, to look again at what Pater, Shaw, and Yeats praised so highly. Important critics such as Ellmann and Frank Kermode have emphasized his place in the emergence of the modern consciousness in literature. Gradually *Dorian Gray* and the comedies receive more attention, although the critical dialogues still receive far too little. But everyone knows some of Wilde's epigrams and paradoxes: most people find many of them irresistible, and are charmed by their defiance of sense and solemnity, their dandiacal levity.

> One would have to have a heart of stone to read the death of Little Nell without . . . laughing.

> If one tells the truth, one is sure, sooner or later, to be found out.

> No artist desires to prove anything. Even things that are true can be proved.

> Art is the only serious thing in the world. And the artist is the only person who is never serious.

> I live in terror of not being misunderstood.

> Dullness is the coming of age of seriousness.

Wilde's witticisms, epigrams, and paradoxes frequently attack sincerity and seriousness, and stress the importance of *not* being earnest. They work to increase the individual's self-awareness. But it is too easy to see Wilde in the light of all this as always flippant, amusing, uncommitted; to identify Wilde with the ageing dandy in *A Woman of No Importance* who says to the solemn and platitudinous MP: 'One should never take sides in anything, Mr Kelvil. Taking sides is the beginning of sincerity, and earnestness follows shortly afterwards, and the human being becomes a bore.' Wilde did take many things seriously, and the chief of these was art.

The collection of Wilde's writing that follows shows that Wilde could and did have very serious opinions about matters other than art, not only when he was in prison and afterwards, but at the height of his writing career in *The Soul of Man*. But the reader will quickly discover that if *The Soul of Man* is serious, it is not solemn, and never earnest. Indeed, Wilde uses witty epigram and spiked cliché as effectively here as in his most sparkling comedies, using them to introduce or sum up an argument with startling effect:

> Charity creates a multitude of sins.

> The fact is, that civilization requires slaves.

> Disobedience, in the eyes of anyone who has read history, is man's original virtue.

> The Lords Temporal say nothing, the Lords Spiritual have nothing to say, and the House of Commons has nothing to say and says it.

Selfishness is not living as one wishes to live, it is asking others to live as one wishes to live.

It is the intention of this volume to present the more serious writings of Wilde together, as they have not been isolated and presented before, to indicate their relationship and to claim for them, as much as for *Intentions, Dorian Gray*, the shorter fiction, and the comedies, classic status. *The Soul of Man* is the only pre-prison work which is at least as concerned with human issues of freedom, authority, Individualism and politics as with art, although a central section of the essay is more characteristically concerned with the artist and the attempts of press and public to curb his freedom. The essay presents a view of life congruent to the views on life and art that we find in the critical dialogues. It grows naturally out of the subject-matter and argument of *The Critic as Artist*, where Gilbert is repeatedly tempted to leave 'the more gracious fields of literature' and to discuss larger and darker general issues. When this essay first appeared in *The Fortnightly Review*, it also contributed effectively and topically to a lively, ongoing debate in the periodical journals, in which political issues of Individualism, Socialism, Anarchism, poverty, philanthropy, and the limitation of freedom were being hotly debated.

It also has a quality that sets it above that debate, a concern to proclaim that the proper aim of human life is not a self-denying altruism but rather a perfecting of the self, Individualism. This quality is achieved by Wilde's developing his own ideas and beliefs about the self, but these are usefully—even crucially—supplemented by the earlier arguments of the great American Transcendentalist, Ralph Waldo Emerson (1803–82). Emerson seems not to be much read by Wilde scholars, who have for too long, perhaps, repeated parrot cries about the most important modern authors for Wilde being Ruskin and Pater, with the occasional mention of Arnold. I think the case for Ruskin as an influence on Wilde has been vastly overstated, whether we consider him as art critic or social reformer. Pater certainly did have enormous influence on Wilde's ideas of art and culture, and perhaps of life, and Ruskin and Pater were the two great figures in the Oxford of Wilde's day. The temptation to see the youthful Wilde oscillating between these two poles has been irresistible: here is part of Ellmann's lengthy account from his biography: 'Though both Ruskin and Pater welcomed beauty, for Ruskin it had to be allied to good, for Pater it might have just a touch of evil. . . . Ruskin appealed to conscience, Pater to imagination. Ruskin invoked disciplined restraint, Pater allowed for a pleasant drift. What Ruskin reviled as vice, Pater caressed as wantonness.' We are left with an impression of literary discipleship, which is rather misleading. Wilde announced his 'new departure from Mr Ruskin' in 1882, and rarely echoed him thereafter.

So Ruskin was not really important for the mature Wilde. Emerson, for too long overlooked, was far more important—even possibly more important as an overall influence than Pater himself. I have pointed out the general nature of Wilde's indebtedness to Emerson in my Introduction and notes to the Oxford Authors *Writings of Oscar Wilde,* but the most important presence of Emerson for Wilde is to be detected in *The Soul of Man,* and indeed in *De Profundis.* Since Emerson's *Essays* were on the very first list of books that Wilde asked for when prison conditions eased, it is not surprising that the influence continues.

Emerson was born in Boston of a long line of ministers, and himself first became a Unitarian preacher, but resigned, unable to sustain even the few dogmas and rituals of that position, and characteristically opting for self-reliance. He became a highly regarded lecturer and thinker, of a very independent cast of mind and often singular expression, and Wilde quotes him widely and refers to him frequently.

One essay of Emerson's meant more to Wilde than all the rest, if we can go by how often he cites or echoes it, and that is 'Self-Reliance'. *The Soul of Man* in particular echoes 'Self-Reliance', and the most striking instances are indicated in the notes here. Attitudes occurring in both works include opposition to all of the following: conformity, consistency, imitation, philanthropy, charity, property, and the mob. Three very brief examples may show the unanimity of Wilde and Emerson here. Wilde says: 'All imitation in morals and in life is wrong': Emerson had said: 'Imitation is suicide', and 'Insist on yourself; never imitate.' Wilde says of the future personality of man: 'Nor will it admit any laws but its own laws.' Emerson wrote: 'No law can be sacred to me but that of my nature.' Wilde declares: 'The true artist is a man who believes absolutely in himself, because he is absolutely himself.' Emerson wrote: 'To believe your own thought, to believe that what is true for you in your private heart, is true for all men,—that is genius.'

No wonder Wilde's political essay, which shows full awareness of the rest of the contemporary periodical debate, none the less has a different flavour. The Individualism in Wilde's essay is much closer to Emerson's Self-Reliance than any of the contemporary political ways of using that ambiguous term. Another Emerson essay particularly important for *The Soul of Man* is 'Considerations by the Way', from *The Conduct of Life*.

I have said that Emerson clearly influenced *De Profundis,* as well as *The Soul of Man.* Indeed, these two works can be seen to have a great deal in common. *De Profundis* is not presented here to be assessed for its biographical accuracy or facts, which Sir Rupert Hart-Davis splendidly provides for in *Selected Letters,* but as a human document. It is a partial autobiography, written in extreme isolation, after a long period of spirit-crushing separation from freedom, friends, and paper. It can be read as a necessary release after this suffering, or, as Ellmann variously sees it, as a dramatic monologue, an elegy for lost greatness, a love-letter. All these are potentially valuable ways of considering it. Here I want to emphasize what it has in common with *The Soul of Man.* Both demonstrate Wilde's great attraction to the person and sayings of Jesus, and a determination to reclaim these sayings, to separate them from a conventional Christianity which has given them a permanent gloss about renunciation, self-sacrifice, and a duty to love one's neighbour. The very first sentence of *The Soul of Man*

signals this: 'The chief advantage that would result from
the establishment of Socialism is, undoubtedly, the fact that
Socialism would relieve us from the sordid necessity of living
for others which, in the present condition of things, presses
so hardly upon almost everybody.' Wilde goes on to claim
Jesus for his own alternative ideals of self-development and
self-realization, self-reliance and Individualism: 'And so he
who would lead a Christ-like life is he who is perfectly and
absolutely himself.' In *De Profundis* he was to return to this
idea with renewed vigour:

To live for others as a definite self-conscious aim was not his
creed. It was not the basis of his creed. When he says 'Forgive
your enemies', it is not for the sake of the enemy but for one's
own sake that he says so . . . But while Christ did not say to men,
'Live for others', he pointed out that there was no difference at all
between the lives of others and one's own life. By this means he
gave to man an extended, a Titan personality. Since his coming the
history of each separate individual is, or can be made, the history
of the world.

Both *The Soul of Man* and *De Profundis* also demonstrate
a great interest in the idea of becoming and remaining free
of convention in all things, of gaining understanding of
one's own nature and refusing to compromise this in other
interests. In *The Soul of Man* there is a forceful attempt to
assert that every human individual—not just the exceptional
man, the artist—can become and express his or her true
self: he believes in 'the great actual Individualism latent
and potential in mankind generally'. And we find this also
in *De Profundis*: 'Every single human being should be the
fulfilment of a prophecy. For every human being should be
the realization of some ideal, either in the mind of God or
in the mind of man.' What makes the reader in spite of
all this feel a great difference between the two works is, I
think, this. In *The Soul of Man* there is an almost reckless
determination that man shall be perfectible, that joy shall
be unconfined. A Utopian future for humanity is forecast.
Stripped of the disabling fetters of property, government,
punishment, authority, and poverty, man will achieve 'true,
beautiful, healthy Individualism', and be free to live and

develop his wonderful personality—the end product will be 'an Individualism expressing itself through joy'. Wilde makes no attempt to show how this Utopian world can be brought about: indeed, he allows that in oppressed countries such as Russia the only self-realization possible as yet is through pain, as was the case, he says, in medieval Europe. But in modern Europe, he asserts, poverty and suffering can be abolished, and man can be 'saner, healthier, more civilized, more himself': 'It will of course be said that such a scheme as is set forth here is quite unpractical, and goes against human nature. This is perfectly true. . . . The conditions will be done away with, and human nature will change.'

Looking back on his earlier life in *De Profundis*, Wilde sees that it was limited by his refusal to experience sorrow: 'I used to live entirely for pleasure. I shunned sorrow and suffering of every kind. I resolved to ignore them as far as possible, to treat them, that is to say, as modes of imperfection. They were not part of my scheme of things. They had no place in my philosophy.' The experience of sorrow comes as a revelation to him: 'One discerns things that one never discerned before. One approaches the whole of history from a different standpoint. What one had felt dimly through instinct, about Art, is intellectually and emotionally realized with perfect clearness of vision and absolute intensity of apprehension.' In his works, as he says, he had prefigured this discovery: he wrote more wisely than he knew.

It is important to read *De Profundis* for what it is, a document written under extraordinary conditions in the later stages of an imprisonment of harsh severity. Wilde was kept to hard labour in silent and solitary confinement throughout. Before his release Major Nelson, the new and merciful governor of Reading Prison, the man who gave him leave to write this document, said to Robert Ross: 'He looks well. But like all men unused to manual labour who receive a sentence of this kind, he will be dead within two years.' It is a mistake, I think, to look at his post-prison career, with all its backslidings, and assume that the humility and self-knowledge, the understanding of his life, achieved in prison and articulated in the letter, were unreal, or illusory. Whatever Wilde achieves in writing the letter—whatever, even, he aspires to—should be given attention for itself. The letter is itself a demonstration of his claims: 'But while to propose to be a better man is a piece of unscientific cant, to have become a *deeper* man is the privilege of those who have suffered. And such I think I have become. You can judge for yourself.'

Wilde aspires further, wanting to believe that one day he will see his prison experience not as an ending but as a 'wonderful beginning'. The Wilde of later letters inevitably descends from these heights, and as inevitably justifies himself. So in February 1898 he wrote to Ross from Paris: 'A patriot put in prison for loving his country loves his country, and a poet in prison for loving boys loves boys.' The post-prison life is essentially irrelevant to *De Profundis*, except that he did attempt, in the two letters to the *Daily Chronicle* and *The Ballad of Reading Gaol*, to fulfil one ambition expressed there: 'The prison-system is absolutely and entirely wrong. I would give anything to be able to alter it when I go out. I intend to try.'

One last important light is cast on the letter by Wilde in a letter to Robert Ross from prison, dated 1 April 1897, a letter intended to accompany the text of *De Profundis*. He expresses the hope that the letter will do Douglas good, and goes on:

> Whether or not the letter does good to his narrow nature and hectic brain, to me it has done great good. I have 'cleansed my bosom of much perilous stuff' . . . I need not remind you that mere expression is to an artist the supreme and only mode of life. It is by utterance that we live. Of the many, many things for which I have to thank the Governor there is none for which I am more grateful than for his permission to write fully to A. D. and at as great length as I desired. For nearly two years I had within me a growing burden of bitterness, much of which I have now got rid of.

The Ballad of Reading Gaol is Wilde's last work of art, the only one he composed after he left prison. It is the only one of his major artworks directly inspired by personal experience. *Selected Letters* gives full details of the murder for which Wooldridge was executed, and the writing and revisions of the poem. It is also the only work in which Wilde speaks for a whole community, and he makes very real the common sufferings and fears of the prisoners. At the same time it briefly stresses his own particular experience as an artist: 'For he who lives more lives than one/ More deaths than one must die.' And it carries a universal and striking message about guilt: 'each man kills the thing he loves', and in part V a condemnation of the prison system: 'every prison that men build/Is built with bricks of shame.' Small wonder that Wilde wrote to Ross: 'With much of your criticism I agree. The poem suffers under the difficulty of a divided aim in style. Some is realistic, some is romantic: some poetry, some propaganda. I feel it keenly, but as a whole I think the production interesting: that it is interesting from more points of view than one is artistically to be regretted.'

The poem has always split its audience. Many of the early reviewers complained about these conflicting elements in the poem, but the most perceptive, Arthur Symons, defended it as 'a romantic artist working on realistic material', and, while acknowledging the divided aim, argued that the message about universal guilt unified the poem. As is clear from Karl Beckson's *Oscar Wilde: The Critical Heritage*, discriminating critics and specialists on the period have admired the poem, and many of these have noticed a family resemblance to *The Soul of Man* or *De Profundis*.

The extreme example of the opposite view is Yeats, who added the poem to his *Oxford Book of Modern Verse* in 1936 only after he had severely pruned it, so severely that only 38 of the 109 stanzas remained. 'A work of art can have but one subject', he pronounced. Details of his version can be found in the notes. The most recent authoritative anthology of the period is that edited by the late Ian Fletcher in 1987, *British Poetry and Prose 1870–1905*. Not an uncritical admirer of the poem, Fletcher nevertheless represents Wilde in his selection with 'The Preface to *Dorian Gray*' and the *Ballad*, describing it as 'a large good-bad poem which needs to be printed virtually in its entirety, quite free of Yeats's editorial purge in his *Oxford Book of Modern Verse*, and of course to be published as a broadside'.

Wilde died in Paris in 1900, newly baptized a Roman Catholic and given the last rites, and in the company of his faithful friends Robert Ross and Reginald Turner. In 1909 his body was moved to the cemetery of Père Lachaise. It is marked by Epstein's monument and four lines from the *Ballad*:

> And alien tears will fill for him
> Pity's long-broken urn
> For his mourners will be outcast men,
> And outcasts always mourn.

NOTE ON THE TEXT

THE text of *The Soul of Man* is taken from the first book edition of that work, privately printed in 1895, and compared with other versions, including the original, published as 'The Soul of Man Under Socialism' in *The Fortnightly Review* in February 1891, and the collected edition by Robert Ross in 1908.

The texts of *De Profundis* and the two letters to the *Daily Chronicle* are those established in Sir Rupert Hart-Davis's edition of *Selected Letters* (1979), used by kind permission. Interested readers are referred to that volume for details of an unusually complex textual—and legal—history.

The text of *The Ballad of Reading Gaol* is the one established by me in *Writings of Oscar Wilde* (1989).

SELECT BIBLIOGRAPHY

MAJOR EDITIONS

[Works] First Collected Edition, ed. Robert Ross in 14 volumes (London, 1908); *The Letters of Oscar Wilde*, ed. Rupert Hart-Davis (London, 1962); *Selected Letters of Oscar Wilde*, ed. Rupert Hart-Davis (Oxford, 1979); *More Letters of Oscar Wilde*, ed. Rupert Hart-Davis (Oxford, 1985); *The Picture of Dorian Gray*, ed. Isobel Murray (Oxford English Novels, Oxford, 1974); *The Picture of Dorian Gray*, ed. Donald L. Lawler (Norton Critical Editions, New York, 1988); *The Complete Shorter Fiction of Oscar Wilde*, ed. Isobel Murray (Oxford, 1979); *The Importance of Being Earnest*, ed. Russell Jackson (New Mermaids, London, 1980); *Lady Windermere's Fan*, ed. Ian Small (New Mermaids, London, 1980); *Two Society Comedies* [*A Woman of No Importance*, ed. Ian Small, and *An Ideal Husband*, ed. Russell Jackson] (New Mermaids, London, 1983); *Oscar Wilde's Oxford Notebooks: A Portrait of Mind in the Making*, ed. Philip E. Smith II and Michael S. Helfand (Oxford, 1989); *Writings of Oscar Wilde*, ed. Isobel Murray (Oxford Authors, Oxford, 1989).

BIBLIOGRAPHIES

Ian Fletcher and John Stokes, 'Oscar Wilde', in *Anglo-Irish Literature: A Review of Research*, ed. Richard J. Finneran (New York, 1976), 48–137; Ian Fletcher and John Stokes, 'Oscar Wilde', in *Recent Research on Anglo-Irish Writers*, ed. Richard J. Finneran (New York, 1983), 21–47 (together these descriptive and evaluative accounts of Wilde scholarship and criticism are by far the best guide to modern scholarship and criticism on Wilde); Stuart Mason [Christopher Millard], *Bibliography of Oscar Wilde* (1914: reprinted 1967); E. H. Mikhail, *Oscar Wilde: An Annotated Bibliography of Criticism*, (London, 1978).

BIOGRAPHY

Richard Ellmann, *Oscar Wilde*, (London, 1987); H. Montgomery Hyde, *Oscar Wilde: A Biography*, (London, 1976).

A CHRONOLOGY OF
OSCAR WILDE

1854   Oscar Wilde born in Dublin, second son of distinguished parents, both authors, Dr (later Sir) William Wilde, leading oculist and ear-surgeon, and Jane Francesca Elgee, poet and translator, who wrote for the Young Ireland movement of the 1840s, under the name Speranza.

1864–71   At Portora Royal School, Enniskillen.

1867   Death of Wilde's younger sister Isola, aged 8.

1871–4   At Trinity College, Dublin, reading Classics.

1873   Publication of the first edition of Pater's *Renäissance*, with its notorious and far-reaching 'Conclusion'.

1874   Berkeley Gold Medal for Greek at Trinity: matriculates, with a scholarship, at Magdalen College, Oxford.

1875   Summer: visits Italy with Dublin professor J. P. Mahaffy.

1876   Death of Sir William Wilde. Wilde takes a First Class in Classical Moderations.

1877   Visits Greece with Mahaffy, returns by Rome.

1878   Wins the Newdigate Prize for his poem *Ravenna*. Takes a First Class in *Litterae Humaniores*.

1879   Settles in London, as 'professor' of aesthetics: regularly lampooned in *Punch* from now on.

1881   *Poems* published. Gilbert and Sullivan's light opera *Patience* produced, satirizing the aesthetes.

1882   Spends year lecturing in the United States and Canada, on such subjects as 'The English Renaissance of Art' and 'The House Beautiful'.

1883   Three months in Paris; lectures in Britain; the early play *Vera* rather unsuccessfully produced in New York.

1884   Marries Constance Lloyd; settles in Chelsea. Begins regular book reviewing, which continues until 1890.

1885   Son Cyril born. Passing of the Criminal Law Amendment Act 1885, which for the first time prohibited indecent relations between consenting males, the offence for which Wilde would serve his years in prison.

1886   Wilde meets Robert Ross. Son Vyvyan born.

1887–9 Edits *The Woman's World*.

1888   *The Happy Prince and Other Tales* published.

1889   'The Portrait of Mr W. H.' published in *Blackwoods*.

1890   The first version of *Dorian Gray* published in *Lippincott's Monthly Magazine*.

1891   Meets Lord Alfred Douglas. An early play *The Duchess of Padua* produced in New York as *Guido Ferranti*. Publishes the revised *Dorian Gray, Intentions, Lord Arthur Savile's Crime and Other Stories, A House of Pomegranates*. 'The Soul of Man under Socialism' published in *The Fortnightly Review*. Irish political leader Parnell, having been vindicated on charges of political murder, is publicly ruined because of his involvement in a divorce suit.

1892   *Lady Windermere's Fan* produced. *Salome* is refused a licence for production in London by Sarah Bernhardt.

1893   *Salome* (original French version) published in Paris. *A Woman of No Importance* is produced in London and *Lady Windermere's Fan* is published.

1894   *Salome* is published in English translation, with illustrations by Aubrey Beardsley. *The Sphinx* and *A Woman of No Importance* published.

1895   *An Ideal Husband* and *The Importance of Being Earnest* produced in London. Wilde charges Lord Alfred Douglas's father, the Marquess of Queensberry, with criminal libel. On Queensberry's acquittal, Wilde is arrested for 'acts of gross indecency with other male persons'. The first trial jury fails to agree a verdict: at the second trial Wilde is found guilty and given the maximum sentence, two years' hard labour, and sent to Pentonville. He is moved to Wandsworth, and finally to Reading Gaol. He is declared bankrupt.

1896   Death of Lady Wilde: Constance Wilde travels from
        Genoa to Reading Gaol to break the news. *Salome*
        produced in Paris.

1897   Writes *De Profundis* (a long letter to Lord Alfred
        Douglas) in gaol. On his release Wilde writes to the
        Daily Chronicle about the treatment of children in gaol.
        He settles first at Berneval, near Dieppe: later he joins
        Lord Alfred Douglas in Italy, causing a new rift with
        his wife.

1898   Moves to Paris. Publishes *The Ballad of Reading Gaol*,
        and writes another long letter about prison conditions to
        the *Daily Chronicle*. Death of Constance Wilde.

1899   *The Importance of Being Earnest* and *An Ideal Husband*
        published. Travels in Europe.

1900   Visits Rome, returns to Paris. During serious illness is
        baptized a Roman Catholic: dies 30 November.

The Soul of Man

THE chief advantage that would result from the establishment of Socialism is, undoubtedly, the fact that Socialism would relieve us from that sordid necessity of living for others* which, in the present condition of things, presses so hardly upon almost everybody. In fact, scarcely anyone at all escapes.

Now and then, in the course of the century, a great man of science, like Darwin;* a great poet, like Keats; a fine critical spirit, like M. Renan;* a supreme artist, like Flaubert, has been able to isolate himself, to keep himself out of reach of the clamorous claims of others, to stand 'under the shelter of the wall', as Plato puts it,* and so to realize the perfection of what was in him,* to his own incomparable gain, and to the incomparable and lasting gain of the whole world. These, however, are exceptions. The majority of people spoil their lives by an unhealthy and exaggerated altruism—are forced, indeed, so to spoil them. They find themselves surrounded by hideous poverty, by hideous ugliness, by hideous starvation. It is inevitable that they should be strongly moved by all this. The emotions of man are stirred more quickly than man's intelligence; and, as I pointed out some time ago in an article on the function of criticism,* it is much more easy to have sympathy with suffering than it is to have sympathy with thought. Accordingly, with admirable, though misdirected intentions, they very seriously and very sentimentally set themselves to the task of remedying the evils that they see. But their remedies do not cure the disease: they merely prolong it. Indeed, their remedies are part of the disease.

They try to solve the problem of poverty, for instance, by keeping the poor alive; or, in the case of a very advanced school, by amusing the poor.*

But this is not a solution: it is an aggravation of the difficulty. The proper aim is to try and reconstruct society on such a basis that poverty will be impossible.* And the altruistic virtues have really prevented the carrying out of this aim. Just as the worst slave-owners were those who were kind to their slaves, and so prevented the horror of the system being realized by those who suffered from it, and understood by those who contemplated it, so, in the present state of things in England, the people who do most harm are the people who try to do most good;* and at last we have had the spectacle of men who have really studied the problem and know the life—educated men who live in the East End—coming forward and imploring the community to restrain its altruistic impulses of charity, benevolence, and the like. They do so on the ground that such charity degrades and demoralizes.* They are perfectly right. Charity creates a multitude of sins.*

There is also this to be said. It is immoral to use private property in order to alleviate the horrible evils that result from the institution of private property. It is both immoral and unfair.

Under Socialism all this will, of course, be altered. There will be no people living in fetid dens and fetid rags, and bringing up unhealthy, hunger-pinched children in the midst of impossible and absolutely repulsive surroundings. The security of society will not depend, as it does now, on the state of the weather. If a frost comes* we shall not have a hundred thousand men out of work, tramping about the streets in a state of disgusting misery, or whining to their neighbours for alms, or crowding round the doors of loathsome shelters to try and secure a hunch of bread and a night's unclean lodging. Each member of the society will share in the general prosperity and happiness of the society, and if a frost comes no one will practically be anything the worse.

Upon the other hand, Socialism itself will be of value simply because it will lead to Individualism.*

Socialism, Communism, or whatever one chooses to call it, by converting private property into public wealth, and substituting co-operation for competition, will restore society to its proper condition of a thoroughly healthy organism, and ensure the material well-being of each member of the community. It will, in fact, give Life its proper basis and its proper environment. But for the full development of Life to its highest mode of perfection, something more is needed. What is needed is Individualism. If the Socialism is Authoritarian; if there are Governments armed with economic power as they are now with political power; if, in a word, we are to have Industrial Tyrannies, then the last state of man will be worse than the first. At present, in consequence of the existence of private property, a great many people are enabled to develop a certain very limited amount of Individualism. They are either under no necessity to work for their living, or are enabled to choose the sphere of activity that is really congenial to them, and gives them pleasure. These are the poets, the philosophers, the men of science, the men of culture—in a word, the real men, the men who have realized themselves, and in whom all Humanity gains a partial realization. Upon the other hand, there are a great many people who, having no private property of their own, and being always on the brink of sheer starvation, are compelled to do the work of beasts of burden, to do work that is quite uncongenial to them, and to which they are forced by the peremptory, unreasonable, degrading Tyranny of want. These are the poor, and amongst them there is no grace of manner, or charm of speech, or civilization, or culture, or refinement in pleasures, or joy of life. From their collective force Humanity gains much in material prosperity. But it is only the material result that it gains, and the man who is poor is in himself absolutely of no importance. He is merely the infinitesimal atom of a force that, so far from regarding him, crushes him: indeed, prefers him crushed, as in that case he is far more obedient.

Of course, it might be said that the Individualism generated under conditions of private property is not always, or even as a rule, of a fine or wonderful type, and that the poor, if they have not culture and charm, have still many virtues. Both these statements would be quite true. The possession of private property is very often extremely demoralizing, and that is, of course, one of the reasons why

Socialism wants to get rid of the institution. In fact, property is really a nuisance. Some years ago people went about the country saying that property has duties. They said it so often and so tediously that, at last, the Church has begun to say it. One hears it now from every pulpit. It is perfectly true. Property not merely has duties,* but has so many duties that its possession to any large extent is a bore. It involves endless claims upon one, endless attention to business, endless bother. If property had simply pleasures, we could stand it; but its duties make it unbearable. In the interest of the rich we must get rid of it. The virtues of the poor may be readily admitted, and are much to be regretted. We are often told that the poor are grateful for charity. Some of them are, no doubt, but the best amongst the poor are never grateful.* They are ungrateful, discontented, disobedient, and rebellious. They are quite right to be so. Charity they feel to be a ridiculously inadequate mode of partial restitution, or a sentimental dole, usually accompanied by some impertinent attempt on the part of the sentimentalist to tyrannize over their private lives. Why should they be grateful for the crumbs that fall from the rich man's table?* They should be seated at the board, and are beginning to know it. As for being discontented, a man who would not be discontented with such surroundings and such a low mode of life would be a perfect brute. Disobedience, in the eyes of any one who has read history, is man's original virtue.* It is through disobedience that progress has been made, through disobedience and through rebellion. Sometimes the poor are praised for being thrifty. But to recommend thrift to the poor is both grotesque and insulting. It is like advising a man who is starving to eat less. For a town or country labourer to practise thrift would be absolutely immoral. Man should not be ready to show that he can live like a badly fed animal. He should decline to live like that, and should either steal or go on the rates, which is considered by many to be a form of stealing. As for begging, it is safer to beg than to take, but it is finer to take than to beg. No: a poor man who is ungrateful, unthrifty, discontented, and rebellious, is probably a real personality, and has much in him. He is at any rate a healthy protest. As for the virtuous poor, one can pity them, of course, but one cannot possibly admire them. They have made private terms with the enemy, and sold their birthright for very bad pottage.* They must also be extraordinarily stupid. I can quite understand a man accepting laws that protect private property, and admit of its accumulation, as long as he himself is able under those conditions to realize some form of beautiful and intellectual life. But it is almost incredible to me how a man whose life is marred and made hideous by such laws can possibly acquiesce in their continuance.

However, the explanation is not really difficult to find. It is simply this. Misery and poverty are so absolutely degrading, and exercise such a paralyzing effect over the nature of men, that no class is ever really conscious of its own suffering. They have to be told of it by other people, and they often entirely disbelieve them. What is said by great employers of labour against agitators is unquestionably true. Agitators are a set of interfering, meddling people, who come down to some perfectly contented class of the community, and sow the seeds of discontent amongst them. That is the reason why agitators are so absolutely necessary. Without them, in our incomplete state, there would be no advance towards civilization. Slavery was put down in America, not in consequence of any action on the part of the slaves, or even any express desire on their part that they should be free. It was put down entirely through the grossly illegal conduct of certain agitators in Boston and elsewhere, who were not slaves themselves, nor owners of slaves, nor had anything to do with the question really. It was, undoubtedly, the Abolitionists* who set the torch alight, who began the whole thing. And it is curious to note that from the slaves themselves they received, not merely very little assistance, but hardly any sympathy even; and when at the close of the war the slaves found themselves free, found themselves indeed so absolutely free that they were free to starve,* many of them bitterly regretted the new state of things. To the thinker, the most tragic fact in the whole of the French Revolution is not that Marie Antoinette was killed for being a queen, but that the starved peasant of the Vendée voluntarily went out to die for the hideous cause of feudalism.

It is clear, then, that no Authoritarian Socialism will do. For while under the present system a very large number of people can lead lives of a certain amount of freedom and expression and happiness, under an industrial-barrack system,* or a system of economic tyranny, nobody would be able to have any such freedom at all. It is to be regretted that a portion of our community should be practically in slavery, but to propose to solve the problem by enslaving the entire community is childish. Every man must be left quite free to choose his own work. No form of compulsion must be exercised over him. If there is, his work will not be good for him, will not be good in itself, and will not be good for others. And by work I simply mean activity of any kind.

I hardly think that any Socialist, nowadays, would seriously propose that an inspector should call every morning at each house to see that each citizen rose up and did manual labour for eight hours. Humanity has got beyond that stage, and reserves such a form of life for the people whom, in a very arbitrary manner, it chooses to call criminals. But I confess that many of the socialistic views that I have come across seem to me to be tainted with ideas of authority, if not of actual compulsion. Of course authority and compulsion are out of the question. All association must be quite voluntary. It is only in voluntary associations that man is fine.*

But it may be asked how Individualism, which is now more or less dependent on the existence of private property for its development, will benefit by the abolition of such private property. The answer is very simple. It is true that, under existing conditions, a few men who have had private means of their own, such as Byron, Shelley, Browning, Victor Hugo, Baudelaire, and others, have been able to realize their personality more or less completely. Not one of these men ever did a single day's work for hire. They were relieved from poverty. They had an immense advantage. The question is whether it would be for the good of Individualism that such an advantage should be taken away. Let us suppose that it is taken away. What happens then to Individualism? How will it benefit?

It will benefit in this way. Under the new conditions Individualism will be far freer, far finer, and far more intensified than it is now. I am not talking of the great imaginatively-realized Individualism of such poets as I have mentioned, but of the great actual Individualism latent and potential in mankind generally. For the recognition of private property has really harmed Individualism, and obscured it, by confusing a man with what he possesses. It has led Individualism entirely astray. It has made gain not growth its aim. So that man thought that the important thing was to have, and did not know that the important thing is to be.* The true perfection of man lies, not in what man has, but in what man is.* Private property has crushed true Individualism, and set up an Individualism that is false. It has debarred one part of the community from being individual by starving them. It has debarred the other part of the community from being individual by putting them on the wrong road, and encumbering them. Indeed, so completely has man's personality been absorbed by his possessions that the English law has always treated offences against a man's property with far more severity than offences against his person, and property is still the test of complete citizenship. The industry necessary for the making of money is also very demoralizing. In a community like ours, where property confers immense distinction, social position, honour, respect, titles, and other pleasant things of the kind, man, being naturally ambitious, makes it his aim to accumulate this property, and goes on wearily and tediously accumulating it long after he has got far more than he wants, or can use, or enjoy, or perhaps even know of. Man will kill himself by overwork in order to secure property, and really, considering the enormous advantages that property brings, one is hardly surprised. One's regret is that society should be constructed on such a basis that man has been forced into a groove in which he cannot freely develop what is wonderful, and fascinating, and delightful in him—in which, in fact, he misses the true pleasure and joy of living. He is also, under existing conditions, very insecure. An enormously wealthy merchant may be—often is—at every moment of his life at the mercy of things that are not under his control. If the wind blows an extra point or so, or the weather suddenly changes, or some trivial thing happens, his ship may go down, his speculations may go wrong, and he finds himself a poor man, with his social position quite gone. Now, nothing should be able to harm a man except himself.* Nothing should be able to rob a man at all. What a man really has, is what is in him. What is outside of him should be a matter of no importance.

With the abolition of private property, then, we shall have true, beautiful, healthy Individualism. Nobody will waste his life in accumulating things, and the symbols for things. One will live. To live is the rarest thing in the world. Most people exist, that is all.

It is a question whether we have ever seen the full expression of a personality, except on the imaginative plane of art. In action, we never have. Caesar, says Mommsen,* was the complete and perfect man. But how tragically insecure was Caesar! Wherever there is a man who exercises authority, there is a man who resists authority. Caesar was very perfect, but his perfection travelled by too dangerous a road. Marcus Aurelius was the perfect man, says Renan.* Yes; the great emperor was a perfect man. But how intolerable were the endless claims upon him! He staggered under the burden of the empire. He was conscious how inadequate one man was to bear the weight of that Titan and too vast orb. What I mean by a perfect man is one who develops under perfect conditions; one who is not wounded, or worried, or maimed, or in danger. Most personalities have been obliged to be rebels. Half their strength has been wasted in friction.* Byron's personality, for instance, was terribly wasted in its battle with the stupidity, and hypocrisy, and Philistinism of the English. Such battles do not always intensify strength: they often exaggerate weakness. Byron was never able to give us what he might have given us. Shelley escaped better. Like

Byron, he got out of England as soon as possible. But he was not so well known. If the English had had any idea of what a great poet he really was, they would have fallen on him with tooth and nail, and made his life as unbearable to him as they possibly could. But he was not a remarkable figure in society, and consequently he escaped, to a certain degree. Still, even in Shelley the note of rebellion is sometimes too strong. The note of the perfect personality is not rebellion, but peace.

It will be a marvellous thing—the true personality of man—when we see it. It will grow naturally and simply, flower-like, or as a tree grows. It will not be at discord. It will never argue or dispute. It will not prove things. It will know everything. And yet it will not busy itself about knowledge. It will have wisdom. Its value will not be measured by material things. It will have nothing. And yet it will have everything, and whatever one takes from it, it will still have, so rich will it be. It will not be always meddling with others, or asking them to be like itself. It will love them because they will be different. And yet while it will not meddle with others it will help all, as a beautiful thing helps us, by being what it is. The personality of man will be very wonderful. It will be as wonderful as the personality of a child.

In its development it will be assisted by Christianity, if men desire that; but if men do not desire that, it will develop none the less surely. For it will not worry itself about the past, nor care whether things happened or did not happen. Nor will it admit any laws but its own laws; nor any authority but its own authority.* Yet it will love those who sought to intensify it, and speak often of them. And of these Christ was one.

'Know thyself' was written over the portal of the antique world.* Over the portal of the new world, 'Be thyself'* shall be written. And the message of Christ to man was simply 'Be thyself'. That is the secret of Christ.

When Jesus talks about the poor he simply means personalities, just as when he talks about the rich he simply means people who have not developed their personalities.*

Jesus moved in a community that allowed the accumulation of private property just as ours does, and the gospel that he preached was not that in such a community it is an advantage for a man to live on scanty, unwholesome food, to wear ragged, unwholesome clothes, to sleep in horrid, unwholesome dwellings, and a disadvantage for a man to live under healthy, pleasant, and decent conditions. Such a view would have been wrong there and then, and would of course be still more wrong now and in England; for as man moves northwards the material necessities of life become of more vital importance, and our society is infinitely more complex, and displays far greater extremes of luxury and pauperism than any society of the antique world. What Jesus meant, was this. He said to man, 'You have a wonderful personality. Develop it. Be yourself. Don't imagine that your perfection lies in accumulating or possessing external things. Your perfection is inside of you. If only you could realize that, you would not want to be rich. Ordinary riches can be stolen from a man. Real riches cannot. In the treasury-house of your soul, there are infinitely precious things, that may not be taken from you. And so, try to so shape your life that external things will not harm you. And try also to get rid of personal property. It involves sordid preoccupation, endless industry, continual wrong. Personal property hinders Individualism at every step.'* It is to be noted that Jesus never says that impoverished people are necessarily good, or wealthy people necessarily bad. That would not have been true. Wealthy people are, as a class, better than impoverished people, more moral, more intellectual, more well-behaved. There is only one class in the community that thinks more about money than the rich, and that is the poor.* The poor can think of nothing else. That is the misery of being poor. What Jesus does say is that man reaches his perfection, not through what he has, not even through what he does, but entirely through what he is. And so the wealthy young man who comes to Jesus* is represented as a thoroughly good citizen, who has broken none of the laws of his state, none of the commandments of his religion. He is quite respectable, in the ordinary sense of that extraordinary word. Jesus says to him, 'You should give up private property. It hinders you from realizing your perfection. It is a drag upon you. It is a burden. Your personality does not need it. It is within you, and not outside of you, that you will find what you really are, and what you really want.' To his own friends he says the same thing. He tells them to be themselves, and not to be always worrying about other things.* What do other things matter? Man is complete in himself. When they go into the world, the world will disagree with them. That is inevitable. The world hates Individualism. But that is not to trouble them. They are to be calm and self-centred. If a man takes their cloak, they are to give him their coat,* just to show that material things are of no importance. If people abuse them, they are not to answer back. What does it signify? The things people say of a man do not alter a man. He is what he is. Public opinion is of no value whatsoever. Even if people employ actual violence, they are not to be violent in turn. That would be to fall to the same low level. After all, even in prison, a man can be quite free. His soul can be free. His personality can be untroubled. He can be at peace. And, above all things, they are not to interfere with other people or judge them in any way. Personality is a very mysterious thing. A man cannot always be estimated by what he does. He may keep the law, and yet be worthless. He may break the law, and yet be fine. He may be bad, without ever doing anything bad. He may commit a sin against society, and yet realize through that sin his true perfection.

There was a woman who was taken in adultery. We are not told the history of her love, but that love must have been very great; for Jesus said that her sins were forgiven her, not because she repented, but because her love was so intense and wonderful. Later on, a short time before his death, as he sat at a feast, the woman came in and poured costly perfumes on his hair. His friends tried to interfere with her, and said that it was an extravagance, and that the money that the perfume cost should have been expended on charitable relief of people in want, or something of that kind. Jesus did not accept that view. He pointed out that the material needs of Man were great and very permanent, but that the spiritual needs of Man were greater still, and that in one divine moment, and by selecting its own mode of expression, a personality might make itself perfect. The world worships the woman, even now, as a saint.*

Yes; there are suggestive things in Individualism. Socialism annihilates family life, for instance. With the abolition of private property, marriage in its present form must disappear. This is part of the programme. Individualism accepts this and makes it fine. It converts the abolition of legal restraint into a form of freedom that will help the full development of personality, and make the love of man and woman more wonderful, more beautiful, and more ennobling. Jesus knew this. He rejected the claims of family life, although they existed in his day and community in a very marked form. 'Who is my mother? Who are my brothers?'* he said, when he was told that they wished to speak to him. When one of his followers asked leave to go and bury his father,* 'Let the dead bury the dead', was his terrible answer. He would allow no claim whatsoever to be made on personality.

And so he who would lead a Christ-like life is he who is perfectly and absolutely himself. He may be a great poet, or a great man of science; or a young student at a University, or one who watches sheep upon a moor; or a maker of dramas, like Shakespeare, or a thinker about God, like Spinoza; or a child who plays in a garden, or a fisherman who throws his nets into the sea. It does not matter what he is, as long as he realizes the perfection of the soul that is within him. All imitation in morals and in life is wrong.* Through the streets of Jerusalem at the present day crawls one who is mad and carries a wooden cross on his shoulders. He is a symbol of the lives that are marred by imitation. Father Damien* was Christ-like when he went out to live with the lepers, because in such service he realized fully what was best in him. But he was not more Christ-like than Wagner,* when he realized his soul in music; or than Shelley, when he realized his soul in song. There is no one type for man. There are as many perfections as there are imperfect men.

And while to the claims of charity a man may yield and yet be free, to the claims of conformity no man may yield and remain free at all.

Individualism, then, is what through Socialism we are to attain to. As a natural result the State must give up all idea of government. It must give it up because, as a wise man once said* many centuries before Christ, there is such a thing as leaving mankind alone; there is no such thing as governing mankind. All modes of government are failures.* Despotism is unjust to everybody, including the despot, who was probably made for better things. Oligarchies are unjust to the many, and ochlocracies* are unjust to the few. High hopes were once formed of democracy; but democracy means simply the bludgeoning of the people by the people for the people.* It has been found out. I must say that it was high time, for all authority is quite degrading. It degrades those who exercise it, and degrades those over whom it is exercised. When it is violently, grossly, and cruelly used, it produces a good effect, by creating, or at any rate bringing out, the spirit of revolt and Individualism that is to kill it. When it is used with a certain amount of kindness, and accompanied by prizes and rewards, it is dreadfully demoralizing. People, in that case, are less conscious of the horrible pressure that is being put on them, and so go through their lives in a sort of coarse comfort, like petted animals, without ever realizing that they are probably thinking other people's thoughts,* living by other people's standards, wearing practically what one may call other people's second-hand clothes, and never being themselves for a single moment. 'He who would be free,' says a fine thinker, 'must not conform.'* And authority, by bribing people to conform, produces a very gross kind of over-fed barbarism amongst us.

With authority, punishment will pass away. This will be a great gain—a gain, in fact, of incalculable value. As one reads history, not in the expurgated editions written for schoolboys and passmen,* but in the original authorities of each time, one is absolutely sickened, not by the crimes that the wicked have committed, but by the punishments that the good have inflicted; and a community is infinitely more brutalized by the habitual employment of punishment, than it is by the occasional occurrence of crime.* It obviously follows that the more punishment is inflicted the more crime is produced, and most modern legislation has clearly recognized this, and has made it its task to diminish punishment as far as it thinks it can. Wherever it has really diminished it, the results have always been extremely good. The less punishment, the less crime. When there is no punishment at all, crime will either cease to exist, or if it occurs, will be treated by physicians as a very distressing form of dementia, to be cured by care and kindness. For what are called criminals nowadays are not criminals at all. Starvation, and not sin, is the parent of modern crime. That indeed is the reason why our criminals are, as a class, so absolutely uninteresting from any psychological point of view. They are not marvellous Macbeths and terrible Vautrins.* They are merely what ordinary, respectable, commonplace people would be if they had not got enough to eat. When private property is abolished there will be no necessity for crime, no demand for it; it will cease to exist. Of course all crimes are not crimes against property, though such are the crimes that the English law, valuing what a man has more than what a man is, punishes with the harshest and most horrible severity, if we except the crime of murder, and regard death as worse than penal servitude,* a point on which our criminals, I believe, disagree. But though a crime may not be against property, it may spring from the misery and rage and depression produced by our wrong system of property-holding, and so, when that system is abolished, will disappear. When each member of the community has sufficient for his wants, and is not interfered with by his neighbour, it will not be an object of any interest to him to interfere with anyone else. Jealousy, which is an extraordinary source of crime in modern life, is an emotion closely bound up with our conceptions of property, and under Socialism and Individualism will die out. It is remarkable that in communistic tribes jealousy is entirely unknown.

Now as the State is not to govern, it may be asked what the State is to do. The State is to be a voluntary association that will organize labour, and be the manufacturer and distributor of necessary commodities. The State is to make what is useful. The individual is to make what is beautiful.* And as I have mentioned the word labour, I cannot help saying that a great deal of nonsense is being written and talked nowadays about the dignity of manual labour. There is nothing necessarily dignified about manual labour at all, and most of it is absolutely degrading. It is mentally and morally injurious to man to do anything in which he does not find pleasure, and many forms of labour are quite pleasureless activities, and should be regarded as such. To sweep a slushy crossing for eight hours on a day when the east wind is blowing is a disgusting occupation. To sweep it with mental, moral, or physical dignity seems to me to be impossible. To sweep it with joy would be appalling. Man is made for something better than disturbing dirt. All work of that kind should be done by a machine.

And I have no doubt that it will be so. Up to the present, man has been, to a certain extent, the slave of machinery, and there is something tragic in the fact that as soon as man had invented a machine to do his work he began to starve. This, however, is, of course, the result of our property system and our system of competition. One man owns a machine which does the work of five hundred men. Five hundred men are, in consequence, thrown out of employment, and having no work to do, become hungry and take to thieving. The one man secures the produce of the machine and keeps it, and has five hundred times as much as he should have, and probably, which is of much more importance, a great deal more than he really wants. Were that machine the property of all, every one would benefit by it. It would be an immense advantage to the community. All unintellectual labour, all monotonous, dull labour, all labour that deals with dreadful things, and involves unpleasant conditions, must be done by machinery. Machinery must work for us in coal mines, and do all sanitary services, and be the stoker of steamers, and clean the streets, and run messages on wet days, and do anything that is tedious or distressing. At present machinery competes against man. Under proper conditions machinery will serve man.* There is no doubt at all that this is the future of machinery, and just as trees grow while the country gentleman is asleep, so while Humanity will be amusing itself, or enjoying cultivated leisure—which, and not labour, is the aim of man—or making beautiful things, or reading beautiful things, or simply contemplating the world with admiration and delight, machinery will be doing all the necessary and unpleasant work. The fact is, that civilization requires slaves. The Greeks were quite right there.* Unless there are slaves to do the ugly, horrible, uninteresting work, culture and contemplation become almost impossible. Human slavery is wrong, insecure, and demoralizing. On mechanical slavery, on the slavery of the machine, the future of the world depends. And when scientific men are no longer called upon to go down to a depressing East End and distribute bad cocoa and worse blankets to starving people, they will have delightful leisure in which to devise wonderful and marvellous things for their own joy and the joy of everyone else. There will be great storages of force for every city, and for every house if required, and this force man will convert into heat, light, or motion, according to his needs. Is this Utopian? A map of the world that does not include Utopia* is not worth even glancing at, for it leaves out the one country at which Humanity is always landing. And when Humanity lands there, it looks out, and, seeing a better country, sets sail. Progress is the realization of Utopias.

Now, I have said that the community by means of organization of machinery will supply the useful things, and that the beautiful things will be made by the individual. This is not merely necessary, but it is the only possible way by which we can get either the one or the other. An individual who has to make things for the use of others, and with reference to their wants and their wishes, does not work with interest, and consequently cannot put into his work what is best in him. Upon the other hand, whenever a community or a powerful section of a community, or a government of any kind, attempts to dictate to the artist what he is to do, Art either entirely vanishes, or becomes stereotyped, or degenerates into a low and ignoble form of craft. A work of art is the unique result of a unique temperament. Its beauty comes from the fact that the author is what he is. It has nothing to do with the fact that other people want what they want.* Indeed, the moment that an artist takes notice of what other people want, and tries to supply the demand, he ceases to be an artist, and becomes a dull or an amusing craftsman, an honest or a dishonest tradesman. He has no further claim to be considered as an artist. Art is the most intense mode of Individualism that the world has known.* I am inclined to say that it is the only real mode of Individualism that the world has known. Crime, which, under certain conditions, may seem to have created Individualism, must take cognizance of other people and interfere with them. It belongs to the sphere of action. But alone, without any reference to his neighbours, without any interference, the artist can fashion a beautiful thing; and if he does not do it solely for his own pleasure, he is not an artist at all.

And it is to be noted that it is the fact that Art is this intense form of Individualism that makes the public try to exercise over it an authority that is as immoral as it is ridiculous, and as corrupting as it is contemptible. It is not quite their fault. The public has always, and in every age, been badly brought up. They are continually asking Art to be popular, to please their want of taste, to flatter their absurd vanity, to tell them what they have been told before, to show them what they ought to be tired of seeing, to amuse them when they feel heavy after eating too much, and to distract their thoughts when they are wearied of their own stupidity. Now Art should never try to be popular. The public should try to make itself artistic.* There is a very wide difference. If a man of science were told that the results of his experiments, and the conclusions that he arrived at, should be of such a character that they would not upset the received popular notions on the subject, or disturb popular prejudice, or hurt the sensibilities of people who knew nothing about science; if a philosopher were told that he had a perfect right to speculate in the highest spheres of thought, provided that he arrived at the same conclusions as were held by those who had never thought in any sphere at all—well, nowadays the man of science and the philosopher would be considerably amused. Yet it is really a very few years since both philosophy and science were subjected to brutal popular control, to authority in fact—the authority of either the general ignorance of the community, or the terror and greed for power of an ecclesiastical or governmental class. Of course, we have to a very great extent got rid of any attempt on the part of the community, or the Church, or the Government, to interfere with the individualism of speculative thought, but the attempt to interfere with the individualism of imaginative art still lingers. In fact, it does more than linger: it is aggressive, offensive, and brutalizing.

In England, the arts that have escaped best are the arts in which the public take no interest.* Poetry is an instance of what I mean. We have been able to have fine poetry in England because the public do not read it, and consequently do not influence it. The public like to insult poets because they are individual, but once they have insulted them, they leave them alone. In the case of the novel and the drama, arts in which the public does take an interest, the result of the exercise of popular authority has been absolutely ridiculous. No country produces such badly written fiction, such tedious, common work in the novel-form, such silly, vulgar plays as in England. It must necessarily be so. The popular standard is of such a character that no artist can get to it. It is at once too easy and too difficult to be a popular novelist. It is too easy, because the requirements of the public as far as plot, style, psychology, treatment of life, and treatment of literature are concerned are within the reach of the very meanest capacity and the most uncultivated mind. It is too difficult, because to meet such requirements the artist would have to do violence to his temperament, would have to write not for the artistic joy of writing, but for the amusement of half-educated people, and so would have to suppress his individualism, forget his culture, annihilate his style, and surrender everything that is valuable in him. In the case of the drama, things are a little better: the theatre-going public like the obvious, it is true, but they do not like the tedious; and burlesque and farcical comedy,* the two most popular forms, are distinct forms of art. Delightful work may be produced under burlesque and farcical conditions, and in work of this kind the artist in England is allowed very great freedom. It is when one comes to the higher forms of the drama that the result of popular control is seen. The one thing that the public dislike is novelty. Any attempt to extend the subject-matter of art is extremely distasteful to the public; and yet the vitality and progress of art depend in a large measure on the continual extension of subject-matter. The public dislike novelty because they are afraid of it. It represents to them a mode of Individualism, an assertion on the part of the artist that he selects his own subject, and treats it as he chooses. The public are quite right in their attitude. Art is Individualism, and Individualism is a disturbing and disintegrating force. Therein lies its immense value. For what it seeks to disturb is monotony of type, slavery of custom, tyranny of habit, and the reduction of man to the level of a machine.* In Art, the public accept what has been, because they cannot alter it, not because they appreciate it. They swallow their classics whole, and never taste them. They endure them as the inevitable, and as they cannot mar them, they mouth about them. Strangely enough, or not strangely, according to one's own views, this acceptance of the classics does a great deal of harm. The uncritical admiration of the Bible and Shakespeare in England is an instance of what I mean. With regard to the Bible, considerations of ecclesiastical authority enter into the matter, so that I need not dwell upon the point.

But in the case of Shakespeare it is quite obvious that the public really see neither the beauties nor the defects of his plays. If they saw the beauties, they would not object to the development of the drama; and if they saw the defects, they would not object to the development of the drama either. The fact is, the public make use of the classics of a country as a means of checking the progress of Art.* They degrade the classics into authorities. They use them as bludgeons for preventing the free expression of Beauty in new forms. They are always asking a writer why he does not write like somebody else, or a painter why he does not paint like somebody else, quite oblivious of the fact that if either of them did anything of the kind he would cease to be an artist. A fresh mode of Beauty is absolutely distasteful to them, and whenever it appears they get so angry and bewildered that they always use two stupid expressions—one is that the work of art is grossly unintelligible; the other, that the work of art is grossly immoral. What they mean by these words seems to me to be this. When they say a work is grossly unintelligible, they mean that the artist has said or made a beautiful thing that is new; when they describe a work as grossly immoral, they mean that the artist has said or made a beautiful thing that is true. The former expression has reference to style; the latter to subject-matter. But they probably use the words very vaguely, as an ordinary mob will use ready-made paving-stones. There is not a single real poet or prose-writer of this century, for instance, on whom the British public have not solemnly conferred diplomas of immorality,* and these diplomas practically take the place, with us, of what in France is the formal recognition of an Academy of Letters,* and fortunately make the establishment of such an institution quite unnecessary in England. Of course the public are very reckless in their use of the word. That they should have called Wordsworth an immoral poet, was only to be expected. Wordsworth was a poet. But that they should have called Charles Kingsley* an immoral novelist is extraordinary. Kingsley's prose was not of a very fine quality. Still, there is the word, and they use it as best they can. An artist is, of course, not disturbed by it. The true artist is a man who believes absolutely in himself, because he is absolutely himself.* But I can fancy that if an artist produced a work of art in England that immediately on its appearance was recognized by the public, through their medium, which is the public press, as a work that was quite intelligible and highly moral, he would begin to seriously question whether in its creation he had really been himself at all, and consequently whether the work was not quite unworthy of him, and either of a thoroughly second-rate order, or of no artistic value whatsoever.

Perhaps, however, I have wronged the public in limiting them to such words as 'immoral', 'unintelligible', 'exotic', and 'unhealthy'. There is one other word that they use. That word is 'morbid'. They do not use it often. The meaning of the word is so simple that they are afraid of using it.* Still, they use it sometimes, and, now and then, one comes across it in popular newspapers. It is, of course, a ridiculous word to apply to a work of art. For what is morbidity but a mood of emotion or a mode of thought that one cannot express? The public are all morbid, because the public can never find expression for anything. The artist is never morbid. He expresses everything.* He stands outside his subject, and through its medium produces incomparable and artistic effects. To call an artist morbid because he deals with morbidity as his subject-matter is as silly as if one called Shakespeare mad because he wrote *King Lear*.

On the whole, an artist in England gains something by being attacked. His individuality is intensified. He becomes more completely himself. Of course the attacks are very gross, very impertinent, and very contemptible.* But then no artist expects grace from the vulgar mind, or style from the suburban intellect. Vulgarity and stupidity are two very vivid facts in modern life. One regrets them, naturally. But there they are. They are subjects for study, like everything else. And it is only fair to state, with regard to modern journalists, that they always apologize to one in private for what they have written against one in public.

Within the last few years two other adjectives, it may be mentioned, have been added to the very limited vocabulary of art-abuse that is at the disposal of the public. One is the word 'unhealthy', and the other is the word 'exotic'. The latter merely expresses the rage of the momentary mushroom against the immortal, entrancing, and exquisitely lovely orchid. It is a tribute, but a tribute of no importance. The word 'unhealthy', however, admits of analysis. It is a rather interesting word. In fact, it is so interesting that the people who use it do not know what it means.

What does it mean? What is a healthy, or an unhealthy work of art? All terms that one applies to a work of art, provided that one applies them rationally, have reference to either its style or its subject, or to both together. From the point of view of style, a healthy work of art is one whose style recognizes the beauty of the material it employs, be that material one of words or of bronze, of colour or of ivory, and uses that beauty as a factor in producing the aesthetic effect. From the point of view of subject, a healthy work of art is one the choice of whose subject is conditioned by the temperament of the artist, and comes directly out of it. In fine, a healthy work of art is one that has both perfection and personality. Of course, form and substance cannot be separated in a work of art; they are always one. But for purposes of analysis, and setting the wholeness of aesthetic impression aside for a moment, we can intellectually so separate them. An unhealthy work of art, on the other hand, is a work whose style is obvious, old-fashioned, and common, and whose subject is deliberately chosen, not because the artist has any pleasure in it, but because he thinks that the public will pay him for it. In fact, the popular novel that the public calls healthy is always a thoroughly unhealthy production; and what the public call an unhealthy novel is always a beautiful and healthy work of art.*

I need hardly say that I am not, for a single moment, complaining that the public and the public press misuse these words. I do not see how, with their lack of comprehension of what Art is, they could possibly use them in the proper sense. I am merely pointing out the misuse; and as for the origin of the misuse and the meaning that lies behind it all, the explanation is very simple. It comes from the barbarous conception of authority. It comes from the natural inability of a community corrupted by authority to understand or appreciate Individualism. In a word, it comes from that monstrous and ignorant thing that is called Public Opinion, which bad and well-meaning as it is when it tries to control action, is infamous and of evil meaning when it tries to control Thought or Art.

Indeed, there is much more to be said in favour of the physical force of the public than there is in favour of the public's opinion. The former may be fine. The latter must be foolish. It is often said that force is no argument. That, however, entirely depends on what one wants to prove. Many of the most important problems of the last few centuries, such as the continuance of personal government in England, or of feudalism in France, have been solved entirely by means of physical force. The very violence of a revolution may make the public grand and splendid for a moment. It was a fatal day when the public discovered that the pen is mightier than the paving-stone,* and can be made as offensive as the brickbat. They at once sought for the journalist, found him, developed him, and made him their industrious and well-paid servant. It is greatly to be regretted, for both their sakes. Behind the barricade there may be much that is noble and heroic. But what is there behind the leading-article but prejudice, stupidity, cant, and twaddle? And when these four are joined together they make a terrible force, and constitute the new authority.

In old days men had the rack. Now they have the press.* That is an improvement certainly. But still it is very bad, and wrong, and demoralizing. Somebody—was it Burke?—called journalism the fourth estate.* That was true at the time, no doubt. But at the present moment it really is the only estate. It has eaten up the other three. The Lords Temporal say nothing, the Lords Spiritual* have nothing to say, and the House of Commons has nothing to say and says it. We are dominated by Journalism. In America the President reigns for four years, and Journalism governs for ever and ever. Fortunately in America journalism has carried its authority to the grossest and most brutal extreme.* As a natural consequence it has begun to create a spirit of revolt. People are amused by it, or disgusted by it, according to their temperaments. But it is no longer the real force it was. It is not seriously treated. In England, Journalism, not, except in a few well-known instances, having been carried to such excesses of brutality, is still a great factor, a really remarkable power. The tyranny that it proposes to exercise over people's private lives seems to me to be quite extraordinary. The fact is, that the public have an insatiable curiosity to know everything, except what is worth knowing.* Journalism, conscious of this, and having tradesmanlike habits, supplies their demands. In centuries before ours the public nailed the ears of journalists to the pump. That was quite hideous. In this century journalists have nailed their own ears to the keyhole. That is much worse. And what aggravates the mischief is that the journalists who are most to blame are not the amusing journalists who write for what are called Society papers. The harm is done by the serious, thoughtful, earnest journalists, who solemnly, as they are doing at present, will drag before the eyes of the public some incident in the private life of a great statesman, of a man who is a leader of political thought as he is a creator of political force, and invite the public to discuss the incident, to exercise authority in the matter, to give their views, and not merely to give their views, but to carry them into action, to dictate to the man upon all other points, to dictate to his party, to dictate to his country, in fact to make themselves ridiculous, offensive, and harmful.* The private lives of men and women should not be told to the public. The public have nothing to do with them at all. In France they manage these things better. There they do not allow the details of the trials that take place in the divorce courts to be published for the amusement or criticism of the public. All that the public are allowed to know is that the divorce has taken place and was granted on petition of one or other or both of the married parties concerned. In France, in fact, they limit the journalist, and allow the artist almost perfect freedom. Here we allow absolute freedom to the journalist, and entirely limit the artist.* English public opinion, that is to say, tries to constrain and impede and warp the man who makes things that are beautiful in effect, and compels the journalist to retail things that are ugly, or disgusting, or revolting in fact, so that we have the most serious journalists in the world, and the most indecent newspapers. It is no exaggeration to talk of compulsion. There are possibly some journalists who take a real pleasure in publishing horrible things, or who, being poor, look to scandals as forming a sort of permanent basis for an income. But there are other journalists, I feel certain, men of education and cultivation, who really dislike publishing these things, who know that it is wrong to do so, and only do it because the unhealthy conditions under which their occupation is carried on oblige them to supply the public with what the public wants, and to compete with other journalists in making that supply as full and satisfying to the gross popular appetite as possible. It is a very degrading position for any body of educated men to be placed in, and I have no doubt that most of them feel it acutely.

However, let us leave what is really a very sordid side of the subject, and return to the question of popular control in the matter of Art, by which I mean Public Opinion dictating to the artist the form which he is to use, the mode in which he is to use it, and the materials with which he is to work. I have pointed out that the arts which have escaped best in England are the arts in which the public have not been interested. They are, however, interested in the drama, and as a certain advance has been made in the drama within the last ten or fifteen years, it is important to point out that this advance is entirely due to a few individual artists refusing to accept the popular want of taste as their standard, and refusing to regard Art as a mere matter of demand and supply. With his marvellous and vivid personality, with a style that has really a true colour-element in it, with his extraordinary power, not over mere mimicry but over imaginative and intellectual creation, Mr. Irving,* had his sole object been to give the public what they wanted, could have produced the commonest plays in the commonest manner, and made as much success and money as a man could possibly desire. But his object was not that. His object was to realize his own perfection as an artist, under certain conditions, and in certain forms of Art. At first he appealed to the few: now he has educated the many. He has created in the public both taste and temperament. The public appreciate his artistic success immensely. I often wonder, however, whether the public understand that that success is entirely due to the fact that he did not accept their standard, but realized his own. With their standard the Lyceum would have been a sort of second-rate booth, as some of the popular theatres in London are at present. Whether they understand it or not the fact however remains, that taste and temperament have, to a certain extent, been created in the public, and that the public is capable of developing these qualities. The problem then is, why do not the public become more civilized? They have the capacity. What stops them?

The thing that stops them, it must be said again, is their desire to exercise authority over the artist and over works of art. To certain theatres, such as the Lyceum and the Haymarket,* the public seem to come in a proper mood. In both of these theatres there have been individual artists, who have succeeded in creating in their audiences—and every theatre in London has its own audience—the temperament to which Art appeals. And what is that temperament? It is the temperament of receptivity. That is all.

If a man approaches a work of art with any desire to exercise authority over it and the artist, he approaches it in such a spirit that he cannot receive any artistic impression from it at all. The work of art is to dominate the spectator: the spectator is not to dominate the work of art.* The spectator is to be receptive. He is to be the violin on which the master is to play. And the more completely he can suppress his own silly views, his own foolish prejudices, his own absurd ideas of what Art should be, or should not be, the more likely he is to understand and appreciate the work of art in question. This is, of course, quite obvious in the case of the vulgar theatre-going public of English men and women. But it is equally true of what are called educated people. For an educated person's ideas of Art are drawn naturally from what Art has been, whereas the new work of art is beautiful by being what Art has never been; and to measure it by the standard of the past is to measure it by a standard on the rejection of which its real perfection depends. A temperament capable of receiving, through an imaginative medium, and under imaginative conditions, new and beautiful impressions, is the only temperament that can appreciate a work of art. And true as this is in the case of the appreciation of sculpture and painting, it is still more true of the appreciation of such arts as the drama. For a picture and a statue are not at war with Time. They take no count of its succession. In one moment their unity may be apprehended. In the case of literature it is different. Time must be traversed before the unity of effect is realized. And so, in the drama, there may occur in the first act of the play something whose real artistic value may not be evident to the spectator till the third or fourth act is reached. Is the silly fellow to get angry and call out, and disturb the play, and annoy the artists? No. The honest man is to sit quietly, and know the delightful emotions of wonder, curiosity, and suspense. He is not to go to the play to lose a vulgar temper. He is to go to the play to realize an artistic temperament. He is to go to the play to gain an artistic temperament. He is not the arbiter of the work of art. He is one who is admitted to contemplate the work of art, and, if the work be fine, to forget in its contemplation all the egotism that mars him—the egotism of his ignorance, or the egotism of his information. This point about the drama is hardly, I think, sufficiently recognized. I can quite understand that were *Macbeth* produced for the first time before a modern London audience, many of the people present would strongly and vigorously object to the introduction of the witches in the first act, with their grotesque phrases and their ridiculous words. But when the play is over one realizes that the laughter of the witches in *Macbeth* is as terrible as the laughter of madness in *Lear,* more terrible than the laughter of Iago in the tragedy of the Moor. No spectator of art needs a more perfect mood of receptivity than the spectator of a play. The moment he seeks to exercise authority he becomes the avowed enemy of Art and of himself. Art does not mind. It is he who suffers.

With the novel it is the same thing. Popular authority and the recognition of popular authority are fatal. Thackeray's *Esmond* is a beautiful work of art because he wrote it to please himself. In his other novels, in *Pendennis,* in *Philip,* in *Vanity Fair* even, at times, he is too conscious of the public, and spoils his work by appealing directly to the sympathies of the public, or by directly mocking at them. A true artist takes no notice whatever of the public. The public are to him non-existent.* He has no poppied or honeyed cakes through which to give the monster sleep or sustenance. He leaves that to the popular novelist. One incomparable novelist we have now in England, Mr. George Meredith.* There are better artists in France, but France has no one whose view of life is so large, so varied, so imaginatively true. There are tellers of stories in Russia who have a more vivid sense of what pain in fiction may be. But to him belongs philosophy in fiction. His people not merely live, but they live in thought. One can see them from myriad points of view. They are suggestive. There is soul in them and around them. They are interpretative and symbolic. And he who made them, those wonderful quickly-moving figures, made them for his own pleasure, and has never asked the public what they wanted, has never cared to know what they wanted, has never allowed the public to dictate to him or influence him in any way, but has gone on intensifying his own personality, and producing his own individual work. At first none came to him. That did not matter. Then the few came to him. That did not change him. The many have come now. He is still the same. He is an incomparable novelist.

With the decorative arts it is not different. The public clung with really pathetic tenacity to what I believe were the direct traditions of the Great Exhibition* of international vulgarity, traditions that were so appalling that the houses in which people lived were only fit for blind people to live in. Beautiful things began to be made, beautiful colours came from the dyer's hand, beautiful patterns from the artist's brain, and the use of beautiful things and their value and importance were set forth. The public were really very indignant. They lost their temper. They said silly things. No one minded. No one was a whit the worse. No one accepted the authority of public opinion. And now it is almost impossible to enter any modern house without seeing some recognition of good taste, some recognition of the value of lovely surroundings,* some sign of appreciation of beauty. In fact, people's houses are, as a rule, quite charming nowadays. People have been to a very great extent civilized. It is only fair to state, however, that the extraordinary success of the revolution in house-decoration and furniture and the like has not really been due to the majority of the public developing a very fine taste in such matters. It has been chiefly due to the fact that the craftsmen of things so appreciated the pleasure of making what was beautiful, and woke to such a vivid consciousness of the hideousness and vulgarity of what the public had previously wanted, that they simply starved the public out. It would be quite impossible at the present moment to furnish a room as rooms were furnished a few years ago, without going for everything to an auction of second-hand furniture from some third-rate lodging-house. The things are no longer made. However they may object to it, people must nowadays have something charming in their surroundings. Fortunately for them, their assumption of authority in these art-matters came to entire grief.

It is evident, then, that all authority in such things is bad. People sometimes inquire what form of government is most suitable for an artist to live under. To this question there is only one answer. The form of government that is most suitable to the artist is no government at all.* Authority over him and his art is ridiculous. It has been stated that under despotisms artists have produced lovely work. This is not quite so. Artists have visited despots, not as subjects to be tyrannized over, but as wandering wonder-makers, as fascinating vagrant personalities, to be entertained and charmed and suffered to be at peace, and allowed to create. There is this to be said in favour of the despot, that he, being an individual, may have culture, while the mob, being a monster, has none. One who is an Emperor and King may stoop down to pick up a brush for a painter, but when the democracy stoops down it is merely to throw mud. And yet the democracy have not so far to stoop as the emperor. In fact, when they want to throw mud they have not to stoop at all. But there is no necessity to separate the monarch from the mob; all authority is equally bad.

There are three kinds of despots. There is the despot who tyrannizes over the body. There is the despot who tyrannizes over the soul. There is the despot who tyrannizes over soul and body alike. The first is called the Prince. The second is called the Pope. The third is called the People.* The Prince may be cultivated. Many Princes have been. Yet in the Prince there is danger. One thinks of Dante at the bitter feast in Verona,* of Tasso* in Ferrara's madman's cell. It is better for the artist not to live with Princes. The Pope may be cultivated. Many Popes have been; the bad Popes have been. The bad Popes loved Beauty, almost as passionately, nay, with as much passion as the good Popes hated Thought. To the wickedness of the Papacy humanity owes much. The goodness of the Papacy owes a terrible debt to humanity.* Yet, though the Vatican has kept the rhetoric of its thunders, and lost the rod of its lightning, it is better for the artist not to live with Popes. It was a Pope who said of Cellini to a conclave of Cardinals that common laws and common authority were not made for men such as he;* but it was a Pope who thrust Cellini into prison, and kept him there till he sickened with rage, and created unreal visions for himself, and saw the gilded sun enter his room, and grew so enamoured of it that he sought to escape, and crept out from tower to tower, and falling through dizzy air at dawn, maimed himself, and was by a vine-dresser covered with vine leaves, and carried in a cart to one who, loving beautiful things, had care of him. There is danger in Popes. And as for the People, what of them and their authority? Perhaps of them and their authority one has spoken enough. Their authority is a thing blind, deaf, hideous, grotesque, tragic, amusing, serious and obscene.* It is impossible for the artist to live with the People. All despots bribe. The people bribe and brutalize. Who told them to exercise authority? They were made to live, to listen, and to love. Some one has done them a great wrong. They have marred themselves by imitation of their inferiors. They have taken the sceptre of the Prince. How should they use it? They have taken the triple tiara of the Pope. How should they carry its burden? They are as a clown whose heart is broken. They are as a priest whose soul is not yet born. Let all who love Beauty pity them. Though they themselves love not Beauty, yet let them pity themselves. Who taught them the trick of tyranny?

There are many other things that one might point out. One might point out how the Renaissance was great, because it sought to solve no social problem, and busied itself not about such things, but suffered the individual to develop freely, beautifully, and naturally, and so had great and individual artists, and great and individual men. One might point out how Louis XIV,* by creating the modern state, destroyed the individualism of the artist, and made things monstrous in their monotony of repetition, and contemptible in their conformity to rule, and destroyed throughout all France all those fine freedoms of expression that had made tradition new in beauty, and new modes one with antique form. But the past is of no importance. The present is of no importance. It is with the future that we have to deal. For the past is what man should not have been. The present is what man ought not to be. The future is what artists are.

It will, of course, be said that such a scheme as is set forth here is quite unpractical, and goes against human nature. This is perfectly true. It is unpractical, and it goes against human nature. This is why it is worth carrying out, and that is why one proposes it. For what is a practical scheme? A practical scheme is either a scheme that is already in existence, or a scheme that could be carried out under existing conditions.* But it is exactly the existing conditions that one objects to; and any scheme that could accept these conditions is wrong and foolish. The conditions will be done away with, and human nature will change. The only thing that one really knows about human nature is that it changes. Change is the one quality we can predicate of it. The systems that fail are those that rely on the permanency of human nature, and not on its growth and development. The error of Louis XIV was that he thought human nature would always be the same. The result of his error was the

French Revolution. It was an admirable result. All the results of the mistakes of governments are quite admirable.

It is to be noted also that Individualism does not come to man with any sickly cant about duty, which merely means doing what other people want because they want it; or any hideous cant about self-sacrifice, which is merely a survival of savage mutilation. In fact, it does not come to man with any claims upon him at all. It comes naturally and inevitably out of man.* It is the point to which all development tends. It is the differentiation to which all organisms grow. It is the perfection that is inherent in every mode of life, and towards which every mode of life quickens. And so Individualism exercises no compulsion over man. On the contrary it says to man that he should suffer no compulsion to be exercised over him. It does not try to force people to be good. It knows that people are good when they are let alone. Man will develop Individualism out of himself. Man is now so developing Individualism. To ask whether Individualism is practical is like asking whether Evolution is practical. Evolution is the law of life, and there is no evolution except towards Individualism.* Where this tendency is not expressed, it is a case of artificially arrested growth, or of disease, or of death.

Individualism will also be unselfish and unaffected. It has been pointed out that one of the results of the extraordinary tyranny of authority is that words are absolutely distorted from their proper and simple meaning, and are used to express the obverse of their right signification. What is true about Art is true about Life. A man is called affected, nowadays, if he dresses as he likes to dress. But in doing that he is acting in a perfectly natural manner. Affectation, in such matters, consists in dressing according to the views of one's neighbour, whose views, as they are the views of the majority, will probably be extremely stupid. Or a man is called selfish if he lives in the manner that seems to him most suitable for the full realization of his own personality; if, in fact, the primary aim of his life is self-development.* But this is the way in which everyone should live. Selfishness is not living as one wishes to live, it is asking others to live as one wishes to live.* And unselfishness is letting other people's lives alone, not interfering with them. Selfishness always aims at creating around it an absolute uniformity of type. Unselfishness recognizes infinite variety of type as a delightful thing, accepts it, acquiesces in it, enjoys it. It is not selfish to think for oneself. A man who does not think for himself does not think at all. It is grossly selfish to require of one's neighbour that he should think in the same way, and hold the same opinions. Why should he? If he can think, he will probably think differently. If he cannot think, it is monstrous to require thought of any kind from him. A red rose is not selfish because it wants to be a red rose. It would be horribly selfish if it wanted all the other flowers in the garden to be both red and roses. Under Individualism people will be quite natural and absolutely unselfish, and will know the meanings of the words, and realize them in their free, beautiful lives. Nor will men be egotistic as they are now. For the egotist is he who makes claims upon others, and the Individualist will not desire to do that. It will not give him pleasure. When man has realized Individualism, he will also realize sympathy and exercise it freely and spontaneously. Up to the present man has hardly cultivated sympathy at all. He has merely sympathy with pain, and sympathy with pain is not the highest form of sympathy. All sympathy is fine, but sympathy with suffering is the least fine mode.* It is tainted with egotism. It is apt to become morbid. There is in it a certain element of terror for our own safety. We become afraid that we ourselves might be as the leper or as the blind, and that no man would have care of us. It is curiously limiting, too. One should sympathize with the entirety of life, not with life's sores and maladies merely, but with life's joy and beauty and energy and health and freedom. The wider sympathy is, of course, the more difficult. It requires more unselfishness. Anybody can sympathize with the sufferings of a friend, but it requires a very fine nature—it requires, in fact, the nature of a true Individualist—to sympathize with a friend's success. In the modern stress of competition and struggle for place, such sympathy is naturally rare, and is also very much stifled by the immoral ideal of uniformity of type and conformity to rule which is so prevalent everywhere, and is perhaps most obnoxious in England.

Sympathy with pain there will, of course, always be. It is one of the first instincts of man. The animals which are individual, the higher animals that is to say, share it with us. But it must be remembered that while sympathy with joy intensifies the sum of joy in the world, sympathy with pain does not really diminish the amount of pain. It may make man better able to endure evil, but the evil remains. Sympathy with consumption does not cure consumption; that is what Science does. And when Socialism has solved the problem of poverty, and Science solved the problem of disease, the area of the sentimentalists will be lessened, and the sympathy of man will be large, healthy, and spontaneous. Man will have joy in the contemplation of the joyous lives of others.

For it is through joy that the Individualism of the future will develop itself. Christ made no attempt to reconstruct society, and consequently the Individualism that he preached to man could be realized only through pain or in solitude.* The ideals that we owe to Christ are the ideals of the man who abandons society entirely, or of the man who resists society absolutely. But man is naturally social. Even the Thebaid became peopled at last. And though the cenobite* realizes his personality, it is often an impoverished personality that he so realizes. Upon the other hand, the terrible truth that pain is a mode through which man may realize himself exercised a wonderful fascination over the world. Shallow speakers and shallow thinkers in pulpits and on platforms often talk about the world's worship of pleasure, and whine against it. But it is rarely in the world's history that its ideal has been one of joy and beauty. The worship of pain has far more often dominated the world. Mediaevalism, with its saints and martyrs, its love of self–torture, its wild passion for wounding itself, its gashing with knives, and its whipping with rods—Mediaevalism is real Christianity, and the mediaeval Christ is the real Christ. When the Renaissance dawned upon the world, and brought with it the new ideals of the beauty of life and the joy of living, men could not understand Christ. Even Art shows us that. The painters of the Renaissance drew Christ as a little boy playing with another boy in a palace or a garden, or lying back in his mother's arms, smiling at her, or at a flower, or at a bright bird; or as a noble stately figure moving nobly through the world; or as a wonderful figure rising in a sort of ecstasy from death to life. Even when they drew him crucified they drew him as a beautiful God on whom evil men had inflicted suffering. But he did not preoccupy them much. What delighted them was to paint the men and women whom they admired, and to show the loveliness of this lovely earth. They painted many religious pictures—in fact, they painted far too many, and the monotony of type and motive is wearisome, and was bad for art. It was the result of the authority of the public in art–matters, and is to be deplored. But their soul was not in the subject. Raphael was a great artist when he painted his portrait of the Pope. When he painted his Madonnas and infant Christs, he is not a great artist at all. Christ had no message for the Renaissance, which was wonderful because it brought an ideal at variance with his, and to find the presentation of the real Christ we must go to mediaeval art. There he is one maimed and marred; one who is not comely to look on, because Beauty is a joy; one who is not in fair raiment, because that may be a joy also: he is a beggar who has a marvellous soul; he is a leper whose soul is divine; he needs neither property nor health; he is a God realizing his perfection through pain.

The evolution of man is slow. The injustice of men is great. It was necessary that pain should be put forward as a mode of self-realization. Even now, in some places in the world, the message of Christ is necessary. No one who lived in modern Russia could possibly realize his perfection except by pain.* A few Russian artists have realized themselves in Art, in a fiction that is mediaeval in character, because its dominant note is the realization of men through suffering. But for those who are not artists, and to whom there is no mode of life but the actual life of fact, pain is the only door to perfection. A Russian who lives happily under the present system of government in Russia must either believe that man has no soul, or that, if he has, it is not worth developing. A Nihilist who rejects all authority, because he knows authority to be evil, and who welcomes all pain, because through that he realizes his personality, is a real Christian. To him the Christian ideal is a true thing.

And yet, Christ did not revolt against authority. He accepted the imperial authority of the Roman Empire and paid tribute. He endured the ecclesiastical authority of the Jewish Church, and would not repel its violence by any violence of his own. He had, as I said before, no scheme for the reconstruction of society. But the modern world has schemes. It proposes to do away with poverty and the suffering that it entails. It desires to get rid of pain, and the suffering that pain entails. It trusts to Socialism and to Science as its methods. What it aims at is an Individualism expressing itself through joy. This Individualism will be larger, fuller, lovelier than any Individualism has ever been. Pain is not the ultimate mode of perfection. It is merely provisional and a protest. It has reference to wrong, unhealthy, unjust surroundings. When the wrong, and the disease, and the injustice are removed, it will have no further place. It will have done its work. It was a great work, but it is almost over. Its sphere lessens every day.

Nor will man miss it. For what man has sought for is, indeed, neither pain nor pleasure, but simply Life.* Man has sought to live intensely, fully, perfectly. When he can do so without exercising restraint on others, or suffering it ever, and his activities are all pleasurable to him, he will be saner, healthier, more civilized, more himself. Pleasure is Nature's test, her sign of approval. When man is happy, he is in harmony with himself* and his environment. The new Individualism, for whose service Socialism, whether it wills it or not, is working, will be perfect harmony. It will be what the Greeks sought for, but could not, except in Thought, realize completely, because they had slaves, and fed them;* it will be what the Renaissance sought for, but could not realize completely except in Art, because they had slaves, and starved them. It will be complete, and through it each man will attain to his perfection. The new Individualism is the new Hellenism.*

De Profundis[*]

To Lord Alfred Douglas

[*January–March 1897*]   *HM Prison, Reading*

Dear Bosie, After long and fruitless waiting I have determined to write to you myself, as much for your sake as
for mine, as I would not like to think that I had passed
through two long years of imprisonment without ever
having received a single line from you, or any news or
message even, except such as gave me pain.

Our ill-fated and most lamentable friendship has ended
in ruin and public infamy for me, yet the memory of our
ancient affection is often with me, and the thought that
loathing, bitterness and contempt should for ever take
that place in my heart once held by love is very sad to
me: and you yourself will, I think, feel in your heart that
to write to me as I lie in the loneliness of prison-life is
better than to publish my letters without my permission
or to dedicate poems to me unasked, though the world
will know nothing of whatever words of grief or passion,
of remorse or indifference you may choose to send as your
answer or your appeal.

I have no doubt that in this letter in which I have to write
of your life and of mine, of the past and of the future, of
sweet things changed to bitterness and of bitter things that
may be turned into joy, there will be much that will wound
your vanity to the quick. If it prove so, read the letter
over and over again till it kills your vanity. If you find
in it something of which you feel that you are unjustly
accused, remember that one should be thankful that there
is any fault of which one can be unjustly accused. If there
be in it one single passage that brings tears to your eyes,
weep as we weep in prison where the day no less than the
night is set apart for tears. It is the only thing that can save
you. If you go complaining to your mother, as you did with
reference to the scorn of you I displayed in my letter to

Robbie, so that she may flatter and soothe you back into self-complacency or conceit, you will be completely lost. If you find one false excuse for yourself, you will soon find a hundred, and be just what you were before. Do you still say, as you said to Robbie in your answer, that I '*attribute unworthy motives*' to you? Ah! you had no motives in life. You had appetites merely. A motive is an intellectual aim. That you were '*very young*' when our friendship began? Your defect was not that you knew so little about life, but that you knew so much. The morning dawn of boyhood with its delicate bloom, its clear pure light, its joy of innocence and expectation you had left far behind. With very swift and running feet you had passed from Romance to Realism. The gutter and the things that live in it had begun to fascinate you. That was the origin of the trouble in which you sought my aid, and I, so unwisely according to the wisdom of this world, out of pity and kindness gave it to you. You must read this letter right through, though each word may become to you as the fire or knife of the surgeon that makes the delicate flesh burn or bleed. Remember that the fool in the eyes of the gods and the fool in the eyes of man are very different. One who is entirely ignorant of the modes of Art in its revolution or the moods of thought in its progress, of the pomp of the Latin line or the richer music of the vowelled Greek, of Tuscan sculpture or Elizabethan song may yet be full of the very sweetest wisdom. The real fool, such as the gods mock or mar, is he who does not know himself. I was such a one too long. You have been such a one too long. Be so no more. Do not be afraid. The supreme vice is shallowness.* Everything that is realised is right.* Remember also that whatever is misery to you to read, is still greater misery to me to set down. To you the Unseen Powers have been very good. They have permitted you to see the strange and tragic shapes of Life as one sees shadows in a crystal. The head of Medusa that turns living men to stone, you have been allowed to look at in a mirror merely. You yourself have walked free among the flowers. From me the beautiful world of colour and motion has been taken away.

I will begin by telling you that I blame myself terribly. As I sit here in this dark cell in convict clothes, a disgraced and ruined man, I blame myself. In the perturbed and fitful nights of anguish, in the long monotonous days of pain, it is myself I blame. I blame myself for allowing an unintellectual friendship, a friendship whose primary aim was not the creation and contemplation of beautiful things, to entirely dominate my life. From the very first there was too wide a gap between us. You had been idle at your school, worse than idle at your university. You did not realise that an artist, and especially such an artist as I am,* one, that is to say, the quality of whose work depends on the intensification of personality, requires for the development of his art the companionship of ideas, and intellectual atmosphere, quiet, peace, and solitude. You admired my work when it was finished: you enjoyed the brilliant successes of my first nights, and the brilliant banquets that followed them: you were proud, and quite naturally so, of being the intimate friend of an artist so distinguished: but you could not understand the conditions requisite for the production of artistic work. I am not speaking in phrases of rhetorical exaggeration but in terms of absolute truth to actual fact when I remind you that during the whole time we were together I never wrote one single line. Whether at Torquay, Goring, London, Florence or elsewhere, my life, as long as you were by my side, was entirely sterile and uncreative. And with but few intervals you were, I regret to say, by my side always.

I remember, for instance, in September '93, to select merely one instance out of many, taking a set of chambers, purely in order to work undisturbed, as I had broken my contract with John Hare for whom I had promised to write a play, and who was pressing me on the subject. During the first week you kept away. We had, not unnaturally indeed, differed on the question of the artistic value of your translation of *Salome*,* so you contented yourself with sending me foolish letters on the subject. In that week I wrote and completed in every detail, as it was ultimately performed, the first act of *An Ideal Husband*.

The second week you returned and my work practically had to be given up. I arrived at St James's Place every morning at 11.30, in order to have the opportunity of thinking and writing without the interruptions inseparable from my own household, quiet and peaceful as that household was. But the attempt was vain. At twelve o'clock you drove up, and stayed smoking cigarettes and chattering till 1.30, when I had to take you out to luncheon at the Café Royal or the Berkeley. Luncheon with its *liqueurs* lasted usually till 3.30. For an hour you retired to White's. At tea-time you appeared again, and stayed till it was time to dress for dinner. You dined with me either at the Savoy or at Tite Street.* We did not separate as a rule till after midnight, as supper at Willis's had to wind up the entrancing day. That was my life for those three months, every single day, except during the four days when you went abroad. I then, of course, had to go over to Calais to fetch you back. For one of my nature and temperament it was a position at once grotesque and tragic.

You surely must realise that now? You must see now that your incapacity of being alone: your nature so exigent in its persistent claim on the attention and time of others: your lack of any power of sustained intellectual concentration: the unfortunate accident—for I like to think it was no more—that you had not yet been able to acquire the 'Oxford temper' in intellectual matters, never, I mean, been one who could play gracefully with ideas but had arrived at violence of opinion merely—that all these things, combined with the fact that your desires and interests were in Life not in Art, were as destructive to your own progress in culture as they were to my work as an artist? When I compare my friendship with you to my friendship with such still younger men as John Gray* and Pierre Louÿs* I feel ashamed. My real life, my higher life was with them and such as they.

Of the appalling results of my friendship with you I don't speak at present. I am thinking merely of its quality while it lasted. It was intellectually degrading to me. You had the rudiments of an artistic temperament in its germ. But I met you either too late or too soon, I don't know which.

When you were away I was all right. The moment, in the early December of the year to which I have been alluding, I had succeeded in inducing your mother to send you out of England, I collected again the torn and ravelled web of my imagination, got my life back into my own hands, and not merely finished the three remaining acts of *An Ideal Husband*, but conceived and had almost completed two other plays of a completely different type, the *Florentine Tragedy* and *La Sainte Courtisane*,* when suddenly, unbidden, unwelcome, and under circumstances fatal to my happiness you returned. The two works left then imperfect I was unable to take up again. The mood that created them I could never recover. You now, having yourself published a volume of verse, will be able to recognise the truth of everything I have said here. Whether you can or not it remains as a hideous truth in the very heart of our friendship. While you were with me you were the absolute ruin of my Art, and in allowing you to stand persistently between Art and myself I give to myself shame and blame in the fullest degree. You couldn't know, you couldn't understand, you couldn't appreciate. I had no right to expect it of you at all. Your interests were merely in your meals and moods. Your desires were simply for amusements, for ordinary or less ordinary pleasures. They were what your temperament needed, or thought it needed for the moment. I should have forbidden you my house and my chambers except when I specially invited you. I blame myself without reserve for my weakness. It was merely weakness. One half-hour with Art was always more to me than a cycle with you. Nothing really at any period of my life was ever of the smallest importance to me compared with Art. But in the case of an artist, weakness is nothing less than a crime, when it is a weakness that paralyses the imagination.

I blame myself again for having allowed you to bring me to utter and discreditable financial ruin. I remember one morning in the early October of '92 sitting in the yellowing woods at Bracknell* with your mother. At that time I knew very little of your real nature. I had stayed from a Saturday to Monday with you at Oxford. You had stayed with me at Cromer* for ten days and played golf. The conversation turned on you, and your mother began to speak to me about your character. She told me of your two chief faults, your vanity, and your being, as she termed it, '*all wrong about money*'. I have a distinct recollection of how I laughed. I had no idea that the first would bring me to prison, and the second to bankruptcy. I thought vanity a sort of graceful flower for a young man to wear; as for extravagance—for I thought she meant no more than extravagance—the virtues of prudence and thrift were not in my own nature or my own race. But before our friendship was one month older I began to see what your mother really meant. Your insistence on a life of reckless profusion: your incessant demands for money: your claim that all your pleasures should be paid for by me whether I was with you or not: brought me after some time into serious monetary difficulties, and what made the extravagances to me at any rate so monotonously uninteresting, as your persistent grasp on my life grew stronger and stronger, was that the money was really spent on little more than the pleasures of eating, drinking, and the like. Now and then it is a joy to have one's table red with wine and roses, but you outstripped all taste and temperance. You demanded without grace and received without thanks. You grew to think that you had a sort of right to live at my expense and in a profuse luxury to which you had never been accustomed, and which for that reason made your appetites all the more keen, and at the end if you lost money gambling in some Algiers Casino you simply telegraphed next morning to me in London to lodge the amount of your losses to your account at your bank, and gave the matter no further thought of any kind.

When I tell you that between the autumn of 1892 and the date of my imprisonment I spent with you and on you more than £5000 in actual money, irrespective of the bills I incurred, you will have some idea of the sort of life on which you insisted. Do you think I exaggerate? My ordinary expenses with you for an ordinary day in London—for luncheon, dinner, supper, amusements, hansoms and the rest of it—ranged from £12 to £20, and the week's expenses were naturally in proportion and ranged from £80 to £130. For our three months at Goring my expenses (rent of course included) were £1340. Step by step with the Bankruptcy Receiver I had to go over every item of my life. It was horrible. '*Plain living and high thinking*'* was, of course, an ideal you could not at that time have appreciated, but such extravagance was a disgrace to both of us. One of the most delightful dinners I remember ever having had is one Robbie and I had together in a little Soho café, which cost about as many shillings as my dinners to you used to cost pounds. Out of my dinner with Robbie came the first and best of all my dialogues.* Idea, title, treatment, mode, everything was struck out at a 3 franc 50c. *table-d'hôte*. Out of the reckless dinners with you nothing remains but the memory that too much was eaten and too much was drunk. And my yielding to your demands was bad for you. You know that now. It made you grasping often: at times not a little unscrupulous: ungracious always. There was on far too many occasions too little joy or privilege in being your host. You forgot—I will not say the formal courtesy of thanks, for formal courtesies will strain a close friendship—but simply the grace of sweet companionship, the charm of pleasant conversation, that τερπνὸν κακόν * as the Greeks called it, and all those gentle humanities that make life lovely, and are an accompaniment to life as music might be, keeping things in tune and filling with melody the harsh or silent places. And though it may seem strange to you that one in the terrible position in which I am situated should find a difference between one disgrace and another, still I frankly admit that the folly of throwing away all this money on you, and letting you squander my fortune to your own hurt as well as to mine, gives to me and in my eyes a note of common profligacy to my Bankruptcy that makes me doubly ashamed of it. I was made for other things.

But most of all I blame myself for the entire ethical degradation I allowed you to bring on me. The basis of character is will-power, and my will-power became

absolutely subject to yours. It sounds a grotesque thing
to say, but it is none the less true. Those incessant scenes
that seemed to be almost physically necessary to you, and
in which your mind and body grew distorted and you
became a thing as terrible to look at as to listen to: that
dreadful mania you inherit from your father, the mania for
writing revolting and loathsome letters: your entire lack of
any control over your emotions as displayed in your long
resentful moods of sullen silence, no less than in the sudden
fits of almost epileptic rage: all these things in reference to
which one of my letters to you, left by you lying about at
the Savoy or some other hotel and so produced in Court by
your father's Counsel, contained an entreaty not devoid of
pathos, had you at that time been able to recognise pathos
either in its elements or its expression:*—these, I say, were
the origin and causes of my fatal yielding to you in your
daily increasing demands. You wore one out. It was the
triumph of the smaller over the bigger nature. It was the
case of that tyranny of the weak over the strong which
somewhere in one of my plays I describe as being 'the only
tyranny that lasts'.*

   And it was inevitable. In every relation of life with others
one has to find some *moyen de vivre*. In your case, one had
either to give up to you or to give you up. There was no
other alternative. Through deep if misplaced affection for
you: through great pity for your defects of temper and
temperament: through my own proverbial good-nature
and Celtic laziness: through an artistic aversion to coarse
scenes and ugly words: through that incapacity to bear
resentment of any kind which at that time characterised
me: through my dislike of seeing life made bitter and
uncomely by what to me, with my eyes really fixed on other
things, seemed to be mere trifles too petty for more than
a moment's thought or interest—through these reasons,
simple as they may sound, I gave up to you always. As
a natural result, your claims, your efforts at domination,
your exactions grew more and more unreasonable. Your
meanest motive, your lowest appetite, your most common
passion, became to you laws by which the lives of others

were to be guided always, and to which, if necessary, they were to be without scruple sacrificed. Knowing that by making a scene you could always have your way, it was but natural that you should proceed, almost unconsciously I have no doubt, to every excess of vulgar violence. At the end you did not know to what goal you were hurrying, or with what aim in view. Having made your own of my genius, my will-power, and my fortune, you required, in the blindness of an inexhaustible greed, my entire existence. You took it. At the one supremely and tragically critical moment of all my life, just before my lamentable step of beginning my absurd action, on the one side there was your father attacking me with hideous cards left at my club, on the other side there was you attacking me with no less loathsome letters. The letter I received from you on the morning of the day I let you take me down to the Police Court to apply for the ridiculous warrant for your father's arrest was one of the worst you ever wrote, and for the most shameful reason. Between you both I lost my head. My judgment forsook me. Terror took its place. I saw no possible escape, I may say frankly, from either of you. Blindly I staggered as an ox into the shambles.* I had made a gigantic psychological error. I had always thought that my giving up to you in small things meant nothing: that when a great moment arrived I could reassert my will-power in its natural superiority. It was not so. At the great moment my will-power completely failed me. In life there is really no small or great thing. All things are of equal value and of equal size. My habit—due to indifference chiefly at first—of giving up to you in everything had become insensibly a real part of my nature. Without my knowing it, it had stereotyped my temperament to one permanent and fatal mood. That is why, in the subtle epilogue to the first edition of his essays, Pater says that 'Failure is to form habits'.* When he said it the dull Oxford people thought the phrase a mere wilful inversion of the somewhat wearisome text of Aristotelian *Ethics*,* but there is a wonderful, a terrible truth hidden in it. I had allowed you to sap my strength of character, and to me the formation of a habit had proved to be not Failure merely but Ruin. Ethically you had been even still more destructive to me than you had been artistically.

The warrant once granted, your will of course directed everything. At a time when I should have been in London taking wise counsel, and calmly considering the hideous trap in which I had allowed myself to be caught—the booby-trap as your father calls it to the present day—you insisted on my taking you to Monte Carlo, of all revolting places on God's earth, that all day, and all night as well, you might gamble as long as the Casino remained open. As for me—baccarat having no charms for me—I was left alone outside to myself. You refused to discuss even for five minutes the position to which you and your father had brought me. My business was merely to pay your hotel expenses and your losses. The slightest allusion to the ordeal awaiting me was regarded as a bore. A new brand of champagne that was recommended to us had more interest for you.

On our return to London those of my friends who really desired my welfare implored me to retire abroad, and not to face an impossible trial. You imputed mean motives to them for giving such advice, and cowardice to me for listening to it. You forced me to stay to brazen it out, if possible, in the box by absurd and silly perjuries. At the end, I was of course arrested and your father became the hero of the hour: more indeed than the hero of the hour merely: your family now ranks, strangely enough, with the Immortals: for with that grotesqueness of effect that is as it were a Gothic element in history, and makes Clio* the least serious of all the Muses, your father will always live among the kind pure-minded parents of Sunday-school literature, your place is with the Infant Samuel,* and in the lowest mire of Malebolge* I sit between Gilles de Retz and the Marquis de Sade.*

Of course I should have got rid of you. I should have shaken you out of my life as a man shakes from his raiment a thing that has stung him. In the most wonderful of all his plays* Aeschylus tells us of the great Lord who brings up in his house the lion-cub, the λέοντος ἳνιν , and loves it because it comes bright-eyed to his call and fawns on him for its food: φαιδρωπὸς ποτὶ χεῖρα, σαίνων τε γαστρὸς ἀνάγκαις. And the thing grows up and shows the nature of its race, ἦθος τὸ πρόσθε τοκήων, and destroys the lord and his house and all that he possesses. I feel that I was such a one as he. But my fault was, not that I did not part from you, but that I parted from you far too often. As far as I can make out I ended my friendship with you every three months regularly, and each time that I did so you managed by means of entreaties, telegrams, letters, the interposition of your friends, the interposition of mine, and the like to induce me to allow you back. When at the end of March '93 you left my house at Torquay I had determined never to speak to you again, or to allow you under any circumstances to be with me, so revolting had been the scene you had made the night before your departure. You wrote and telegraphed from Bristol to beg me to forgive you and meet you. Your tutor, who had stayed behind, told me that he thought that at times you were quite irresponsible for what you said and did, and that most, if not all, of the men at Magdalen were of the same opinion. I consented to meet you, and of course I forgave you. On the way up to town you begged me to take you to the Savoy. That was indeed a visit fatal to me.

Three months later, in June, we are at Goring. Some of your Oxford friends come to stay from a Saturday to Monday. The morning of the day they went away you made a scene so dreadful, so distressing that I told you that we must part. I remember quite well, as we stood on the level croquet-ground with the pretty lawn all round us, pointing out to you that we were spoiling each other's lives, that you were absolutely ruining mine and that I evidently was not making you really happy, and that an irrevocable parting, a complete separation was the one wise philosophic thing to do. You went sullenly after luncheon, leaving one of your most offensive letters behind with the butler to be handed to me after your departure. Before three days had elapsed you were telegraphing from London to beg to be forgiven and allowed to return. I had taken the place to please you. I had engaged your own servants at your request. I was always terribly sorry for the hideous temper to which you were really a prey. I was fond of you. So I let you come back and forgave you. Three months later still, in September, new scenes occurred, the occasion of them being my pointing out the schoolboy faults of your attempted translation of *Salome**. You must by this time be a fair enough French scholar to know that the translation was as unworthy of you, as an ordinary Oxonian, as it was of the work it sought to render. You did not of course know it then, and in one of the violent letters you wrote to me on the point you said that you were under '*no intellectual obligation of any kind*' to me. I remember that when I read that statement, I felt that it was the one really true thing you had written to me in the whole course of our friendship. I saw that a less cultivated nature would really have suited you much better. I am not saying this in bitterness at all, but simply as a fact of companionship. Ultimately the bond of all companionship, whether in marriage or in friendship, is conversation, and conversation must have a common basis, and between two people of widely different culture the only common basis possible is the lowest level. The trivial in thought and action is charming. I had made it the keystone of a very brilliant philosophy expressed in plays and paradoxes. But the froth and the folly of our life grew often very wearisome to me: it was only in the mire that we met: and fascinating, terribly fascinating though the one topic round which your talk invariably centred was, still at the end it became quite monotonous to me. I was often bored to death by it, and accepted it as I accepted your passion for going to music-halls, or your mania for absurd extravagances in eating and drinking, or any other of your to me less attractive characteristics, as a thing, that is to say, that one simply had to put up with, a part of the high price one paid for knowing you. When after leaving Goring I went to Dinard for a fortnight you were extremely angry with me for not taking you with me, and, before my departure there, made some very unpleasant scenes on the subject at the Albemarle Hotel, and sent me some equally unpleasant telegrams to a country house I was staying at for a few days. I told you, I remember, that I thought it was your duty to be with your own people for a little, as you had passed the whole season away from them. But in reality, to be perfectly frank with you, I could not under any circumstances have let you be with me. We had been together for nearly twelve weeks. I required rest and freedom from the terrible strain of your companionship. It was necessary for me to be a little by myself. It was intellectually necessary. And so I confess I saw in your letter, from which I have quoted, a very good opportunity for ending the fatal friendship that had sprung up between us, and ending it without bitterness, as I had indeed tried to do on that bright June morning at Goring, three months before. It was however represented to me—I am bound to say candidly by one of my own friends* to whom you had gone in your difficulty—that you would be much hurt, perhaps almost humiliated at having your work sent back to you like a schoolboy's exercise; that I was expecting far too much intellectually from you; and that, no matter what you wrote or did, you were absolutely and entirely devoted to me. I did not want to be the first to check or discourage you in your beginnings in literature: I knew quite well that no translation, unless one done by a poet, could render the colour and cadence of my work in any adequate measure: devotion seemed to me, seems to me still, a wonderful thing, not to be lightly thrown away: so I took the translation and you back. Exactly three months later, after a series of scenes culminating in one more than usually revolting, when you came one Monday evening to my rooms accompanied by two of your friends, I found myself actually flying abroad next morning to escape from you, giving my family* some absurd reason for my sudden departure, and leaving a false address with my servant for fear you might follow me by the next train. And I remember that afternoon, as I was in the railway-carriage whirling up to Paris, thinking what an impossible, terrible, utterly wrong state my life had got into, when I, a man of world-wide reputation, was actually forced to run away from England, in order to try and get rid of a friendship that was entirely destructive of everything fine in me either from the intellectual or ethical point of view: the person from whom I was flying being no terrible creature sprung from sewer or mire into modern life with whom I had entangled my days, but you yourself, a young man of my own social rank and position, who had been at my own college at Oxford, and was an incessant guest at my house. The usual telegrams of entreaty and remorse followed: I disregarded them. Finally you threatened that unless I consented to meet you, you would under no circumstances consent to proceed to Egypt. I had myself, with your knowledge and concurrence, begged your mother to send you to Egypt away from England, as you were wrecking your life in London. I knew that if you did not go it would be a terrible disappointment to her, and for her sake I did meet you, and under the influence of great emotion, which even you cannot have forgotten, I forgave the past; though I said nothing at all about the future.

On my return to London next day I remember sitting in my room and sadly and seriously trying to make up my mind whether or not you really were what you seemed to me to be, so full of terrible defects, so utterly ruinous both to yourself and to others, so fatal a one to know even or to be with. For a whole week I thought about it, and wondered if after all I was not unjust and mistaken in my estimate of you. At the end of the week a letter from your mother is handed in. It expressed to the full every feeling I myself had about you. In it she spoke of your blind exaggerated vanity which made you despise your home, and treat your elder brother—that *candidissima anima*— 'as a Philistine':* of your temper which made her afraid to speak to you about your life, the life she felt, she knew, you were leading: about your conduct in money matters, so distressing to her in more ways than one: of the degeneration and change that had taken place in you. She saw, of course, that heredity had burdened you with a terrible legacy, and frankly admitted it, admitted it with terror: he is 'the one of my children who has inherited the fatal Douglas temperament', she wrote of you. At the end she stated that she felt bound to declare that your friendship with me, in her opinion, had so intensified your vanity that it had become the source of all your faults, and earnestly begged me not to meet you abroad. I wrote to her at once, in reply, and told her that I agreed entirely with every word she had said. I added much more. I went as far as I could possibly go. I told her that the origin of our friendship was you in your undergraduate days at Oxford coming to beg me to help you in very serious trouble of a very particular character. I told her that your life had been continually in the same manner troubled. The reason of your going to Belgium you had placed to the fault of your companion in that journey, and your mother had reproached me with having introduced you to him. I replaced the fault on the right shoulders, on yours. I assured her at the end that I had not the smallest intention of meeting you abroad, and begged her to try to keep you there, either as an honorary *attaché*,* if that were possible, or to learn modern languages, if it were not; or for any reason she chose, at least during two or three years, and for your sake as well as for mine.

In the meantime you are writing to me by every post from Egypt. I took not the smallest notice of any of your communications. I read them, and tore them up. I had quite settled to have no more to do with you. My mind was made up, and I gladly devoted myself to the Art whose progress I had allowed you to interrupt. At the end of three months, your mother, with that unfortunate weakness of will that characterises her, and that in the tragedy of my life has been an element no less fatal than your father's violence, actually writes to me herself——I have no doubt, of course, at your instigation——tells me that you are extremely anxious to hear from me, and in order that I should have no excuse for not communicating with you, sends me your address in Athens, which, of course, I knew perfectly well. I confess I was absolutely astounded at her letter. I could not understand how, after what she had written to me in December, and what I in answer had written to her, she could in any way try to repair or to renew my unfortunate friendship with you. I acknowledged her letter, of course, and again urged her to try and get you connected with some Embassy abroad,* so as to prevent your returning to England, but I did not write to you, or take any more notice of your telegrams then I did before your mother had written to me. Finally you actually telegraphed to my wife begging her to use her influence with me to get me to write to you. Our friendship had always been a source of distress to her: not merely because she had never liked you personally, but because she saw how your continual companionship altered me, and not for the better: still, just as she had always been most gracious and hospitable to you, so she could not bear the idea of my being in any way unkind—for so it seemed to her—to any of my friends. She thought, knew indeed, that it was a thing alien to my character. At her request I did communicate with you. I remember the wording of my telegram quite well. I said that time healed every wound but that for many months to come I would neither write to you nor see you. You started without delay for Paris, sending me passionate telegrams on the road to beg me to see you once, at any rate. I declined. You arrived in Paris late on a Saturday night, and found a brief letter from me waiting for you at your hotel stating that I would not see you. Next morning I received in Tite Street a telegram of some ten or eleven pages in length from you. You stated in it that no matter what you had done to me you could not believe that I would absolutely decline to see you: you reminded me that for the sake of seeing me even for one hour you had travelled six days and nights across Europe without stopping once on the way: you made what I must admit was a most pathetic appeal, and ended with what seemed to me a threat of suicide, and one not thinly veiled. You had yourself often told me how many of your race there had been who had stained their hands in their own blood; your uncle certainly, your grandfather possibly; many others in the mad, bad line from which you come.* Pity, my old affection for you, regard for your mother to whom your death under such dreadful circumstances would have been a blow almost too great for her to bear, the horror of the idea that so young a life, and one that amidst all its ugly faults had still promise of beauty in it, should come to so revolting an end, mere humanity itself—all these, if excuses be necessary, must serve as my excuse for consenting to accord you one last interview. When I arrived in Paris, your tears, breaking out again and again all through the evening, and falling over your cheeks like rain as we sat, at dinner first at Voisin's, at supper at Paillard's afterwards: the unfeigned joy you evinced at seeing me, holding my hand whenever you could, as though you were a gentle and penitent child: your contrition, so simple and sincere, at the moment: made me consent to renew our friendship. Two days after we had returned to London, your father saw you having luncheon with me at the Café Royal, joined my table, drank of my wine, and that afternoon, through a letter addressed to you, began his first attack on me.*

It may be strange, but I had once again, I will not say the chance, but the duty of separating from you forced on me. I need hardly remind you that I refer to your conduct to me at Brighton from October 10th to 13th, 1894. Three years ago is a long time for you to go back. But we who live in prison, and in whose lives there is no event but sorrow, have to measure time by throbs of pain, and the record of bitter moments. We have nothing else to think of. Suffering—curious as it may sound to you—is the means by which we exist, because it is the only means by which we become conscious of existing; and the remembrance of suffering in the past is necessary to us as the warrant, the evidence, of our continued identity. Between myself and the memory of joy lies a gulf no less deep than that between myself and joy in its actuality. Had our life together been as the world fancied it to be, one simply of pleasure, profligacy and laughter, I would not be able to recall a single passage in it. It is because it was full of moments and days tragic, bitter, sinister in their warnings, dull or dreadful in their monotonous scenes and unseemly violences, that I can see or hear each separate incident in its detail, can indeed see or hear little else. So much in this place do men live by pain that my friendship with you, in the way through which I am forced to remember it, appears to me always as a prelude consonant with those varying modes of anguish which each day I have to realise; nay more, to necessitate them even; as though my life, whatever it had seemed to myself and to others, had all the while been a real Symphony of Sorrow, passing through its rhythmically-linked movements to its certain resolution, with that inevitableness that in Art characterises the treatment of every great theme.

I spoke of your conduct to me on three successive days, three years ago, did I not? I was trying to finish my last play at Worthing by myself. The two visits you had paid to me had ended. You suddenly appeared a third time bringing with you a companion whom you actually proposed should stay in my house. I (you must admit now quite properly) absolutely declined. I entertained you, of course; I had no option in the matter: but elsewhere, and not in my own home. The next day, a Monday, your companion returned to the duties of his profession, and you stayed with me. Bored with Worthing, and still more, I have no doubt, with my fruitless efforts to concentrate my attention on my play, the only thing that really interested me at the moment, you insist on being taken to the Grand Hotel at Brighton. The night we arrive you fall ill with that dreadful low fever that is foolishly called the influenza, your second, if not third attack. I need not remind you how I waited on you, and tended you, not merely with every luxury of fruit, flowers, presents, books, and the like that money can procure, but with that affection, tenderness and love that, whatever you may think, is not to be procured for money. Except for an hour's walk in the morning, an hour's drive in the afternoon, I never left the hotel. I got special grapes from London for you, as you did not care for those the hotel supplied, invented things to please you, remained either with you or in the room next to yours, sat with you every evening to quiet or amuse you.

After four or five days you recover, and I take lodgings in order to try and finish my play. You, of course, accompany me. The morning after the day on which we were installed I feel extremely ill. You have to go to London on business, but promise to return in the afternoon. In London you meet a friend, and do not come back to Brighton till late the next day, by which time I am in a terrible fever, and the doctor finds I have caught the influenza from you. Nothing could have been more uncomfortable for anyone ill than the lodgings turn out to be. My sitting-room is on the first floor, my bedroom on the third. There is no manservant to wait on one, not even anyone to send out on a message, or to get what the doctor orders. But you are there. I feel no alarm. The next two days you leave me entirely alone without care, without attendance, without anything. It was not a question of grapes, flowers, and charming gifts: it was a question of mere necessaries: I could not even get the milk the doctor had ordered for me: lemonade was pronounced an impossibility: and when I begged you to procure me a book at the bookseller's, or if they had not got whatever I had fixed on to choose something else, you never even take the trouble to go there. And when I was left all day without anything to read in consequence, you calmly tell me that you bought me the book and that they promised to sent it down, a statement which I found out by chance afterwards to have been entirely untrue from beginning to end. All the while you are of course living at my expense, driving about, dining at the Grand Hotel, and indeed only appearing in my room for money. On the Saturday night, you having left me completely unattended and alone since the morning, I asked you to come back after dinner, and sit with me for a little. With irritable voice and ungracious manner you promise to do so. I wait till eleven o'clock and you never appear. I then left a note for you in your room just reminding you of the promise you had made me, and how you had kept it. At three in the morning, unable to sleep, and tortured with thirst, I made my way, in the dark and cold, down to the sitting-room in the hopes of finding some water there. I found *you*. You fell on me with every hideous word an intemperate mood, an undisciplined and untutored nature could suggest. By the terrible alchemy of egotism you converted your remorse into rage. You accused me of selfishness in expecting you to be with me when I was ill; of standing between you and your amusements; of trying to deprive you of your pleasures. You told me, and I know it was quite true, that you had come back at midnight simply in order to change your dress-clothes, and go out again to where you hoped new pleasures were waiting for you, but that by leaving for you a letter in which I had reminded you that you had neglected me the whole day and the whole evening, I had really robbed you of your desire for more enjoyments, and diminished your actual capacity for fresh delights. I went back upstairs in disgust, and remained sleepless till dawn, nor till long after dawn was I able to get anything to quench the thirst of the fever that was on me. At eleven o'clock you came into my room. In the previous scene I could not help observing that by my letter I had, at any rate, checked you in a night of more than usual excess. In the morning you were quite yourself. I waited naturally to hear what excuses you had to make, and in what way you were going to ask for the forgiveness that you knew in your heart was invariably waiting for you, no matter what you did; your absolute trust that I would always forgive you being the thing in you that I always really liked the best, perhaps the best thing in you to like. So far from doing that, you began to repeat the same scene with renewed emphasis and more violent assertion. I told you at length to leave the room: you pretended to do so, but when I lifted up my head from the pillow in which I had buried it, you were still there, and with brutality of laughter and hysteria of rage you moved suddenly towards me. A sense of horror came over me, for what exact reason I could not make out; but I got out of my bed at once, and bare-footed and just as I was, made my way down the two flights of stairs to the sitting-room, which I did not leave till the owner of the lodgings—whom I had rung for—had assured me that you had left my bedroom, and promised to remain within call, in case of necessity. After an interval of an hour, during which time the doctor had come and found me, of course, in a state of absolute nervous prostration, as well as in a worse condition of fever than I had been at the outset, you returned silently, for money: took what you could find on the dressing-table and mantelpiece, and left the house with your luggage. Need I tell you what I thought of you during the two wretched lonely days of illness that followed? Is it necessary for me to state that I saw clearly that it would be a dishonour to myself to continue even an acquaintance with such a one as you had showed yourself to be? That I recognised that the ultimate moment had come, and recognised it as being really a great relief? And that I knew that for the future my Art and Life would be freer and better and more beautiful in every possible way? Ill as I was, I felt at ease. The fact that the separation was irrevocable gave me peace. By Tuesday the fever had left me, and for the first time I dined downstairs. Wednesday was my birthday.* Amongst the telegrams and communications on my table was a letter in your handwriting. I opened it with a sense of sadness over me. I knew that the time had gone by when a pretty phrase, an expression of affection, a word of sorrow would make me take you back. But I was entirely deceived. I had underrated you. The letter you sent to me on my birthday was an elaborate repetition of the two scenes, set cunningly and carefully down in black and white! You mocked me with common jests. Your one satisfaction in the whole affair was, you said, that you retired to the Grand Hotel, and entered your luncheon to my account before you left for town. You congratulated me on my prudence in leaving my sickbed, on my sudden flight downstairs. '*It was an ugly moment for you*,' you said, '*uglier than you imagine.*' Ah! I felt it but too well. What it had really meant I did not know: whether you had with you the pistol you had bought to try and frighten your father with, and that, thinking it to be unloaded, you had onced fired off in a public restaurant in my company: whether your hand was moving towards a common dinner-knife that by chance was lying on the table between us: whether, forgetting in your rage your low stature and inferior strength, you had thought of some specially personal insult, or attack even, as I lay ill there: I could not tell. I do not know to the present moment. All I know is that a feeling of utter horror had come over me, and that I had felt that unless I left the room at once, and got away, you would have done, or tried to do, something that would have been, even to you, a source of lifelong shame. Only once before in my life had I experienced such a feeling of horror at any human being. It was when in my library at Tite Street, waving his small hands in the air in epileptic fury, your father, with his bully, or his friend, between us, had stood uttering every foul word his foul mind could think of, and screaming the loathsome threats he afterwards with such cunning carried out. In the latter case he, of course, was the one who had to leave the room first. I drove him out. In your case I went. It was not the first time I had been obliged to save you from yourself.

You concluded your letter by saying: '*When you are not on your pedestal you are not interesting. The next time you are ill I will go away at once.*' Ah! what coarseness of fibre does that reveal! What an entire lack of imagination! How callous, how common had the temperament by that time become! '*When you are not on your pedestal you are not interesting. The next time you are ill I will go away at once.*' How often have those words come back to me in the wretched solitary cell of the various prisons I have been sent to. I have said them to myself over and over again, and seen in them, I hope unjustly, some of the secret of your strange silence. For you to write thus to me, when the very illness and fever from which I was suffering I had caught from tending you, was of course revolting in its coarseness and crudity; but for any human being in the whole world to write thus to another would be a sin for which there is no pardon, were there any sin for which there is none.

I confess that when I had finished your letter I felt almost polluted, as if by associating with one of such a nature I had soiled and shamed my life irretrievably. I had, it is true, done so, but I was not to learn how fully till just six months later on in life. I settled with myself to go back to London on the Friday, and see Sir George Lewis personally and request him to write to your father to state that I had determined never under any circumstances to allow you to enter my house, to sit at my board, to talk to me, walk with me, or anywhere and at any time to be my companion at all. This done I would have written to you just to inform you of the course of action I had adopted; the reasons you would inevitably have realised for yourself. I had everything arranged on Thursday night, when on Friday morning, as I was sitting at breakfast before starting, I happened to open the newspaper and saw in it a telegram stating that your elder brother, the real head of the family, the heir to the title, the pillar of the house, had been found dead in a ditch with his gun lying discharged beside him.* The horror of the circumstances of the tragedy, now known to have been an accident, but then stained with a darker suggestion; the pathos of the sudden death of one so loved by all who knew him, and almost on the eve, as it were, of his marriage; my idea of what your own sorrow would, or should be; my consciousness of the misery awaiting your mother at the loss of the one to whom she clung for comfort and joy in life, and who, as she told me once herself, had from the very day of his birth never caused her to shed a single tear; my consciousness of your own isolation, both your other brothers being out of Europe, and you consequently the only one to whom your mother and sister could look, not merely for companionship in their sorrow, but also for those dreary responsibilities of dreadful detail that Death always brings with it; the mere sense of the *lacrimae rerum*,* of the tears of which the world is made, and of the sadness of all human things—out of the confluence of these thoughts and emotions crowding into my brain came infinite pity for you and your family. My own griefs and bitterness against you I forgot. What you had been to me in my sickness, I could not be to you in your bereavement. I telegraphed at once to you my deepest sympathy, and in the letter that followed invited you to come to my house as soon as you were able. I felt that to abandon you at that particular moment, and formally through a solicitor, would have been too terrible for you.

On your return to town from the actual scene of the tragedy to which you had been summoned, you came at once to me very sweetly and very simply, in your suit of woe, and with your eyes dim with tears. You sought consolation and help, as a child might seek it. I opened to you my house, my home, my heart. I made your sorrow mine also, that you might have help in bearing it. Never, even by one word, did I allude to your conduct towards me, to the revolting scenes, and the revolting letter. Your grief, which was real, seemed to me to bring you nearer to me than you had ever been. The flowers you took from me to put on your brother's grave were to be a symbol not merely of the beauty of his life, but of the beauty that in all lives lies dormant and may be brought to light.

The gods are strange. It is not of our vices only they make instruments to scourge us.* They bring us to ruin through what in us is good, gentle, humane, loving. But for my pity and affection for you and yours, I would not now be weeping in this terrible place.

Of course I discern in all our relations, not Destiny merely, but Doom: Doom that walks always swiftly, because she goes to the shedding of blood. Through your father you come of a race, marriage with whom is horrible, friendship fatal, and that lays violent hands either on its own life or on the lives of others. In every little circumstance in which the ways of our lives met; in every point of great, or seemingly trivial import in which you came to me for pleasure or for help; in the small chances, the slight accidents that look, in their relation to life, to be no more than the dust that dances in a beam, or the leaf that flutters from a tree, Ruin followed, like the echo of a bitter cry, or the shadow that hunts with the beast of prey. Our friendship really begins with your begging me in a most pathetic and charming letter to assist you in a position appalling to anyone, doubly so to a young man at Oxford: I do so, and ultimately through your using my name as your friend with Sir George Lewis, I begin to lose his esteem and friendship, a friendship of fifteen years' standing. When I was deprived of his advice and help and regard I was deprived of the one great safeguard of my life.

You send me a very nice poem, of the undergraduate school of verse, for my approval: I reply by a letter of fantastic literary conceits:* I compare you to Hylas, or Hyacinth, Jonquil or Narcisse,* or someone whom the great god of Poetry favoured, and honoured with his love. The letter is like a passage from one of Shakespeare's sonnets, transposed to a minor key. It can only be understood by those who have read the *Symposium*￼* of Plato, or caught the spirit of a certain grave mood made beautiful for us in Greek marbles. It was, let me say frankly, the sort of letter I would, in a happy if wilful moment, have written to any graceful young man of either University* who had sent me a poem of his own making, certain that he would have sufficient wit or culture to interpret rightly its fantastic phrases. Look at the history of that letter! It passes from you into the hands of a loathsome companion: from him to a gang of blackmailers: copies of it are sent about London to my friends, and to the manager of the theatre where my work is being performed: every construction but the right one is put on it: Society is thrilled with the absurd rumours that I have had to pay a huge sum of money for having written an infamous letter to you: this forms the basis of your father's worst attack: I produce the original letter myself in Court to show what it really is: it is denounced by your father's Counsel as a revolting and insidious attempt to corrupt Innocence: ultimately it forms part of a criminal charge: the Crown takes it up: the Judge sums up on it with little learning and much morality: I go to prison for it at last. That is the result of writing you a charming letter.

While I am staying with you at Salisbury you are terribly alarmed at a threatening communication from a former companion of yours: you beg me to see the writer and help you: I do so: the result is Ruin to me. I am forced to take everything you have done on my own shoulders and answer for it. When, having failed to take your degree, you have to go down from Oxford, you telegraph to me in London to beg me to come to you. I do so at once: you ask me to take you to Goring, as you did not like, under the circumstances, to go home: at Goring you see a house that charms you: I take it for you: the result from every point of view is Ruin to me. One day you come to me and ask me, as a personal favour to you, to write something for an Oxford undergraduate magazine, about to be started by some friend of yours, whom I had never heard of in all my life, and knew nothing at all about. To please you—what did I not do always to please you?—I sent him a page of paradoxes destined originally for the *Saturday Review*.* A few months later I find myself standing in the dock of the Old Bailey on account of the character of the magazine. It forms part of the Crown charge against me. I am called upon to defend your friend's prose and your own verse. The former I cannot palliate; the latter I, loyal to the bitter extreme, to your youthful literature as to your youthful life, do very strongly defend, and will not hear of your being a writer of indecencies. But I go to prison, all the same, for your friend's undergraduate magazine, and 'the Love that dares not tell its name'.* At Christmas I give you a 'very pretty present', as you described it in your letter of thanks, on which I knew you had set your heart, worth some £40 or £50 at most. When the crash of my life comes, and I am ruined, the bailiff who seizes my library, and has it sold, does so to pay for the 'very pretty present'. It was for that the execution was put into my house. At the ultimate and terrible moment when I am taunted, and spurred-on by your taunts, to take an action against your father and have him arrested, the last straw to which I clutch in my wretched efforts to escape is the terrible expense. I tell the solicitor in your presence that I have no funds, that I cannot possibly afford the appalling costs, that I have no money at my disposal. What I said was, as you know, perfectly true. On that fatal Friday* instead of being in Humphreys's office weakly consenting to my own ruin, I would have been happy and free in France, away from you and your father, unconscious of his loathsome card, and indifferent to your letters, if I had been able to leave the Avondale Hotel. But the hotel people absolutely refused to allow me to go. You had been staying with me for ten days: indeed you had ultimately, to my great and, you will admit, rightful indignation, brought a companion of yours to stay with me also: my bill for the ten days was nearly

£140. The proprietor said he could not allow my luggage to be removed from the hotel till I had paid the account in full. That is what kept me in London. Had it not been for the hotel bill I would have gone to Paris on Thursday morning.

When I told the solicitor I had no money to face the gigantic expense, you interposed at once. You said that your own family would be only too delighted to pay all the necessary costs: that your father had been an incubus to them all: that they had often discussed the possibility of getting him put into a lunatic asylum so as to keep him out of the way: that he was a daily source of annoyance and distress to your mother and to everyone else: that if I would only come forward to have him shut up I would be regarded by the family as their champion and their benefactor: and that your mother's rich relations themselves would look on it as a real delight to be allowed to pay all costs and expenses that might be incurred in any such effort. The solicitor closed at once, and I was hurried to the Police Court. I had no excuse left for not going. I was forced into it. Of course your family don't pay the costs, and, when I am made bankrupt, it is by your father, and *for* the costs—the meagre balance of them—some £700.* At the present moment my wife, estranged from me over the important question of whether I should have £3 or £3.10 a week to live on, is preparing a divorce suit, for which, of course, entirely new evidence and an entirely new trial, to be followed perhaps by more serious proceedings, will be necessary. I, naturally, know nothing of the details. I merely know the name of the witness on whose evidence my wife's solicitors rely. It is your own Oxford servant, whom at your special request I took into my service for our summer at Goring.

But, indeed, I need not go on further with more instances of the strange Doom you seem to have brought on me in all things big or little. It makes me feel sometimes as if you yourself had been merely a puppet worked by some secret and unseen hand to bring terrible events to a terrible issue. But puppets themselves have passions. They will bring a new plot into what they are presenting, and twist the ordered issue of vicissitude to suit some whim or appetite of their own. To be entirely free, and at the same time entirely dominated by law, is the eternal paradox of human life that we realise at every moment; and this, I often think, is the only explanation possible of your nature, if indeed for the profound and terrible mysteries of a human soul there is any explanation at all, except one that makes the mystery more marvellous still.

Of course you had your illusions, lived in them indeed, and through their shifting mists and coloured veils saw all things changed. You thought, I remember quite well, that your devoting yourself to me, to the entire exclusion of your family and family life, was a proof of your wonderful appreciation of me, and your great affection. No doubt to you it seemed so. But recollect that with me was luxury, high living, unlimited pleasure, money without stint. Your family life bored you. The 'cold cheap wine of Salisbury', to use a phrase of your own making, was distasteful to you. On my side, and along with my intellectual attractions, were the fleshpots of Egypt.* When you could not find me to be with, the companions whom you chose as substitutes were not flattering.

You thought again that in sending a lawyer's letter to your father to say that, rather than sever your eternal friendship with me, you would give up the allowance of £250 a year which, with I believe deductions for your Oxford debts, he was then making you, you were realising the very chivalry of friendship, touching the noblest note of self-denial. But your surrender of your little allowance did not mean that you were ready to give up even one of your most superfluous luxuries, or most unnecessary extravagances. On the contrary. Your appetite for luxurious living was never so keen. My expenses for eight days in Paris for myself, you, and your Italian servant were nearly £150: Paillard alone absorbing £85. At the rate at which you wished to live, your entire income for a whole year, if you had taken your meals alone, and been especially economical in your selection of the cheaper form of pleasures, would hardly have lasted you for three weeks. The fact that in what was merely a pretence of bravado you had surrendered your allowance, such as it was, gave you at last a plausible reason for your claim to live at my expense, or what you thought a plausible reason: and on many occasions you seriously availed yourself of it, and gave the very fullest expression to it: and the continued drain, principally of course on me, but also to a certain extent, I know, on your mother, was never so distressing, because in my case at any rate, never so completely unaccompanied by the smallest word of thanks, or sense of limit.

You thought again that in attacking your own father with dreadful letters, abusive telegrams, and insulting postcards you were really fighting your mother's battles, coming forward as her champion, and avenging the no doubt terrible wrongs and sufferings of her married life. It was quite an illusion on your part; one of your worst indeed. The way for you to have avenged your mother's wrongs on your father, if you considered it part of a son's duty to do so, was by being a better son to your mother than you had been: by not making her afraid to speak to you on serious things: by not signing bills the payment of which devolved on her: by being gentler to her, and not bringing sorrow into her days. Your brother Francis* made great amends to her for what she had suffered, by his sweetness and goodness to her through the brief years of his flower-like life. You should have taken him as your model. You were wrong even in fancying that it would have been an absolute delight and joy to your mother if you *had* managed through me to get your father put into prison. I feel sure you were wrong. And if you want to know what a woman really feels when her husband, and the father of her children, is in prison dress, in a prison cell, write to my wife and ask her. She will tell you.

I also had my illusions. I thought life was going to be a brilliant comedy, and that you were to be one of many graceful figures in it. I found it to be a revolting and repellent tragedy, and that the sinister occasion of the great catastrophe, sinister in its concentration of aim and intensity of narrowed will-power, was yourself, stripped of that mask of joy and pleasure by which you, no less than I, had been deceived and led astray.

You can now understand—can you not?—a little of what I am suffering. Some paper, the *Pall Mall Gazette* I think, describing the dress-rehearsal of one of my plays, spoke of you as following me about like my shadow: the memory of our friendship is the shadow that walks with me here: that seems never to leave me: that wakes me up at night to tell me the same story over and over till its wearisome iteration makes all sleep abandon me till dawn: at dawn it begins again: it follows me into the prison-yard and makes me talk to myself as I tramp round: each detail that accompanied each dreadful moment I am forced to recall: there is nothing that happened in those ill-starred years that I cannot recreate in that chamber of the brain which is set apart for grief or for despair: every strained note of your voice, every twitch and gesture of your nervous hands, every bitter word, every poisonous phrase comes back to me: I remember the street or river down which we passed, the wall or woodland that surrounded us, at what figure on the dial stood the hands of the clock, which way went the wings of the wind, the shape and colour of the moon.

There is, I know, one answer to all that I have said to you, and that is that you loved me: that all through those two and a half years during which the Fates were weaving into one scarlet pattern the threads of our divided lives you really loved me. Yes: I know you did. No matter what your conduct to me was I always felt that at heart you really did love me. Though I saw quite clearly that my position in the world of Art, the interest my personality had always excited, my money, the luxury in which I lived, the thousand and one things that went to make up a life so charmingly, so wonderfully improbable as mine was, were, each and all of them, elements that fascinated you and made you cling to me: yet besides all this there was something more, some strange attraction for you: you loved me far better than you loved anybody else. But you, like myself, have had a terrible tragedy in your life, though one of an entirely opposite character to mine. Do you want to learn what it was? It was this. In you Hate was always stronger than Love. Your hatred of your father was of such stature that it entirely outstripped, o'erthrew, and overshadowed your love of me. There was no struggle between them at all, or but little; of such dimensions was your Hatred and of such monstrous growth. You did not realise that there is no room for both passions in the same soul. They cannot live together in that fair carven house. Love is fed by the imagination, by which we become wiser than we know, better than we feel, nobler than we are: by which we can see Life as a whole: by which, and by which alone, we can understand others in their real as in their ideal relations. Only what is fine, and finely conceived, can feed Love. But anything will feed Hate. There was not a glass of champagne you drank, not a rich dish you ate of in all those years, that did not feed your Hate and make it fat. So to gratify it, you gambled with my life, as you gambled with my money, carelessly, recklessly, indifferent to the consequence. If you lost, the loss would not, you fancied, be yours. If you won, yours, you knew, would be the exultation, and the advantages of victory.

Hate blinds people. You were not aware of that. Love can read the writing on the remotest star, but Hate so blinded you that you could see no further than the narrow, walled-in, and already lust-withered garden of your common desires. Your terrible lack of imagination, the one really fatal defect of your character, was entirely the result of the Hate that lived in you. Subtly, silently, and in secret, Hate gnawed at your nature, as the lichen bites at the root of some sallow plant, till you grew to see nothing but the most meagre interests and the most petty aims. That faculty in you which Love would have fostered, Hate poisoned and paralysed. When your father first began to attack me it was as your private friend, and in a private letter to you. As soon as I had read the letter, with its obscene threats and coarse violences, I saw at once that a terrible danger was looming on the horizon of my troubled days: I told you I would not be the catspaw between you both in your ancient hatred of each other: that I in London was naturally much bigger game for him than a Secretary for Foreign Affairs at Homburg:* that it would be unfair to me to place me even for a moment in such a position: and that I had something better to do with my life than to have scenes with a man drunken, *déclassé*, and half-witted as he was. You could not be made to see this. Hate blinded you. You insisted that the quarrel had really nothing to do with me: that you would not allow your father to dictate to you in your private friendships: that it would be most unfair of me to interfere. You had already, before you saw me on the subject, sent your father a foolish and vulgar telegram, as your answer.* That of course committed you to a foolish and vulgar course of action to follow. The fatal errors of life are not due to man's being unreasonable: an unreasonable moment may be one's finest moment. They are due to man's being logical. There is a wide difference. That telegram conditioned the whole of your subsequent relations with your father, and consequently the whole of my life. And the grotesque thing about it is that it was a telegram of which the commonest street-boy would have been ashamed. From pert telegrams to priggish lawyers' letters was a natural progress, and the result of your lawyer's letters to your father was, of course, to urge him on still further. You left him no option but to go on. You forced it on him as a point of honour, or of dishonour rather, that your appeal should have the more effect. So the next time he attacks me, no longer in a private letter and as your private friend, but in public and as a public man. I have to expel him from my house. He goes from restaurant to restaurant looking for me, in order to insult me before the whole world, and in such a manner that if I retaliated I would be ruined, and if I did not retaliate I would be ruined also. *Then* surely was the time when *you* should have come forward, and said that you would not expose me to such hideous attacks, such infamous persecution, on your account, but would, readily and at once, resign any claim you had to my friendship? You feel that now, I suppose. But it never even occurred to you then. Hate blinded you. All you could think of (besides of course writing to him insulting letters and telegrams) was to buy a ridiculo pistol that goes off in the Berkeley under circumstances that create a worse scandal than ever came to *your* ears. Indeed the idea of your being the object of a terrible quarrel between your father and a man of my position seemed to delight you. It, I suppose very naturally, pleased your vanity, and flattered your self-importance. That your father might have had your body, which did not interest me, and left me your soul, which did not interest him, would have been to you a distressing solution of the question. You scented the chance of a public scandal and flew to it. The prospect of a battle in which you would be safe delighted you. I never remember you in higher spirits than you were for the rest of that season. Your only disappointment seemed to be that nothing actually happened, and that no further meeting or fracas had taken place between us. You consoled yourself by sending him telegrams of such a character that at last the wretched man wrote to you and said that he had given orders to his servants that no telegram was to be brought to him under any pretence whatsoever. That did not daunt you. You saw the immense opportunities afforded by the open postcard, and availed yourself of them to the full. You hounded him on in the chase still more. I do not suppose he would ever really have given it up. Family instincts were strong in him. His hatred of you was just as persistent as your hatred of him, and I was the stalking-horse for both of you, and a mode of attack as well as a mode of shelter. His very passion for notoriety was not merely individual but racial. Still, if his interest had flagged for a moment your letters and postcards would soon have quickened it to its ancient flame. They did so. And he naturally went on further still. Having assailed me as a private gentleman and in private, as a public man and in public, he ultimately determines to make his final and great attack on me as an artist, and in the place where my Art is being represented. He secures by fraud a seat for the first night of one of my plays,* and contrives a plot to interrupt the performance, to make a foul speech about me to the audience, to insult my actors, to throw offensive or indecent missiles at me when I am called before the curtain at the close, utterly in some hideous way to ruin me through my work. By the merest chance, in the brief and accidental sincerity of a more than usually intoxicated mood, he boasts of his intention before others. Information is given to the police, and he is kept out of the theatre. You had your chance then. Then was your opportunity. Don't you realise now that you should have seen it, and come forward and said that you would not have my Art, at any rate, ruined for your sake? You knew what my Art was to me, the great primal note by which I had revealed, first myself to myself, and then myself to the world; the real passion of my life; the love to which all other loves were as marsh-water to red wine, or the glow-worm of the marsh to the magic mirror of the moon. Don't you understand now that your lack of imagination was the one really fatal defect of your character? What you had to do was quite simple, and quite clear before you, but Hate had blinded you, and you could see nothing. I could not apologise to your father for his having insulted me and persecuted me in the most loathsome manner for nearly nine months. I could not get rid of you out of my life. I had tried it again and again. I had gone so far as actually leaving England and going abroad in the hope of escaping from you. It had all been of no use. You were the only person who could have done anything. The key of the situation rested entirely with yourself. It was the one great opportunity you had of making some slight return to me for all the love and affection and kindness and generosity and care I had shown you. Had you appreciated me even at a tenth of my value as an artist you would have done so. But Hate blinded you. The faculty 'by which, and by which alone, we can understand others in their real as in their ideal relations' was dead in you. You thought simply of how to get your father into prison. To see him 'in the dock', as you used to say: that was your one idea. The phrase became one of the many *scies* * of your daily conversation. One heard it at every meal. Well, you had your desire gratified. Hate granted you every single thing you wished for. It was an indulgent Master to you. It is so, indeed, to all who serve it. For two days you sat on a high seat with the Sheriffs, and feasted your eyes with the spectacle of your father standing in the dock of the Central Criminal Court. And on the third day I took his place. What had occurred? In your hideous game of hate together, you had both thrown dice for my soul, and you happened to have lost. That was all.

You see that I have to write your life to you, and you have to realise it. We have known each other now for more than four years. Half of the time we have been together: the other half I have had to spend in prison as the result of our friendship. Where you will receive this letter, if indeed it ever reaches you, I don't know. Rome, Naples, Paris, Venice, some beautiful city on sea or river, I have no doubt, holds you. You are surrounded, if not with all the useless luxury you had with me, at any rate with everything that is pleasurable to eye, ear, and taste. Life is quite lovely to you. And yet, if you are wise, and wish to find Life much lovelier still, and in a different manner, you will let the reading of this terrible letter—for such I know it is—prove to you as important a crisis and turning-point of your life as the writing of it is to me. Your pale face used to flush easily with wine or pleasure. If, as you read what is here written, it from time to time becomes scorched, as though by a furnace-blast, with shame, it will be all the better for you. The supreme vice is shallowness. Whatever is realised is right.

I have now got as far as the House of Detention, have I not? After a night passed in the Police Cells I am sent there in the van. You were most attentive and kind. Almost every afternoon, if not actually every afternoon till you go abroad, you took the trouble to drive up to Holloway to see me. You also wrote very sweet and nice letters. But that it was not your father but you who had put me into prison, that from beginning to end you were the responsible person, that it was through you, for you, and by you that I was there, never for one instant dawned upon you. Even the spectacle of me behind the bars of a wooden cage could not quicken that dead unimaginative nature. You had the sympathy and the sentimentality of the spectator of a rather pathetic play. That you were the true author of the hideous tragedy did not occur to you. I saw that you realised nothing of what you had done. I did not desire to be the one to tell you what your own heart should have told you, what it indeed would have told you if you had not let Hate harden it and make it insensate. Everything must come to one out of one's own nature.* There is no use in telling a person a thing that they don't feel and can't understand. If I write to you now as I do it is because your own silence and conduct during my long imprisonment have made it necessary. Besides, as things had turned out, the blow had fallen upon me alone. That was a source of pleasure to me. I was content for many reasons to suffer, though there was always to my eyes, as I watched you, something not a little contemptible in your complete and wilful blindness. I remember your producing with absolute pride a letter you had published in one of the halfpenny newspapers about me.* It was a very prudent, temperate, indeed commonplace production. You appealed to the '*English sense of fair play*', or something very dreary of that kind, on behalf of '*a man who was down*'. It was the sort of letter you might have written had a painful charge been brought against some respectable person with whom personally you had been quite unacquainted. But you thought it a wonderful letter. You looked on it as a proof of almost quixotic chivalry. I am aware that you wrote other letters to other newspapers that they did not publish. But then they were simply to say that you hated your father. Nobody cared if you did or not. Hate, you have yet to learn, is, intellectually considered, the Eternal Negation. Considered from the point of view of the emotions it is a form of Atrophy, and kills everything but itself. To write to the papers to say that one hates someone else is as if one were to write to the papers to say that one had some secret and shameful malady: the fact that the man you hated was your own father, and that the feeling was thoroughly reciprocated, did not make your Hate noble or fine in any way. If it showed anything it was simply that it was a... hereditary disease.

I remember again, when an execution was put into my house, and my books and furniture were seized and advertised to be sold,* and Bankruptcy was impending, I

naturally wrote to tell you about it. I did not mention
that it was to pay for some gifts of mine to you that
the bailiffs had entered the home where you had so often
dined. I thought, rightly or wrongly, that such news might
pain you a little. I merely told you the bare facts. I thought
it proper that you should know them. You wrote back from
Boulogne in a strain of almost lyrical exultation. You said
that you knew your father was 'hard up for money', and
had been obliged to raise £1500 for the expenses of the
trial, and that my going bankrupt was really a 'splendid
score' off him, as he would not then be able to get any of
his costs out of me! Do you realise now what Hate blinding
a person is? Do you recognise now that when I described
it as an Atrophy destructive of everything but itself, I was
scientifically describing a real psychological fact? That all
my charming things were to be sold: my Burne-Jones
drawings: my Whistler drawings: my Monticelli: my
Simeon Solomons: my china: my Library with its collection
of presentation volumes from almost every poet of my time,
from Hugo to Whitman, from Swinburne to Mallarmé, from
Morris to Verlaine; with its beautifully bound editions of
my father's and mother's works; its wonderful array of
college and school prizes, its *éditions de luxe*, and the like;
was absolutely nothing to you. You said it was a great bore:
that was all. What you really saw in it was the possibility that
your father might ultimately lose a few hundred pounds, and
that paltry consideration filled you with ecstatic joy. As for
the costs of the trial, you may be interested to know that your
father openly said in the Orleans Club that if it had cost him
£20,000 he would have considered the money thoroughly
well spent, he had extracted such enjoyment, and delight,
and triumph out of it all. The fact that he was able not
merely to put me into prison for two years, but to take me
out for an afternoon and make me a public bankrupt was an
extra-refinement of pleasure that he had not expected. It was
the crowning-point of my humiliation, and of his complete
and perfect victory. Had your father had no claim for his
costs on me, you, I know perfectly well, would, as far as
words go, at any rate have been most sympathetic about

the entire loss of my library, a loss irreparable to a man of letters, the one of all my material losses the most distressing to me. You might even, remembering the sums of money I had lavishly spent on you and how you had lived on me for years, have taken the trouble to buy in some of my books for me. The best all went for less than £150: about as much as I would spend on you in an ordinary week. But the mean small pleasure of thinking that your father was going to be a few pence out of pocket made you forget all about trying to make me a little return, so slight, so easy, so inexpensive, so obvious, and so enormously welcome to me, had you brought it about. Am I right in saying that Hate blinds people? Do you see it now? If you don't, try to see it.

How clearly I saw it then, as now, I need not tell you. But I said to myself: '*At all costs I must keep Love in my heart. If I go into prison without Love what will become of my soul?*' The letters I wrote to you at that time from Holloway were my efforts to keep Love as the dominant note of my own nature. I could if I had chosen have torn you to pieces with bitter reproaches. I could have rent you with maledictions. I could have held up a mirror to you, and shown you such an image of yourself that you would not have recognised it as your own till you found it mimicking back your gestures of horror, and then you would have known whose shape it was, and hated it and yourself for ever. More than that indeed. The sins of another were being placed to my account. Had I so chosen, I could on either trial have saved myself at his expense, not from shame indeed but from imprisonment. Had I cared to show that the Crown witnesses—the three most important—had been carefully coached by your father and his solicitors, not in reticences merely, but in assertions, in the absolute transference, deliberate, plotted, and rehearsed, of the actions and doings of someone else on to me, I could have had each one of them dismissed from the box by the Judge, more summarily than even wretched perjured Atkins was.* I could have walked out of Court with my tongue in my cheek, and my hands in my pockets, a free man. The strongest pressure was put upon me to do so. I was earnestly advised, begged, entreated to do so by people whose sole interest was my welfare, and the welfare of my house. But I refused. I did not choose to do so. I have never regretted my decision for a single moment, even in the most bitter periods of my imprisonment. Such a course of action would have been beneath me. Sins of the flesh are nothing. They are maladies for physicians to cure, if they should be cured. Sins of the soul alone are shameful. To have secured my acquittal by such means would have been a life-long torture to me. But do you really think that you were worthy of the love I was showing you then, or that for a single moment I thought you were? Do you really think that at any period in our friendship you were worthy of the love I showed you, or that for a single moment I thought you were? I knew you were not. But Love does not traffic in a marketplace, nor use a huckster's scales. Its joy, like the joy of the intellect, is to feel itself alive. The aim of Love is to love: no more, and no less. You were my enemy: such an enemy as no man ever had. I had given you my life, and to gratify the lowest and most contemptible of all human passions, Hatred and Vanity and Greed, you had thrown it away. In less than three years you had entirely ruined me from every point of view. For my own sake there was nothing for me to do but to love you. I knew, if I allowed myself to hate you, that in the dry desert of existence over which I had to travel, and am travelling still, every rock would lose its shadow, every palm tree be withered, every well or water prove poisoned at its source. Are you beginning now to understand a little? Is your imagination wakening from the long lethargy in which it has lain? You know already what Hate is. Is it beginning to dawn on you what Love is, and what is the nature of Love? It is not too late for you to learn, though to teach it to you I may have had to go to a convict's cell.

After my terrible sentence, when the prison-dress was on me, and the prison-house closed, I sat amidst the ruins of my wonderful life, crushed by anguish, bewildered with terror, dazed through pain. But I would not hate you. Every day I said to myself, '*I must keep Love in my heart today, else how shall I live through the day*'. I reminded myself that you meant no evil, to me at any rate: I set myself to think that you had but drawn a bow at a venture, and that the arrow had pierced a King between the joints of the harness.* To have weighed you against the smallest of my sorrows, the meanest of my losses, would have been, I felt, unfair. I determined I would regard you as one suffering too. I forced myself to believe that at last the scales had fallen from your long-blinded eyes. I used to fancy, and with pain, what your horror must have been when you contemplated your terrible handiwork. There were times, even in those dark days, the darkest of all my life, when I actually longed to console you. So sure was I that at last you had realised what you had done.

It did not occur to me then that you could have the supreme vice, shallowness. Indeed, it was a real grief to me when I had to let you know that I was obliged to reserve for family business my first opportunity of receiving a letter: but my brother-in-law had written to me to say that if I would only write once to my wife she would, for my own sake and for our children's sake, take no action for divorce. I felt my duty was to do so. Setting aside other reasons, I could not bear the idea of being separated from Cyril, that beautiful, loving, loveable child of mine, my friend of all friends, my companion beyond all companions, one single hair of whose little golden head should have been dearer and of more value to me than, I will not merely say you from top to toe, but the entire chrysolite of the whole world:* was so indeed to me always, though I failed to understand it till too late.

Two weeks after your application, I get news of you. Robert Sherard,* that bravest and most chivalrous of all brilliant beings, comes to see me, and amongst other things tells me that in that ridiculous *Mercure de France*, with its absurd affectation of being the true centre of literary corruption, you are about to publish an article on me with specimens of my letters. He asks me if it really was by my wish. I was greatly taken aback, and much annoyed, and gave orders that the thing was to be stopped at once. You had left my letters lying about for blackmailing companions to steal, for hotel servants to pilfer, for housemaids to sell.

That was simply your careless want of appreciation of what
I had written to you. But that you should seriously propose
to publish selections from the balance was almost incredible
to me. And which of my letters were they? I could get no
information. That was my first news of you. It displeased
me.

The second piece of news followed shortly afterwards.
Your father's solicitors had appeared in the prison, and
served me personally with a Bankruptcy notice, for a paltry
£700, the amount of their taxed costs. I was adjudged a
public insolvent, and ordered to be produced in Court. I
felt most strongly, and feel still, and will revert to the subject
again, that these costs should have been paid by your family.
You had taken personally on yourself the responsibility of
stating that your family would do so. It was that which
had made the solicitor take up the case in the way he did.
You were absolutely responsible. Even irrespective of your
engagement on your family's behalf you should have felt
that as you had brought the whole ruin on me, the least
that could have been done was to spare me the additional
ignominy of bankruptcy for an absolutely contemptible
sum of money, less than half of what I spent on you in
three brief summer months at Goring. Of that, however, no
more here. I did through the solicitor's clerk, I fully admit,
receive a message from you on the subject, or at any rate in
connection with the occasion. The day he came to receive my
depositions and statements, he leant across the table—the
prison warder being present—and having consulted a piece
of paper which he pulled from his pocket, said to me in a
low voice: 'Prince Fleur-de-Lys* wishes to be remembered
to you.' I stared at him. He repeated the message again.
I did not know what he meant. 'The gentleman is abroad
at present,' he added mysteriously. It all flashed across me,
and I remember that, for the first and last time in my entire
prison-life, I laughed. In that laugh was all the scorn of
all the world. Prince Fleur-de-Lys! I saw—and subsequent
events showed me that I rightly saw—that nothing that had
happened had made you realise a single thing. You were in
your own eyes still the graceful prince of a trivial comedy,

not the sombre figure of a tragic show. All that had occurred was but as a feather for the cap that gilds a narrow head, a flower to pink the doublet that hides a heart that Hate, and Hate alone, can warm, that Love, and Love alone, finds cold. Prince Fleur-de-Lys! You were, no doubt, quite right to communicate with me under an assumed name. I myself, at that time, had no name at all. In the great prison where I was then incarcerated I was merely the figure and letter of a little cell in a long gallery, one of a thousand lifeless numbers, as of a thousand lifeless lives. But surely there were many real names in real history which would have suited you much better, and by which I would have had no difficulty at all in recognising you at once? I did not look for you behind the spangles of a tinsel vizard only suitable for an amusing masquerade. Ah! had your soul been, as for its own perfection even it should have been, wounded with sorrow, bowed with remorse, and humble with grief, such was not the disguise it would have chosen beneath whose shadow to seek entrance to the House of Pain! The great things of life are what they seem to be, and for that reason, strange as it may sound to you, are often difficult to interpret. But the little things of life are symbols. We receive our bitter lessons most easily through them. Your seemingly casual choice of a feigned name was, and will remain, symbolic. It reveals you.

Six weeks later a third piece of news arrives. I am called out of the Hospital Ward, where I was lying wretchedly ill, to receive a special message from you through the Governor of the Prison. He reads me out a letter you had addressed to him in which you stated that you proposed to publish an article 'on the case of Mr Oscar Wilde', in the *Mercure de France* ('a magazine', you added for some extraordinary reason, 'corresponding to our English *Fortnightly Review*') and were anxious to obtain my permission to publish extracts and selections from—what letters? The letters I had written to you from Holloway Prison! The letters that should have been to you things sacred and secret beyond anything in the whole world! These actually were the letters you proposed to publish for the jaded *décadent* to wonder at, for the greedy *feuilletoniste* to chronicle, for the little lions of the *Quartier Latin* to gape and mouth at! Had there been nothing in your own heart to cry out against so vulgar a sacrilege you might at least have remembered the sonnet he wrote who saw with such sorrow and scorn the letters of John Keats sold by public auction in London and have understood at last the real meaning of my lines

> I think they love not Art
> Who break the crystal of a poet's heart
> That small and sickly eyes may glare or gloat.*

For what was your article to show? That I had been too fond of you? The Paris *gamin* was quite aware of the fact. They all read the newspapers, and most of them write for them. That I was a man of genius? The French understood that, and the peculiar quality of my genius, much better than you did, or could have been expected to do. That along with genius goes often a curious perversity of passion and desire? Admirable: but the subject belongs to Lombroso* rather than to you. Besides, the pathological phenomenon in question is also found amongst those who have not genius. That in your war of hate with your father I was at once shield and weapon to each of you? Nay more, that in that hideous hunt for my life, that took place when the war was over, he never could have reached me had not your nets been already about my feet? Quite true: but I am told that Henri Bauër had already done it extremely well.* Besides, to corroborate his view, had such been your intention, you did not require to publish my letters; at any rate those written from Holloway Prison.

Will you say, in answer to my questions, that in one of my Holloway letters I had myself asked you to try, as far as you were able, to set me a little right with some small portion of the world? Certainly, I did so. Remember how and why I am here, at this very moment. Do you think I am here on account of my relations with the witnesses on my trial? My relations, real or supposed, witn people of that kind were matters of no interest to either the Government or Society. They knew nothing of them, and cared less. I am here for having tried to put your father into prison. My attempt failed of course. My own Counsel threw up their briefs. Your father completely turned the tables on me, and had *me* in prison, has me there still. That is why there is contempt felt for me. That is why people despise me. That is why I have to serve out every day, every hour, every minute of my dreadful imprisonment. That is why my petitions have been refused.

You were the only person who, and without in any way exposing yourself to scorn or danger or blame, could have given another colour to the whole affair: have put the matter in a different light: have shown to a certain degree how things really stood. I would not of course have expected, nor indeed wished you to have stated how and for what purpose you had sought my assistance in your trouble at Oxford: or how, and for what purpose, if you had a purpose at all, you had practically never left my side for nearly three years. My incessant attempts to break off a friendship that was so ruinous to me as an artist, as a man of position, as a member of society even, need not have been chronicled with the accuracy with which they have been set down here. Nor would I have desired you to have described the scenes you used to make with such almost monotonous recurrence: nor to have reprinted your wonderful series of telegrams to me with their strange mixture of romance and finance; nor to have quoted from your letters the more revolting or heartless passages, as I have been forced to do. Still, I thought it would have been good, as well for you as for me, if you had made some protest against your father's version of our friendship, one no less grotesque than venomous, and as absurd in its reference to you as it was dishonouring in its reference to me. That version has now actually passed into serious history: it is quoted, believed, and chronicled: the preacher has taken it for his text, and the moralist for his barren theme: and I who appealed to all the ages have had to accept my verdict from one who is an ape and a buffoon. I have said, and with some bitterness, I admit, in this letter that such was the irony of things that your father would live to be the hero of a Sunday-school tract: that you would rank with the infant Samuel: and that my place would be between Gilles de Retz and the Marquis de Sade. I dare say it is best so. I have no desire to complain. One of the many lessons that one learns in prison is that things are what they are, and will be what they will be. Nor have I any doubt but that the leper of mediaevalism, and the author of *Justine*, will prove better company than *Sandford and Merton.*

But at the time I wrote to you I felt that for both our sakes it would be a good thing, a proper thing, a right thing *not* to accept the account your father had put forward through his Counsel for the edification of a Philistine world, and that is why I asked you to think out and write something that would be nearer the truth. It would at least have been better for you than scribbling to the French papers about the domestic life of your parents. What did the French care whether or not your parents had led a happy domestic life? One cannot conceive a subject more entirely uninteresting to them. What did interest them was how an artist of my distinction, one who by the school and movement of which he was the incarnation had exercised a marked influence on the direction of French thought, could, having led such a life, have brought such an action. Had you proposed for your article to publish the letters, endless I fear in number, in which I had spoken to you of the ruin you were bringing on my life, of the madness of moods of rage that you were allowing to master you to your own hurt as well as to mine, and of my desire, nay, my determination to end a friendship so fatal to me in every way, I could have understood it, though I would not have allowed such letters to be published: when your father's Counsel desiring to catch me in a contradiction suddenly produced in Court a letter of mine, written to you in March '93, in which I stated that, rather than endure a repetition of the hideous scenes you seemed to take such a terrible pleasure in making, I would readily consent to be 'blackmailed by every renter in London',* it was a very real grief to me that that side of my friendship with you should incidentally be revealed to the common gaze: but that you should have been so slow to see, so lacking in all sensitiveness, and so dull in apprehension of what is rare, delicate and beautiful, as to propose yourself to publish the letters in which, and through which, I was trying to keep alive the very spirit and soul of Love, that it might dwell in my body through the long years of that body's humiliation—this was, and still is to me, a source of the very deepest pain, the most poignant disappointment. Why you did so, I fear I know but too well. If Hate blinded your eyes, Vanity sewed your eyelids together with threads of iron. The faculty 'by which, and by which alone, one can understand others in their real as in their ideal relations', your narrow egotism had blunted, and long disuse had made of no avail. The imagination was as much in prison as I was. Vanity had barred up the windows, and the name of the warder was Hate.

All this took place in the early part of November of the year before last. A great river of life flows between you and a date so distant. Hardly, if at all, can you see across so wide a waste. But to me it seems to have occurred, I will not say yesterday, but today. Suffering is one long moment. We cannot divide it by seasons. We can only record its moods, and chronicle their return. With us time itself does not progress. It revolves. It seems to circle round one centre of pain. The paralysing immobility of a life, every circumstance of which is regulated after an unchangeable pattern, so that we eat and drink and walk and lie down and pray, or kneel at least for prayer, according to the inflexible laws of an iron formula: this immobile quality, that makes each dreadful day in the very minutest detail like its brother, seems to communicate itself to those external forces the very essence of whose existence is ceaseless change. Of seed-time or harvest, of the reapers bending over the corn, or the grape-gatherers threading through the vines, of the grass in the orchard made white with broken blossoms, or strewn with fallen fruit, we know nothing, and can know nothing. For us there is only one season, the season of Sorrow. The very sun and moon seem taken from us. Outside, the day may be blue and gold, but the light that creeps down through the thickly-muffled glass of the small iron-barred window beneath which one sits is grey and niggard. It is always twilight in one's cell, as it is always midnight in one's heart. And in the sphere of thought, no less than in the sphere of time, motion is no more. The thing that you personally have long ago forgotten, or can easily forget, is happening to me now, and will happen to me again to-morrow. Remember this, and you will be able to understand a little of why I am writing to you, and in this manner writing.

A week later, I am transferred here. Three more months go over and my mother dies. You knew, none better, how deeply I loved and honoured her. Her death was so terrible to me that I, once a lord of language, have no words in which to express my anguish and my shame. Never, even in the most perfect days of my development as an artist, could I have had words fit to bear so august a burden, or to move with sufficient stateliness of music through the purple pageant of my incommunicable woe. She and my father had bequeathed me a name they had made noble and honoured not merely in Literature, Art, Archaeology and Science, but in the public history of my own country in its evolution as a nation. I had disgraced that name eternally. I had made it a low byword among low people. I had dragged it through the very mire. I had given it to brutes that they might make it brutal, and to fools that they might turn it into a synonym for folly. What I suffered then, and still suffer, is not for pen to write or paper to record. My wife, at that time kind and gentle to me, rather than that I should hear the news from indifferent or alien lips, travelled, ill as she was, all the way from Genoa to England to break to me herself the tidings of so irreparable, so irredeemable a loss. Messages of sympathy reached me from all who had still affection for me. Even people who had not known me personally, hearing what a new sorrow had come into my broken life, wrote to ask that some expression of their condolence should be conveyed to me. You alone stood aloof, sent me no message, and wrote me no letter. Of such actions, it is best to say what Virgil says to Dante of those whose lives have been barren in noble impulse and shallow of intention: '*Non ragioniam di lor, ma guarda, e passa.*'*

Three more months go over. The calendar of my daily conduct and labour that hangs on the outside of my cell-door, with my name and sentence written upon it, tells me that it is Maytime. My friends come to see me again. I enquire, as I always do, after you. I am told that you are in your villa at Naples, and are bringing out a volume of poems. At the close of the interview it is mentioned casually that you are dedicating them to me. The tidings seemed to give me a sort of nausea of life. I said nothing, but silently went back to my cell with contempt and scorn in my heart. How could you dream of dedicating a volume of poems to me without first asking my permission? Dream, do I say? How could you dare to do such a thing? Will you give as your answer that in the days of my greatness and fame I had consented to receive the dedication of your early work? Certainly, I did so; just as I would have accepted the homage of any other young man beginning the difficult and beautiful art of literature. All homage is delightful to an artist, and doubly sweet when youth brings it. Laurel and bay leaf wither when aged hands pluck them. Only youth has a right to crown an artist. That is the real privilege of being young, if youth only knew it. But the days of abasement and infamy are different from those of greatness and of fame. You have yet to learn that Prosperity, Pleasure and Success may be rough of grain and common in fibre, but that Sorrow is the most sensitive of all created things. There is nothing that stirs in the whole world of thought or motion to which Sorrow does not vibrate in terrible if exquisite pulsation. The thin beaten-out leaf of tremulous gold that chronicles the direction of forces that the eye cannot see is in comparison coarse.* It is a wound that bleeds when any hand but that of Love touches it and even then must bleed again, though not for pain.

You could write to the Governor of Wandsworth Prison to ask my permission to publish my letters in the *Mercure de France*, '*corresponding to our* English *Fortnightly Review*'. Why not have written to the Governor of the Prison at Reading to ask my permission to dedicate your poems to me, whatever fantastic description you may have chosen to give of them? Was it because in the one case the magazine in question had been prohibited by me from publishing letters, the legal copyright of which, as you are of course perfectly well aware, was and is vested entirely in me, and in the other you thought that you could enjoy the wilfulness of your own way without my knowing anything about it till it was too late to interfere? The mere fact that I was a man disgraced, ruined, and in prison should have made you, if you desired to write my name on the fore-page of your work, beg it of me as a favour, an honour, a privilege. That is the way in which one should approach those who are in distress and sit in shame.

Where there is Sorrow there is holy ground. Some day you will realise what that means. You will know nothing of life till you do. Robbie, and natures like his, can realise it. When I was brought down from my prison to the Court of Bankruptcy between two policemen, Robbie waited in the long dreary corridor, that before the whole crowd, whom an action so sweet and simple hushed into silence, he might gravely raise his hat to me, as handcuffed and with bowed head I passed him by. Men have gone to heaven for smaller things than that. It was in this spirit, and with this mode of love that the saints knelt down to wash the feet of the poor, or stooped to kiss the leper on the cheek. I have never said one single word to him about what he did. I do not know to the present moment whether he is aware that I was even conscious of his action. It is not a thing for which one can render formal thanks in formal words. I store it in the treasury-house of my heart. I keep it there as a secret debt that I am glad to think I can never possibly repay. It is embalmed and kept sweet by the myrrh and cassia of many tears. When Wisdom has been profitless to me, and Philosophy barren, and the proverbs and phrases of those who have sought to give me consolation as dust and ashes in my mouth, the memory of that little lowly silent act of Love has unsealed for me all the wells of pity, made the desert blossom like a rose, and brought me out of the bitterness of lonely exile into harmony with the wounded, broken and great heart of the world. When you are able to understand, not merely how beautiful Robbie's action was, but why it meant so much to me, and always will mean so much, then, perhaps, you will realise how and in what spirit you should have approached me for permission to dedicate to me your verses.

It is only right to state that in any case I would not have accepted the dedication. Though, possibly, it would under other circumstances have pleased me to have been asked, I would have refused the request for *your* sake, irrespective of any feelings of my own. The first volume of poems that in the very springtime of his manhood a young man sends forth to the world should be like a blossom or flower of spring, like the white thorn in the meadow at Magdalen, or the cowslips in the Cumnor fields. It should not be burdened by the weight of a terrible, a revolting tragedy, a terrible, a revolting scandal. If I had allowed my name to serve as herald to the book it would have been a grave artistic error. It would have brought a wrong atmosphere round the whole work, and in modern art atmosphere counts for so much. Modern life is complex and relative. Those are its two distinguishing notes. To render the first we require atmosphere with its subtlety of *nuances*, of suggestion, of strange perspectives: as for the second we require background. That is why Sculpture has ceased to be a representative art; and why Music *is* a representative art; and why Literature is, and has been, and always will remain the supreme representative art.

Your little book should have brought with it Sicilian and Arcadian airs, not the pestilent foulness of the criminal dock or the close breath of the convict cell. Nor would such a dedication as you proposed have been merely an error of taste in Art; it would from other points of view have been entirely unseemly. It would have looked like a continuance of your conduct before and after my arrest. It would have given people the impression of being an attempt at foolish bravado: an example of that kind of courage that is sold cheap and bought cheap in the streets of shame. As far as our friendship is concerned Nemesis has crushed us both like flies. The dedication of verses to me when I was in prison would have seemed a sort of silly effort at smart repartee, an accomplishment on which in your old days of dreadful letter-writing—days never, I sincerely hope for your sake, to return—you used openly to pride yourself and about which it was your joy to boast. It would not have produced the serious, the beautiful effect which I trust—I believe indeed—you had intended. Had you consulted me, I would have advised you to delay the publication of your verses for a little; or, if that proved displeasing to you, to publish anonymously at first, and then when you had won lovers by your song—the only sort of lovers really worth the winning—you might have turned round and said to the world 'These flowers that you admire are of my sowing, and now I offer them to one whom you regard as a pariah and an outcast, as my tribute to what I love and reverence and admire in him.' But you chose the wrong method and the wrong moment. There is a tact in love, and a tact in literature: you were not sensitive to either.

I have spoken to you at length on this point in order that you should grasp its full bearings, and understand why I wrote at once to Robbie in terms of such scorn and contempt of you,* and absolutely prohibited the dedication, and desired that the words I had written of you should be copied out carefully and sent to you. I felt that at last the time had come when you should be made to see, to recognise, to realise a little of what you had done. Blindness may be carried so far that it becomes grotesque, and an unimaginative nature, if something be not done to rouse it, will become petrified into absolute insensibility, so that while the body may eat, and drink, and have its pleasures, the soul, whose house it is, may, like the soul of Branca d'Oria in Dante, be dead absolutely.* My letter seems to have arrived not a moment too soon. It fell on you, as far as I can judge, like a thunderbolt. You describe yourself, in your answer to Robbie, as being 'deprived of all power of thought and expression.' Indeed, apparently, you can think of nothing better than to write to your mother to complain. Of course, she, with that blindness to your real good that has been her ill-starred fortune and yours, gives you every comfort she can think of, and lulls you back, I suppose, into your former unhappy, unworthy condition; while as far as I am concerned, she lets my friends know that she is 'very much annoyed' at the severity of my remarks about you. Indeed it is not merely to my friends that she conveys her sentiments of annoyance, but also to those—a very much larger number, I need hardly remind you—who are not my friends: and I am informed now, and through channels very kindly-disposed to you and yours, that in consequence of this a great deal of the sympathy that, by reason of my distinguished genius and terrible sufferings, had been gradually but surely growing up for me, has been entirely taken away. People say 'Ah! he first tried to get the kind father put into prison and failed: now he turns round and blames the innocent son for his failure. How right we were to despise him! How worthy of contempt he is!' It seems to me that, when my name is mentioned in your mother's presence, if she has no word of sorrow or regret for her share—no slight one—in the ruin of my house, it would be more seemly if she remained silent. And as for you—don't you think now that, instead of writing to *her* to complain, it would have been better for you, in every way, to have written to *me* directly, and to have had the courage to say to me whatever you had or fancied you had to say? It is nearly a year ago now since I wrote that letter. You cannot have remained during that entire time 'deprived of all power of thought and expression'. Why did you not write to me? You saw by my letter how deeply wounded, how outraged I was by your whole conduct. More than that; you saw your entire friendship with me set before you, at last, in its true light, and by a mode not to be mistaken. Often in old days I had told you that you were ruining my life. You had always laughed. When Edwin Levy at the very beginning of our friendship, seeing your manner of putting me forward to bear the brunt, and annoyance, and expense even of that unfortunate Oxford mishap of yours, if we must so term it, in reference to which his advice and help had been sought, warned me for the space of a whole hour against knowing you, you laughed, as at Bracknell I described to you my long and impressive interview with him. When I told you how even that unfortunate young man who ultimately stood beside me in the Dock* had warned me more than once that you would prove far more fatal in bringing me to utter destruction than any even of the common lads whom I was foolish enough to know, you laughed, though not with such sense of amusement. When my more prudent or less well-disposed friends either warned me or left me, on account of my friendship with you, you laughed with scorn. You laughed immoderately when, on the occasion of your father writing his first abusive letter to you about me, I told you that I knew I would be the mere catspaw of your dreadful quarrel and come to some evil between you. But every single thing had happened as I had said it would happen, as far as the result goes. You had no excuse for not seeing how all things had come to pass. Why did you not write to me? Was it cowardice? Was it callousness? What was it? The fact that I was outraged with you, and had expressed my sense of the outrage, was all the more reason for writing. If you thought my letter just, you should have written. If you thought it in the smallest point unjust, you should have written. I waited for a letter. I felt sure that at last you would see that, if old affection, much-protested love, the thousand acts of ill-requited kindness I had showered on you, the thousand unpaid debts of gratitude you owed me—that if all these were nothing to you, mere duty itself, most barren of all bonds between man and man, should have made you write. You cannot say that you seriously thought I was obliged to receive none but business communications from members of my family. You knew perfectly well that every twelve weeks Robbie was writing to me a little budget of literary news. Nothing can be more charming than his letters, in their wit, their clever concentrated criticism, their light touch: they are real letters: they are like a person talking to one: they have the quality of a French *causerie intime*:* and in his delicate modes of deference to me, appealing at one time to my judgment, at another to my sense of humour, at another to my instinct for beauty or to my culture, and reminding me in a hundred subtle ways that once I was to many an arbiter of style in Art, the supreme arbiter to some, he shows how he has the tact of love as well as the tact of literature. His letters have been the little messengers between me and that beautiful unreal world of Art where once I was King, and would have remained King, indeed, had I not let myself be lured into the imperfect world of coarse uncompleted passions, of appetite without distinction, desire without limit, and formless greed. Yet, when all is said, surely you might have been able to understand, or conceive, at any rate, in your own mind, that, even on the ordinary grounds of mere psychological curiosity, it would have been more interesting to me to hear from *you* than to learn that Alfred Austin was trying to bring out a volume of poems, or that Street was writing dramatic criticisms for the *Daily Chronicle*, or that by one who cannot speak a panegyric without stammering Mrs Meynell had been pronounced to be the new Sibyl of Style.*

Ah! had *you* been in prison—I will not say through any fault of mine, for that would be a thought too terrible for me to bear—but through fault of your own, error of your own, faith in some unworthy friend, slip in sensual mire, trust misapplied, or love ill-bestowed, or none, or all of these—do you think that I would have allowed you to eat your heart away in darkness and solitude without trying in some way, however slight, to help you to bear the bitter burden of your disgrace? Do you think that I would not have let you know that if you suffered, I was suffering too: that if you wept, there were tears in my eyes also: and that if you lay in the house of bondage and were despised of men, I out of my very griefs had built a house in which to dwell until your coming, a treasury in which all that men had denied to you would be laid up for your healing, one hundredfold in increase? If bitter necessity, or prudence, to *me* more bitter still, had prevented my being near you, and robbed me of the joy of your presence, though seen through prison-bars and in a shape of shame, I would have written to you in season and out of season in the hope that some mere phrase, some single word, some broken echo even of Love might reach you. If you had refused to receive my letters, I would have written none the less, so that you should have known that at any rate there were always letters waiting for you. Many have done so to me. Every three months people write to me, or propose to write to me. Their letters and communications are kept. They will be handed to me when I go out of prison. I know that they are there. I know the names of the people who have written them. I know that they are full of sympathy, and affection, and kindness. That is sufficient for me. I need to know no more. Your silence has been horrible. Nor has it been a silence of weeks and months merely, but of years; of years even as they have to count them who, like yourself, live swiftly in happiness, and can hardly catch the gilt feet of the days as they dance by, and are out of breath in the chase after pleasure. It is a silence without excuse; a silence without palliation. I knew you had feet of clay. Who knew it better? When I wrote, among my aphorisms, that it was simply the feet of clay that made the gold of the image precious,* it was of you I was thinking. But it is no gold image with clay feet that you have made of yourself. Out of the very dust of the common highway that the hooves of horned things pash into mire you have moulded your perfect semblance for me to look at, so that, whatever my secret desire might have been, it would be impossible for me now to have for you any feeling other than that of contempt and scorn, for myself any feeling other than that of contempt and scorn either. And setting aside all other reasons, your indifference, your worldly wisdom, your callousness, your prudence, whatever you may choose to call it, has been made doubly bitter to me by the peculiar circumstances that either accompanied or followed my fall.

Other miserable men, when they are thrown into prison, if they are robbed of the beauty of the world, are at least safe, in some measure, from the world's most deadly slings, most awful arrows. They can hide in the darkness of their cells, and of their very disgrace make a mode of sanctuary. The world, having had its will, goes its way, and they are left to suffer undisturbed. With me it has been different. Sorrow after sorrow has come beating at the prison doors in search of me. They have opened the gates wide and let them in. Hardly, if at all, have my friends been suffered to see me. But my enemies have had full access to me always. Twice in my public appearances at the Bankruptcy Court, twice again in my public transferences from one prison to another, have I been shown under conditions of unspeakable humiliation to the gaze and mockery of men. The messenger of Death has brought me his tidings and gone his way, and in entire solitude, and isolated from all that could give me comfort, or suggest relief, I have had to bear the intolerable burden of misery and remorse that the memory of my mother placed upon me, and places on me still. Hardly has that wound been dulled, not healed, by time, when violent and bitter and harsh letters come to me from my wife through her solicitor. I am, at once, taunted and threatened with poverty. That I can bear. I can school myself to worse than that. But my two children are taken from me by legal procedure.* That is and always will remain to me a source of infinite distress, of infinite pain, of grief without end or limit. That the law should decide, and take upon itself to decide, that I am one unfit to be with my own children is something quite horrible to me. The disgrace of prison is as nothing compared to it. I envy the other men who tread the yard along with me. I am sure that their children wait for them, look for their coming, will be sweet to them.

The poor are wiser, more charitable, more kind, more sensitive than we are. In their eyes prison is a tragedy in a man's life, a misfortune, a casualty, something that calls for sympathy in others. They speak of one who is in prison as of one who is '*in trouble*' simply. It is the phrase they always use, and the expression has the perfect wisdom of Love in it. With people of our rank it is different. With us prison makes a man a pariah. I, and such as I am, have hardly any right to air and sun. Our presence taints the pleasures of others. We are unwelcome when we reappear. To revisit the glimpses of the moon* is not for us. Our very children are taken away. Those lovely links with humanity are broken. We are doomed to be solitary, while our sons still live. We are denied the one thing that might heal us and help us, that might bring balm to the bruised heart, and peace to the soul in pain.

And to all this has been added the hard, small fact that by your actions and by your silence, by what you have done and by what you have left undone, you have made every day of my long imprisonment still more difficult for me to live through. The very bread and water of prison fare you have by your conduct changed. You have rendered the one bitter and the other brackish to me. The sorrow you should have shared you have doubled, the pain you should have sought to lighten you have quickened to anguish. I have no doubt that you did not mean to do so. I know that you did not mean to do so. It was simply that 'one really fatal defect of your character, your entire lack of imagination'.

And the end of it all is that I have got to forgive you. I must do so. I don't write this letter to put bitterness into your heart, but to pluck it out of mine. For my own sake I must forgive you. One cannot always keep an adder in one's breast to feed on one, nor rise up every night to sow thorns in the garden of one's soul. It will not be difficult at all for me to do so, if you help me a little. Whatever you did to me in old days I always readily forgave. It did you no good then. Only one whose life is without stain of any kind can forgive sins. But now when I sit in humiliation and disgrace it is different. My forgiveness should mean a great deal to you now. Some day you will realise it. Whether you do so early or late, soon or not at all, my way is clear before me. I cannot allow you to go through life bearing in your heart the burden of having ruined a man like me. The thought might make you callously indifferent, or morbidly sad. I must take the burden from you and put it on my own shoulders.

I must say to myself that neither you nor your father, multiplied a thousand times over, could possibly have ruined a man like me: that I ruined myself: and that nobody, great or small, can be ruined except by his own hand.* I am quite ready to do so. I am trying to do so, though you may not think it at the present moment. If I have brought this pitiless indictment against you, think what an indictment I bring without pity against myself. Terrible as what you did to me was, what I did to myself was far more terrible still.

I was a man who stood in symbolic relations to the art and culture of my age. I had realised this for myself at the very dawn of my manhood, and had forced my age to realise it afterwards. Few men hold such a position in their own lifetime and have it so acknowledged. It is usually discerned, if discerned at all, by the historian, or the critic, long after both the man and his age have passed away. With me it was different. I felt it myself, and made others feel it. Byron was a symbolic figure, but his relations were to the passion of his age and its weariness of passion. Mine were to something more noble, more permanent, of more vital issue, of larger scope.

The gods had given me almost everything. I had genius, a distinguished name, high social position, brilliancy, intellectual daring: I made art a philosophy, and philosophy an art: I altered the minds of men and the colours of things: there was nothing I said or did that did not make people wonder: I took the drama, the most objective form known to art, and made it as personal a mode of expression as the lyric or the sonnet, at the same time that I widened its range and enriched its characterisation: drama, novel, poem in rhyme, poem in prose, subtle or fantastic dialogue, whatever I touched I made beautiful in a new mode of beauty: to truth itself I gave what is false no less than what is true as its rightful province, and showed that the false and the true are merely forms of intellectual existence. I treated Art as the supreme reality, and life as a mere mode of fiction: I awoke the imagination of my century so that it created myth and legend around me: I summed up all systems in a phrase, and all existence in an epigram.

Along with these things, I had things that were different. I let myself be lured into long spells of senseless and sensual ease. I amused myself with being a *flâneur,** a dandy, a man of fashion. I surrounded myself with the smaller natures and the meaner minds. I became the spendthrift of my own genius, and to waste an eternal youth gave me a curious joy. Tired of being on the heights I deliberately went to the depths in the search for new sensations. What the paradox was to me in the sphere of thought, perversity became to me in the sphere of passion. Desire, at the end, was a malady, or a madness, or both. I grew careless of the lives of others. I took pleasure where it pleased me and passed on. I forgot that every little action of the common day makes or unmakes character, and that therefore what one has done in the secret chamber one has some day to cry aloud on the housetops. I ceased to be Lord over myself. I was no longer the Captain of my Soul,* and did not know it. I allowed you to dominate me, and your father to frighten me. I ended in horrible disgrace. There is only one thing for me now, absolute Humility: just as there is only one thing for you, absolute Humility also. You had better come down into the dust and learn it beside me.

I have lain in prison for nearly two years. Out of my nature has come wild despair; an abandonment to grief that was piteous even to look at: terrible and impotent rage: bitterness and scorn: anguish that wept aloud: misery that could find no voice: sorrow that was dumb. I have passed through every possible mood of suffering. Better than Wordsworth himself I know what Wordsworth meant when he said:

> Suffering is permanent, obscure, and dark
> And has the nature of Infinity.*

But while there were times when I rejoiced in the idea that my sufferings were to be endless, I could not bear them to be without meaning. Now I find hidden away in my nature something that tells me that nothing in the whole world is meaningless, and suffering least of all. That something hidden away in my nature, like a treasure in a field, is Humility.

It is the last thing left in me, and the best: the ultimate discovery at which I have arrived: the starting-point for a fresh development. It has come to me right out of myself, so I know that it has come at the proper time. It could not have come before, nor later. Had anyone told me of it, I would have rejected it. Had it been brought to me, I would have refused it. As I found it, I want to keep it. I must do so. It is the one thing that has in it the elements of life, of a new life, a *Vita Nuova** for me. Of all things it is the strangest. One cannot give it away, and another may not give it to one. One cannot acquire it, except by surrendering everything that one has. It is only when one has lost all things, that one knows that one possesses it.

Now that I realise that it is in me, I see quite clearly what I have got to do, what, in fact, I must do. And when I use such a phrase as that, I need not tell you that I am not alluding to any external sanction or command. I admit none. I am far more of an individualist than I ever was. Nothing seems to me of the smallest value except what one gets out of oneself.* My nature is seeking a fresh mode of self-realisation. That is all I am concerned with. And the first thing that I have got to do is to free myself from any possible bitterness of feeling against you.

I am completely penniless, and absolutely homeless. Yet there are worse things in the world than that. I am quite candid when I tell you that rather than go out from this prison with bitterness in my heart against you or against the world I would gladly and readily beg my bread from door to door. If I got nothing at the house of the rich, I would get something at the house of the poor. Those who have much are often greedy. Those who have little always share. I would not a bit mind sleeping in the cool grass in summer, and when winter came on sheltering myself by the warm close-thatched rick, or under the penthouse of a great barn, provided I had love in my heart. The external things of life seem to me now of no importance at all. You can see to what intensity of individualism I have arrived, or am arriving rather, for the journey is long, and 'where I walk there are thorns'.*

Of course I know that to ask for alms on the highway is not to be my lot, and that if ever I lie in the cool grass at night-time it will be to write sonnets to the Moon. When I go out of prison, Robbie will be waiting for me on the other side of the big iron-studded gate, and he is the symbol not merely of his own affection, but of the affection of many others besides. I believe I am to have enough to live on for about eighteen months at any rate, so that, if I may not write beautiful books, I may at least read beautiful books, and what joy can be greater? After that, I hope to be able to recreate my creative faculty. But were things different: had I not a friend left in the world: were there not a single house open to me even in pity: had I to accept the wallet and ragged cloak of sheer penury: still as long as I remained free from all resentment, hardness, and scorn, I would be able to face life with much more calm and confidence than I would were my body in purple and fine linen, and the soul within it sick with hate. And I shall really have no difficulty in forgiving you. But to make it a pleasure for me you must feel that you want it. When you really want it you will find it waiting for you.

I need not say that my task does not end there. It would be comparatively easy if it did. There is much more before me. I have hills far steeper to climb, valleys much darker to pass through. And I have to get it all out of myself. Neither Religion, Morality, nor Reason can help me at all.

Morality does not help me. I am a born antinomian. I am one of those who are made for exceptions, not for laws. But while I see that there is nothing wrong in what one does, I see that there is something wrong in what one becomes. It is well to have learned that.

Religion does not help me. The faith that others give to what is unseen, I give to what one can touch, and look at. My Gods dwell in temples made with hands, and within the circle of actual experience is my creed made perfect and complete: too complete it may be, for like many or all of those who have placed their Heaven in this earth, I have found in it not merely the beauty of Heaven, but the horror of Hell also. When I think about Religion at all, I feel as if I would like to found an order for those who cannot believe: the Confraternity of the Fatherless one might call it, where on an altar, on which no taper burned, a priest, in whose heart peace had no dwelling, might celebrate with unblessed bread and a chalice empty of wine. Everything to be true must become a religion. And agnosticism should have its ritual no less than faith. It has sown its martyrs, it should reap its saints, and praise God daily for having hidden Himself from man. But whether it be faith or agnosticism, it must be nothing external to me. Its symbols must be of my own creating. Only that is spiritual which makes its own form. If I may not find its secret within myself, I shall never find it. If I have not got it already, it will never come to me.

Reason does not help me. It tells me that the laws under which I am convicted are wrong and unjust laws, and the system under which I have suffered a wrong and unjust system. But, somehow, I have got to make both of these things just and right to me. And exactly as in Art one is only concerned with what a particular thing is at a particular moment to oneself, so it is also in the ethical evolution of one's character. I have got to make everything that has happened to me good for me. The plank-bed, the loathsome food, the hard ropes shredded into oakum till one's fingertips grow dull with pain, the menial offices with which each day begins and finishes, the harsh orders that routine seems to necessitate, the dreadful dress that makes sorrow grotesque to look at, the silence, the solitude, the shame—each and all of these things I have to transform into a spiritual experience. There is not a single degradation of the body which I must not try and make into a spiritualising of the soul.

I want to get to the point when I shall be able to say, quite simply and without affectation, that the two great turning-points of my life were when my father sent me to Oxford, and when society sent me to prison. I will not say that it is the best thing that could have happened to me, for that phrase would savour of too great bitterness towards myself. I would sooner say, or hear it said of me, that I was so typical a child of my age that in my perversity, and for that perversity's sake, I turned the good things of my life to evil, and the evil things of my life to good. What is said, however, by myself or by others matters little. The important thing, the thing that lies before me, the thing that I have to do, or be for the brief remainder of my days one maimed, marred, and incomplete, is to absorb into my nature all that has been done to me, to make it part of me, to accept it without complaint, fear, or reluctance. The supreme vice is shallowness. Whatever is realised is right.

When first I was put into prison some people advised me to try and forget who I was. It was ruinous advice. It is only by realising what I am that I have found comfort of any kind. Now I am advised by others to try on my release to forget that I have ever been in a prison at all. I know that would be equally fatal. It would mean that I would be always haunted by an intolerable sense of disgrace, and that those things that are meant as much for me as for anyone else—the beauty of the sun and the moon, the pageant of the seasons, the music of daybreak and the silence of great nights, the rain falling through the leaves, or the dew creeping over the grass and making it silver—would all be tainted for me, and lose their healing power and their power of communicating joy. To reject one's own experiences is to arrest one's own development. To deny one's own experiences is to put a lie into the lips of one's own life. It is no less than a denial of the Soul. For just as the body absorbs things of all kinds, things common and unclean no less than those that the priest or a vision has cleansed, and converts them into swiftness or strength, into the play of beautiful muscles and the moulding of fair flesh, into the curves and colours of the hair, the lips, the eye: so the Soul, in its turn, has its nutritive functions also, and can transform into noble moods of thought, and passions of high import, what in itself is base, cruel, and degrading: nay more, may find in these its most august modes of assertion, and can often reveal itself most perfectly through what was intended to desecrate or destroy.

The fact of my having been the common prisoner of a common gaol I must frankly accept, and, curious as it may seem to you, one of the things I shall have to teach myself is not to be ashamed of it. I must accept it as a punishment, and if one is ashamed of having been punished, one might just as well never have been punished at all. Of course there are many things of which I was convicted that I had not done, but then there are many things of which I was convicted that I had done, and a still greater number of things in my life for which I never was indicted at all. And as for what I have said in this letter, that the gods are strange, and punish us for what is good and humane in us as much as for what is evil and perverse, I must accept the fact that one is punished for the good as well as for the evil that one does. I have no doubt that it is quite right one should be. It helps one, or should help one, to realise both, and not to be too conceited about either. And if I then am not ashamed of my punishment, as I hope not to be, I shall be able to think, and walk, and live with freedom.

Many men on their release carry their prison along with them into the air, hide it as a secret disgrace in their hearts, and at length like poor poisoned things creep into some hole and die. It is wretched that they should have to do so, and it is wrong, terribly wrong, of Society that it should force them to do so. Society takes upon itself the right to inflict appalling punishments on the individual, but it also has the supreme vice of shallowness, and fails to realise what it has done. When the man's punishment is over, it leaves him to himself: that is to say it abandons him at the very moment when its highest duty towards him begins. It is really ashamed of its own actions, and shuns those whom it has punished, as people shun a creditor whose debt they cannot pay, or one on whom they have inflicted an irreparable, an irredeemable wrong. I claim on my side that if I realise what I have suffered, Society should realise what it has inflicted on me: and that there should be no bitterness or hate on either side.

Of course I know that from one point of view things will be made more difficult for me than for others; must indeed, by the very nature of the case, be made so. The poor thieves and outcasts who are imprisoned here with me are in many respects more fortunate than I am. The little way in grey city or green field that saw their sin is small: to find those who know nothing of what they have done they need go no further than a bird might fly between the twilight before dawn and dawn itself: but for me 'the world is shrivelled to a handsbreadth',* and everywhere I turn my name is written on the rocks in lead. For I have come, not from obscurity into the momentary notoriety of crime, but from a sort of eternity of fame to a sort of eternity of infamy, and sometimes seem to myself to have shown, if indeed it required showing, that between the famous and the infamous there is but one step, if so much as one.

Still, in the very fact that people will recognise me wherever I go, and know all about my life, as far as its follies go, I can discern something good for me. It will force on me the necessity of again asserting myself as an artist, and as soon as I possibly can. If I can produce even one more beautiful work of art I shall be able to rob malice of its venom, and cowardice of its sneer, and to pluck out the tongue of scorn by the roots. And if life be, as it surely is, a problem to me, I am no less a problem to Life. People must adopt some attitude towards me, and so pass judgment both on themselves and me. I need not say I am not talking of particular individuals. The only people I would care to be with now are artists and people who have suffered: those who know what Beauty is, and those who know what Sorrow is: nobody else interests me. Nor am I making any demands on Life. In all that I have said I am simply concerned with my own mental attitude towards life as a whole: and I feel that not to be ashamed of having been punished is one of the first points I must attain to, for the sake of my own perfection, and because I am so imperfect.

Then I must learn how to be happy. Once I knew it, or thought I knew it, by instinct. It was always springtime once in my heart. My temperament was akin to joy. I filled my life to the very brim with pleasure, as one might fill a cup to the very brim with wine. Now I am approaching life from a completely new standpoint, and even to conceive happiness is often extremely difficult for me. I remember during my first term at Oxford reading in Pater's *Renaissance**—that book which has had such a strange influence over my life—how Dante places low in the Inferno those who wilfully live in sadness, and going to the College Library and turning to the passage in the *Divine Comedy* where beneath the dreary marsh lie those who were 'sullen in the sweet air', saying for ever through their sighs:

Tristi fummo
nell' aer dolce che dal sol s'allegra.[*]

I knew the Church condemned *accidia,* but the whole idea seemed to me quite fantastic, just the sort of sin, I fancied, a priest who knew nothing about real life would invent. Nor could I understand how Dante, who says that 'sorrow remarries us to God',[*] could have been so harsh to those who were enamoured of melancholy, if any such there really were. I had no idea that some day this would become to me one of the greatest temptations of my life.

While I was in Wandsworth Prison I longed to die. It was my one desire. When after two months in the Infirmary I was transferred here, and found myself growing gradually better in physical health, I was filled with rage. I determined to commit suicide on the very day on which I left prison. After a time that evil mood passed away, and I made up my mind to live, but to wear gloom as a King wears purple: never to smile again: to turn whatever house I entered into a house of mourning: to make my friends walk slowly in sadness with me: to teach them that melancholy is the true secret of life: to maim them with an alien sorrow: to mar them with my own pain. Now I feel quite differently. I see it would be both ungrateful and unkind of me to pull so long a face that when my friends came to see me they would have to make their faces still longer in order to show their sympathy, or, if I desired to entertain them, to invite them to sit down silently to bitter herbs and funeral baked meats. I must learn how to be cheerful and happy.

The last two occasions on which I was allowed to see my friends here I tried to be as cheerful as possible, and to show my cheerfulness in order to make them some slight return for their trouble in coming all the way from town to visit me. It is only a slight return, I know, but it is the one, I feel certain, that pleases them most. I saw Robbie for an hour on Saturday week, and I tried to give the fullest possible expression to the delight I really felt at our meeting. And that, in the views and ideas I am here shaping for myself, I am quite right is shown to me by the fact that now for the first time since my imprisonment I have a real desire to live.

There is before me so much to do that I would regard it as a terrible tragedy if I died before I was allowed to complete at any rate a little of it. I see new developments in Art and Life, each one of which is a fresh mode of perfection. I long to live so that I can explore what is no less than a new world to me. Do you want to know what this new world is? I think you can guess what it is. It is the world in which I have been living.

Sorrow, then, and all that it teaches one, is my new world. I used to live entirely for pleasure. I shunned sorrow and suffering of every kind. I hated both. I resolved to ignore them as far as possible, to treat them, that is to say, as modes of imperfection. They were not part of my scheme of life. They had no place in my philosophy. My mother, who knew life as a whole, used often to quote to me Goethe's lines—written by Carlyle in a book he had given her years ago—and translated, I fancy, by him also:

> Who never ate his bread in sorrow,
>   Who never spent the midnight hours
> Weeping and waiting for the morrow,
>   He knows you not, ye Heavenly Powers.*

They were the lines that noble Queen of Prussia, whom Napoleon treated with such coarse brutality, used to quote in her humiliation and exile:* they were lines my mother often quoted in the troubles of her later life: I absolutely declined to accept or admit the enormous truth hidden in them. I could not understand it. I remember quite well how I used to tell her that I did not want to eat my bread in sorrow, or to pass any night weeping and watching for a more bitter dawn. I had no idea that it was one of the special things that the Fates had in store for me; that for a whole year of my life, indeed, I was to do little else. But so has my portion been meted out to me; and during the last few months I have, after terrible struggles and difficulties, been able to comprehend some of the lessons hidden in the heart of pain. Clergymen, and people who use phrases without wisdom, sometimes talk of suffering as a mystery. It is really a revelation. One discerns things that one never discerned before. One approaches the whole of history from a different standpoint. What one had felt dimly through instinct, about Art, is intellectually and emotionally realised with perfect clearness of vision and absolute intensity of apprehension.

I now see that sorrow, being the supreme emotion of which man is capable, is at once the type and test of all great Art. What the artist is always looking for is that mode of existence in which soul and body are one and indivisible: in which the outward is expressive of the inward: in which Form reveals. Of such modes of existence there are not a few: youth and the arts preoccupied with youth may serve as a model for us at one moment: at another, we may like to think that, in its subtlety and sensitiveness of impression, its suggestion of a spirit dwelling in external things and making its raiment of earth and air, of mist and city alike, and in the morbid sympathy of its moods, and tones and colours, modern landscape art is realising for us pictorially what was realised in such plastic perfection by the Greeks. Music, in which all subject is absorbed in expression and cannot be separated from it, is a complex example, and a flower or a child a simple example of what I mean: but Sorrow is the ultimate type both in life and Art.

Behind Joy and Laughter there may be a temperament, coarse, hard and callous. But behind Sorrow there is always Sorrow. Pain, unlike Pleasure, wears no mask. Truth in Art is not any correspondence between the essential idea and the accidental existence; it is not the resemblance of shape to shadow, or of the form mirrored in the crystal to the form itself: it is no Echo coming from a hollow hill, any more than it is the well of silver water in the valley that shows the Moon to the Moon and Narcissus to Narcissus. Truth in Art is the unity of a thing with itself: the outward rendered expressive of the inward: the soul made incarnate: the body instinct with spirit. For this reason there is no truth comparable to Sorrow. There are times when Sorrow seems to me to be the only truth. Other things may be illusions of the eye or the appetite, made to blind the one and cloy the other, but out of Sorrow have the worlds been built, and at the birth of a child or a star there is pain.

More than this, there is about Sorrow an intense, an extraordinary reality. I have said of myself that I was one who stood in symbolic relations to the art and culture of my age. There is not a single wretched man in this wretched place along with me who does not stand in symbolic relations to the very secret of life. For the secret of life is suffering. It is what is hidden behind everything. When we begin to live, what is sweet is so sweet to us, and what is bitter so bitter, that we inevitably direct all our desires towards pleasure, and seek not merely for 'a month or twain to feed on honeycomb',* but for all our years to taste no other food, ignorant the while that we may be really starving the soul.

I remember talking once on this subject to one of the most beautiful personalities I have ever known: a woman, whose sympathy and noble kindness to me both before and since the tragedy of my imprisonment have been beyond power and description: one who has really assisted me, though she does not know it, to bear the burden of my troubles more than anyone else in the whole world has: and all through the mere fact of her existence: through her being what she is, partly an ideal and partly an influence, a suggestion of what one might become, as well as a real help towards becoming it, a soul that renders the common air sweet, and makes what is spiritual seem as simple and natural as sunlight or the sea, one for whom Beauty and Sorrow walk hand in hand and have the same message. On the occasion of which I am thinking I recall distinctly how I said to her that there was enough suffering in one narrow London lane to show that God did not love man, and that wherever there was any sorrow, though but that of a child in some little garden weeping over a fault that it had or had not committed, the whole face of creation was completely marred. I was entirely wrong. She told me so, but I could not believe her. I was not in the sphere in which such belief was to be attained to. Now it seems to me that Love of some kind is the only possible explanation of the extraordinary amount of suffering that there is in the world. I cannot conceive any other explanation. I am convinced that there is no other, and that if the worlds have indeed, as I have said, been built out of Sorrow, it has been by the hands of Love, because in no other way could the Soul of man for whom the worlds are made reach the full stature of its perfection. Pleasure for the beautiful body, but Pain for the beautiful Soul.

When I say that I am convinced of these things I speak with too much pride. Far off, like a perfect pearl, one can see the city of God. It is so wonderful that it seems as if a child could reach it in a summer's day. And so a child could. But with me and such as I am it is different. One can realise a thing in a single moment, but one loses it in the long hours that follow with leaden feet. It is so difficult to keep 'heights that the soul is competent to gain'.* We think in Eternity, but we move slowly through Time: and how slowly time goes with us who lie in prison I need not speak again, nor of the weariness and despair that creep back into one's cell, and into the cell of one's heart, with such strange insistence that one has, as it were, to garnish and sweep one's house for their coming, as for an unwelcome guest, or a bitter master, or a slave whose slave it is one's chance or choice to be. And, though at present you may find it a thing hard to believe, it is true none the less that for you, living in freedom and idleness and comfort, it is more easy to learn the lessons of Humility than it is for me, who begin the day by going down on my knees and washing the floor of my cell. For prison-life, with its endless privations and restrictions, makes one rebellious. The most terrible thing about it is not that it breaks one's heart—hearts are made to be broken—but that it turns one's heart to stone. One sometimes feels that it is only with a front of brass and a lip of scorn that one can get through the day at all. And he who is in a state of rebellion cannot receive grace, to use the phrase of which the Church is so fond—so rightly fond, I dare say—for in life, as in Art, the mood of rebellion closes up the channels of the soul, and shuts out the airs of heaven. Yet I must learn these lessons here, if I am to learn them anywhere, and must be filled with joy if my feet are on the right road, and my face set towards the 'gate which is called Beautiful,'* though I may fall many times in the mire, and often in the mist go astray.

This new life, as through my love of Dante I like sometimes to call it, is, of course, no new life at all, but simply the continuance, by means of development, and evolution, of my former life. I remember when I was at Oxford saying to one of my friends—as we were strolling round Magdalen's narrow bird-haunted walks one morning in the June before I took my degree—that I wanted to eat of the fruit of all the trees in the garden of the world,* and that I was going out into the world with that passion in my soul. And so, indeed, I went out, and so I lived. My only mistake was that I confined myself so exclusively to the trees of what seemed to me the sun-gilt side of the garden, and shunned the other side for its shadow and its gloom. Failure, disgrace, poverty, sorrow, despair, suffering, tears even, the broken words that come from the lips of pain, remorse that makes one walk in thorns, conscience that condemns, self-abasement that punishes, the misery that puts ashes on its head, the anguish that chooses sackcloth for its raiment and into its own drink puts gall—all these were things of which I was afraid. And as I had determined to know nothing of them, I was forced to taste each one of them in turn, to feed on them, to have for a season, indeed, no other food at all. I don't regret for a single moment having lived for pleasure. I did it to the full, as one should do everything that one does to the full. There was no pleasure I did not experience. I threw the pearl of my soul into a cup of wine.* I went down the primrose path* to the sound of flutes.* I lived on honeycomb. But to have continued the same life would have been wrong because it would have been limiting. I had to pass on. The other half of the garden had its secrets for me also.

Of course all this is foreshadowed and prefigured in my art. Some of it is in 'The Happy Prince': some of it in 'The

Young King', notably in the passage where the Bishop says
to the kneeling boy, 'Is not He who made misery wiser than
thou art?'* a phrase which when I wrote it seemed to me little
more than a phrase: a great deal of it is hidden away in the
note of Doom that like a purple thread runs through the
gold cloth of *Dorian Gray*: in 'The Critic as Artist' it is set
forth in many colours: in *The Soul of Man* it is written down
simply and in letters too easy to read: it is one of the refrains
whose recurring *motifs* make *Salome* so like a piece of music
and bind it together as a ballad: in the prose-poem of the
man who from the bronze of the image of the 'Pleasure that
liveth for a Moment' has to make the image of the 'Sorrow
that abideth for Ever' it is incarnate.* It could not have been
otherwise. At every single moment of one's life one is what
one is going to be no less than what one has been. Art is a
symbol, because man is a symbol.

   It is, if I can fully attain to it, the ultimate realisation
of the artistic life. For the artistic life is simple self-
development. Humility in the artist is his frank acceptance
of all experiences, just as Love in the artist is simply that
sense of Beauty that reveals to the world its body and its
soul. In *Marius the Epicurean* Pater seeks to reconcile the
artistic life with the life of religion in the deep, sweet and
austere sense of the word. But Marius is little more than a
spectator:* an ideal spectator indeed, and one to whom it is
given 'to contemplate the spectacle of life with appropriate
emotions', which Wordsworth defines as the poet's true
aim:* yet a spectator merely, and perhaps a little too much
occupied with the comeliness of the vessels of the Sanctuary
to notice that it is the Sanctuary of Sorrow that he is gazing
at.

   I see a far more intimate and immediate connection
between the true life of Christ and the true life of the
artist, and I take a keen pleasure in the reflection that long
before Sorrow had made my days her own and bound me
to her wheel I had written in *The Soul of Man* that he who
would lead a Christ-like life must be entirely and absolutely
himself,* and had taken as my types not merely the shepherd
on the hillside and the prisoner in his cell but also the painter

to whom the world is a pageant and the poet for whom the world is a song. I remember saying once to André Gide, as we sat together in some Paris café, that while Metaphysics had but little real interest for me, and Morality absolutely none, there was nothing that either Plato or Christ had said that could not be transferred immediately into the sphere of Art, and there find its complete fulfilment. It was a generalisation as profound as it was novel.

Nor is it merely that we can discern in Christ that close union of personality with perfection which forms the real distinction between classical and romantic Art and makes Christ the true precursor of the romantic movement in life, but the very basis of his nature was the same as that of the nature of the artist, an intense and flamelike imagination. He realised in the entire sphere of human relations that imaginative sympathy which in the sphere of Art is the sole secret of creation. He understood the leprosy of the leper, the darkness of the blind, the fierce misery of those who live for pleasure, the strange poverty of the rich. You can see now—can you not?—that when you wrote to me in my trouble, 'When you are not on your pedestal you are not interesting. The next time you are ill I will go away at once', you were as remote from the true temper of the artist as you were from what Matthew Arnold calls 'the secret of Jesus'.* Either would have taught you that whatever happens to another happens to oneself, and if you want an inscription to read at dawn and at night-time and for pleasure or for pain, write up on the wall of your house in letters for the sun to gild and the moon to silver '*Whatever happens to another happens to oneself*', and should anyone ask you what such an inscription can possibly mean you can answer that it means 'Lord Christ's heart and Shakespeare's brain'.*

Christ's place indeed is with the poets. His whole conception of Humanity sprang right out of the imagination and can only be realised by it. What God was to the Pantheist, man was to him. He was the first to conceive the divided races as a unity. Before his time there had been gods and men. He alone saw that on the hills of life there

were but God and Man, and, feeling through the mysticism
of sympathy that in himself each had been made incarnate,
he calls himself the Son of the One or the son of the
other, according to his mood. More than anyone else in
history he wakes in us that temper of wonder to which
Romance always appeals. There is still something to me
almost incredible in the idea of a young Galilean peasant
imagining that he could bear on his own shoulders the
burden of the entire world: all that had been already done
and suffered, and all that was yet to be done and suffered:
the sins of Nero, of Caesar Borgia, of Alexander VI, and
of him who was Emperor of Rome and Priest of the Sun:*
the sufferings of those whose name is Legion and whose
dwelling is among the tombs,* oppressed nationalities,
factory children, thieves, people in prison, outcasts, those
who are dumb under oppression and whose silence is heard
only of God: and not merely imagining this but actually
achieving it, so that at the present moment all who come in
contact with his personality, even though they may neither
bow to his altar nor kneel before his priest, yet somehow
find that the ugliness of their sins is taken away and the
beauty of their sorrow revealed to them.

I have said of him that he ranks with the poets. That is
true. Shelley and Sophocles are of his company. But his
entire life also is the most wonderful of poems. For 'pity
and terror'* there is nothing in the entire cycle of Greek
Tragedy to touch it. The absolute purity of the protagonist
raises the entire scheme to a height of romantic art from
which the sufferings of 'Thebes and Pelops' line'* are by
their very horror excluded, and shows how wrong Aristotle
was when he said in his treatise on the Drama that it would
be impossible to bear the spectacle of one blameless in
pain.* Nor in Aeschylus or Dante, those stern masters of
tenderness, in Shakespeare, the most purely human of all
the great artists, in the whole of Celtic myth and legend
where the loveliness of the world is shown through a mist
of tears, and the life of a man is no more than the life of a
flower, is there anything that for sheer simplicity of pathos
wedded and made one with sublimity of tragic effect can

be said to equal or approach even the last act of Christ's Passion. The little supper with his companions, one of whom had already sold him for a price: the anguish in the quiet moonlit olive-garden: the false friend coming close to him so as to betray him with a kiss: the friend who still believed in him and on whom as on a rock he had hoped to build a House of Refuge for Man denying him as the bird cried to the dawn: his own utter loneliness, his submission, his acceptance of everything: and along with it all such scenes as the high priest of Orthodoxy rending his raiment in wrath, and the Magistrate of Civil Justice calling for water in the vain hope of cleansing himself of that stain of innocent blood that makes him the scarlet figure of History: the coronation-ceremony of Sorrow, one of the most wonderful things in the whole of recorded time: the crucifixion of the Innocent One before the eyes of his mother and of the disciple whom he loved: the soldiers gambling and throwing dice for his clothes: the terrible death by which he gave the world its most eternal symbol: and his final burial in the tomb of the rich man, his body swathed in Egyptian linen with costly spices and perfumes as though he had been a King's son—when one contemplates all this from the point of view of Art alone one cannot but be grateful that the supreme office of the Church should be the playing of the tragedy without the shedding of blood, the mystical presentation by means of dialogue and costume and gesture even of the Passion of her Lord, and it is always a source of pleasure and awe to me to remember that the ultimate survival of the Greek Chorus, lost elsewhere to art, is to be found in the servitor answering the priest at Mass.

Yet the whole life of Christ—so entirely may Sorrow and Beauty be made one in their meaning and manifestation—is really an idyll,* though it ends with the veil of the temple being rent, and the darkness coming over the face of the earth, and the stone rolled to the door of the sepulchre. One always thinks of him as a young bridegroom with his companions, as indeed he somewhere describes himself, or as a shepherd straying through a valley with his sheep in search of green meadow or cool stream, or as a singer trying to build out of music the walls of the city of God, or as a lover for whose love the whole world was too small. His miracles seem to me as exquisite as the coming of Spring, and quite as natural. I see no difficulty at all in believing that such was the charm of his personality that his mere presence could bring peace to souls in anguish, and that those who touched his garments or his hands forgot their pain: or that as he passed by on the highway of life people who had seen nothing of life's mysteries saw them clearly, and others who had been deaf to every voice but that of Pleasure heard for the first time the voice of Love and found it as 'musical as is Apollo's lute':* or that evil passions fled at his approach, and men whose dull unimaginative lives had been but a mode of death rose as it were from the grave when he called them: or that when he taught on the hillside the multitude forgot their hunger and thirst and the cares of this world, and that to his friends who listened to him as he sat at meat the coarse food seemed delicate, and the water had the taste of good wine, and the whole house became full of the odour and sweetness of nard.

Renan in his *Vie de Jésus*—that gracious Fifth Gospel, the Gospel according to St Thomas one might call it*—says somewhere that Christ's great achievement was that he made himself as much loved after his death as he had been during his lifetime.* And certainly, if his place is among the poets, he is the leader of all the lovers. He saw that love was that lost secret of the world for which the wise men had been looking, and that it was only through love that one could approach either the heart of the leper or the feet of God.

And, above all, Christ is the most supreme of Individualists. Humility, like the artistic acceptance of all experiences, is merely a mode of manifestation. It is man's soul that Christ is always looking for. He calls it 'God's Kingdom' —ἡ βασιλεία τοῦ θεοῦ—and finds it in everyone. He compares it to little things, to a tiny seed, to a handful of leaven, to a pearl. That is because one only realises one's soul by getting rid of all alien passions, all acquired culture, and all external possessions be they good or evil.*

I bore up against everything with some stubbornness of will and much rebellion of nature till I had absolutely nothing left in the world but Cyril. I had lost my name, my position, my happiness, my freedom, my wealth. I was a prisoner and a pauper. But I had still one beautiful thing left, my own eldest son. Suddenly he was taken away from me by the law. It was a blow so appalling that I did not know what to do, so I flung myself on my knees, and bowed my head, and wept and said 'The body of a child is as the body of the Lord: I am not worthy of either'. That moment seemed to save me. I saw then that the only thing for me was to accept everything. Since then—curious as it will no doubt sound to you—I have been happier.

It was of course my soul in its ultimate essence that I had reached. In many ways I had been its enemy, but I found it waiting for me as a friend. When one comes in contact with the soul it makes one simple as a child, as Christ said one should be. It is tragic how few people ever 'possess their souls' before they die.* 'Nothing is more rare in any man,' says Emerson, 'than an act of his own.'* It is quite true. Most people are other people. Their thoughts are someone else's opinions, their life a mimicry, their passions a quotation. Christ was not merely the supreme Individualist, but he was the first in History. People have tried to make him out an ordinary Philanthropist, like the dreadful philanthropists of the nineteenth century, or ranked him as an Altruist with the unscientific and sentimental. But he was really neither one nor the other. Pity he has, of course, for the poor, for those who are shut up in prisons, for the lowly, for the wretched, but he has far more pity for the rich, for the hard Hedonists, for those who waste their freedom in becoming slaves to things, for those who wear soft raiment and live in Kings' houses. Riches and Pleasure seemed to him to be really greater tragedies than Poverty and Sorrow. And as for Altruism, who knew better than he that it is vocation not volition that determines us, and that one cannot gather grapes off thorns or figs from thistles?*

To live for others as a definite self-conscious aim was not his creed.* It was not the basis of his creed. When he says

'Forgive your enemies', it is not for the sake of the enemy but for one's own sake that he says so, and because Love is more beautiful than Hate. In his entreaty to the young man whom when he looked on he loved, 'Sell all that thou hast and give it to the poor',* it is not of the state of the poor that he is thinking but of the soul of the young man, the lovely soul that wealth was marring. In his view of life he is one with the artist who knows that by the inevitable law of self-perfection the poet must sing, and the sculptor think in bronze, and the painter make the world a mirror for his moods, as surely and as certainly as the hawthorn must blossom in Spring, and the corn burn to gold at harvest-time, and the Moon in her ordered wanderings change from shield to sickle, and from sickle to shield.

But while Christ did not say to men, 'Live for others', he pointed out that there was no difference at all between the lives of others and one's own life. By this means he gave to man an extended, a Titan personality. Since his coming the history of each separate individual is, or can be made, the history of the world.* Of course Culture has intensified the personality of man. Art has made us myriad-minded. Those who have the artistic temperament go into exile with Dante and learn how salt is the bread of others and how steep their stairs:* they catch for a moment the serenity and calm of Goethe, and yet know but too well why Baudelaire cried to God:

> O Seigneur, donnez-moi la force et le courage
> De contempler mon corps et mon coeur sans dégout.*

Out of Shakespeare's sonnets they draw, to their own hurt it may be, the secret of his love and make it their own: they look with new eyes on modern life because they have listened to one of Chopin's nocturnes, or handled Greek things, or read the story of the passion of some dead man for some dead woman whose hair was like threads of fine gold and whose mouth was as a pomegranate. But the sympathy of the artistic temperament is necessarily with what has found expression. In words or in colour, in music or in marble, behind the painted masks of an Aeschylean play or

through some Sicilian shepherd's pierced and jointed reeds
the man and his message must have been revealed.

To the artist, expression is the only mode under which
he can conceive life at all. To him what is dumb is dead.
But to Christ it was not so. With a width and wonder
of imagination, that fills one almost with awe, he took
the entire world of the inarticulate, the voiceless world
of pain, as his kingdom, and made of himself its eternal
mouthpiece. Those of whom I have spoken, who are
dumb under oppression and 'whose silence is heard only
of God', he chose as his brothers. He sought to become
eyes to the blind, ears to the deaf, and a cry on the lips
of those whose tongue had been tied. His desire was to
be to the myriads who had found no utterance a very
trumpet through which they might call to Heaven. And
feeling, with the artistic nature of one to whom Sorrow
and Suffering were modes through which he could realise
his conception of the Beautiful, that an idea is of no value
till it becomes incarnate and is made an image, he makes
of himself the image of the Man of Sorrows, and as such
has fascinated and dominated Art as no Greek god ever
succeeded in doing.

For the Greek gods, in spite of the white and red of their
fair fleet limbs, were not really what they appeared to be.*
The curved brow of Apollo was like the sun's disk crescent
over a hill at dawn, and his feet were as the wings of the
morning, but he himself had been cruel to Marsyas and
had made Niobe childless: in the steel shields of the eyes
of Pallas there had been no pity for Arachne: the pomp and
peacocks of Hera were all that was really noble about her:
and the Father of the Gods himself had been too fond of the
daughters of men. The two deep suggestive figures of Greek
mythology were, for religion, Demeter, an earth-goddess,
not one of the Olympians, and, for art, Dionysus, the son
of a mortal woman to whom the moment of his birth had
proved the moment of her death also.

But Life itself from its lowliest and most humble sphere
produced one far more marvellous than the mother of
Proserpina or the son of Semele. Out of the carpenter's shop

at Nazareth had come a personality infinitely greater than any made by myth or legend, and one, strangely enough, destined to reveal to the world the mystical meaning of wine and the real beauty of the lilies of the field as none, either on Cithaeron or at Enna,* had ever done it.

The song of Isaiah, '*He is despised and rejected of men, a man of sorrows and acquainted with grief: and we hid as it were our faces from him*',* had seemed to him to be a prefiguring of himself, and in him the prophecy was fulfilled. We must not be afraid of such a phrase. Every single work of art is the fulfilment of a prophecy. For every work of art is the conversion of an idea into an image. Every single human being should be the fulfilment of a prophecy. For every human being should be the realisation of some ideal, either in the mind of God or in the mind of man. Christ found the type, and fixed it, and the dream of a Virgilian poet, either at Jerusalem or at Babylon, became in the long progress of the centuries incarnate in him for whom the world was waiting.* '*His visage was marred more than any man's, and his form more than the sons of men*',* are among the signs noted by Isaiah as distinguishing the new ideal, and as soon as Art understood what was meant it opened like a flower at the presence of one in whom truth in Art was set forth as it had never been before. For is not truth in Art, as I have said, 'that in which the outward is expressive of the inward; in which the soul is made flesh, and the body instinct with spirit: in which Form reveals'?*

To me one of the things in history the most to be regretted is that the Christ's own renaissance which had produced the Cathedral of Chartres, the Arthurian cycle of legends, the life of St Francis of Assisi, the art of Giotto, and Dante's *Divine Comedy*, was not allowed to develop on its own lines but was interrupted and spoiled by the dreary classical Renaissance that gave us Petrarch, and Raphael's frescoes, and Palladian architecture, and formal French tragedy, and St Paul's Cathedral, and Pope's poetry, and everything that is made from without and by dead rules, and does not spring from within through some spirit informing it. But wherever there is a romantic movement in Art, there somehow, and under some form, is Christ, or the soul of Christ. He is in *Romeo and Juliet*, in the *Winter's Tale*, in Provençal poetry, in 'The Ancient Mariner', in 'La Belle Dame sans Merci', and in Chatterton's 'Ballad of Charity'.

We owe to him the most diverse things and people. Hugo's *Les Misérables*, Baudelaire's *Fleurs du Mal*, the note of pity in Russian novels, the stained glass and tapestries and quattrocento work of Burne-Jones and Morris, Verlaine and Verlaine's poems, belong to him no less than the Tower of Giotto, Lancelot and Guinevere, Tannhäuser, the troubled romantic marbles of Michael Angelo, pointed architecture, and the love of children and flowers—for both of whom, indeed, in classical art there was but little place, hardly enough for them to grow or play in, but who from the twelfth century down to our own day have been continually making their appearance in art, under various modes and at various times, coming fitfully and wilfully as children and flowers are apt to do, Spring always seeming to one as if the flowers had been hiding, and only came out into the sun because they were afraid that grown-up people would grow tired of looking for them and give up the search, and the life of a child being no more than an April day on which there is both rain and sun for the narcissus.

And it is the imaginative quality of Christ's own nature that makes him this palpitating centre of romance. The strange figures of poetic drama and ballad are made by the imagination of others, but out of his own imagination entirely did Jesus of Nazareth create himself. The cry of Isaiah had really no more to do with his coming than the song of the nightingale has to do with the rising of the moon—no more, though perhaps no less. He was the denial as well as the affirmation of prophecy. For every expectation that he fulfilled, there was another that he destroyed. In all beauty, says Bacon, there is 'some strangeness of proportion',* and of those who are born of the spirit, of those, that is to say, who like himself are dynamic forces, Christ says that they are like the wind that 'bloweth where it listeth and no man can tell whence it cometh or whither it goeth'.* That is why he is so fascinating to artists.

He has all the colour-elements of life: mystery, strangeness, pathos, suggestion, ecstasy, love. He appeals to the temper of wonder, and creates that mood by which alone he can be understood.

And it is to me a joy to remember that if he is 'of imagination all compact',* the world itself is of the same substance. I said in *Dorian Gray* that the great sins of the world take place in the brain, but it is in the brain that everything takes place.* We know now that we do not see with the eye or hear with the ear. They are merely channels for the transmission, adequate or inadequate, of sense-impressions. It is in the brain that the poppy is red, that the apple is odorous, that the skylark sings.

Of late I have been studying the four prose-poems about Christ with some diligence. At Christmas I managed to get hold of a Greek Testament, and every morning, after I have cleaned my cell and polished my tins, I read a little of the Gospels, a dozen verses taken by chance anywhere. It is a delightful way of opening the day. To you, in your turbulent, ill-disciplined life, it would be a capital thing if you would do the same. It would do you no end of good, and the Greek is quite simple. Endless repetition, in and out of season, has spoiled for us the *naïveté*, the freshness, the simple romantic charm of the Gospels. We hear them read far too often, and far too badly, and all repetition is anti-spiritual. When one returns to the Greek it is like going into a garden of lilies out of some narrow and dark house.

And to me the pleasure is doubled by the reflection that it is extremely probable that we have the actual terms, the *ipsissima verba,* used by Christ. It was always supposed that Christ talked in Aramaic. Even Renan thought so. But now we know that the Galilean peasants, like the Irish peasants of our own day, were bilingual,* and that Greek was the ordinary language of intercourse all over Palestine, as indeed all over the Eastern world. I never liked the idea that we only knew of Christ's own words through a translation of a translation. It is a delight to me to think that as far as his conversation was concerned, Charmides* might have listened to him, and Socrates reasoned with him, and Plato understood

him: that he really said ἐγώ εἰμι ὁ ποιμὴν ὁ καλός:* that when
he thought of the lilies of the field, and how they neither
toil nor spin, his absolute expression was καταμάθετε
τὰ κρίνα τοῦ ἀγροῦ πῶς αὐξάνει· οὐ κοπιᾷ οὐδὲ νήθει,* and
that his last word when he cried out 'My life has been
completed, has reached its fulfilment, has been perfected,'
was exactly as St John tells us it was: τετέλεσται:* no more.

And while in reading the Gospels—particularly that
of St John himself, or whatever early Gnostic took his
name and mantle—I see this continual assertion of the
imagination as the basis of all spiritual and material life,
I see also that to Christ imagination was simply a form of
Love, and that to him Love was Lord in the fullest meaning
of the phrase. Some six weeks ago I was allowed by the
Doctor to have white bread to eat instead of the coarse
black or brown bread of ordinary prison fare. It is a great
delicacy. To you it will sound strange that dry bread could
possibly be a delicacy to anyone. I assure you that to me it
is so much so that at the close of each meal I carefully eat
whatever crumbs may be left on my tin plate, or have fallen
on the rough towel that one uses as a cloth so as not to soil
one's table: and do so not from hunger—I get now quite
sufficient food—but simply in order that nothing should be
wasted of what is given to me. So one should look on love.

Christ, like all fascinating personalities, had the power
not merely of saying beautiful things himself, but of making
other people say beautiful things to him; and I love the
story St Mark tells us about the Greek woman—the γυνὴ
Ἑλληνίς — who, when as a trial of her faith he said to
her that he could not give her the bread of the children of
Israel, answered him that the little dogs— κυνάρια, 'little
dogs' it should be rendered—who are under the table eat of
the crumbs that the children let fall.* Most people live for
love and admiration. But it is by love and admiration that we
should live.* If any love is shown us we should recognise that
we are quite unworthy of it. Nobody is worthy to be loved.
The fact that God loves man shows that in the divine order
of ideal things it is written that eternal love is to be given to
what is eternally unworthy. Or if that phrase seems to you

a bitter one to hear, let us say that everyone is worthy of love, except he who thinks that he is. Love is a sacrament that should be taken kneeling, and *Domine, non sum dignus* should be on the lips and in the hearts of those who receive it.* I wish you would sometimes think of that. You need it so much.

If I ever write again, in the sense of producing artistic work, there are just two subjects on which and through which I desire to express myself: one is 'Christ, as the precursor of the Romantic movement in life': the other is 'the Artistic life considered in its relation to Conduct'. The first is, of course, intensely fascinating, for I see in Christ not merely the essentials of the supreme romantic type, but all the accidents, the wilfulnesses even, of the romantic temperament also. He was the first person who ever said to people that they should live 'flower-like' lives. He fixed the phrase. He took children as the type of what people should try to become. He held them up as examples to their elders, which I myself have always thought the chief use of children, if what is perfect should have a use. Dante describes the soul of man as coming from the hand of God 'weeping and laughing like a little child', and Christ also saw that the soul of each one should be '*a guisa di fanciulla, che piangendo e ridendo pargoleggia*'.* He felt that life was changeful, fluid, active, and that to allow it to be stereotyped into any form was death. He said that people should not be too serious over material, common interests: that to be unpractical was a great thing: that one should not bother too much over affairs. 'The birds didn't, why should man?' He is charming when he says, 'Take no thought for the morrow. Is not the *soul* more than meat? Is not the *body* more than raiment?'* A Greek might have said the latter phrase. It is full of Greek feeling. But only Christ could have said both, and so summed up life perfectly for us.

His morality is all sympathy, just what morality should be. If the only thing he had ever said had been 'Her sins are forgiven her because she loved much', it would have been worth while dying to have said it.* His justice is all poetical justice, exactly what justice should be. The beggar goes to heaven because he had been unhappy. I can't conceive a better reason for his being sent there. The people who work for an hour in the vineyard in the cool of the evening receive just as much reward as those who had toiled there all day long in the hot sun. Why shouldn't they? Probably no one deserved anything. Or perhaps they were a different kind of people. Christ had no patience with the dull lifeless mechanical systems that treat people as if they were things, and so treat everybody alike: as if anybody, or anything for that matter, was like aught else in the world. For him there were no laws: there were exceptions merely.

That which is the very keynote of romantic art was to him the proper basis of actual life. He saw no other basis. And when they brought him one taken in the very act of sin and showed him her sentence written in the law and asked him what was to be done, he wrote with his finger on the ground as though he did not hear them, and finally, when they pressed him again and again, looked up and said 'Let him of you who has never sinned be the first to throw the stone at her.' It was worth while living to have said that.

Like all poetical natures, he loved ignorant people. He knew that in the soul of one who is ignorant there is always room for a great idea. But he could not stand stupid people, especially those who are made stupid by education—people who are full of opinions not one of which they can understand, a peculiarly modern type, and one summed up by Christ when he describes it as the type of one who has the key of knowledge,* can't use it himself, and won't allow other people to use it, though it may be made to open the gate of God's Kingdom. His chief war was against the Philistines. That is the war every child of light has to wage.* Philistinism was the note of the age and community in which he lived. In their heavy inaccessibility to ideas, their dull respectability, their tedious orthodoxy, their worship of vulgar success, their entire preoccupation with the gross materialistic side of life, and their ridiculous estimate of themselves and their importance, the Jew of Jerusalem in Christ's day was the exact counterpart of the

British Philistine of our own. Christ mocked at the 'whited sepulchres'* of respectability, and fixed that phrase for ever. He treated worldly success as a thing to be absolutely despised. He saw nothing in it at all. He looked on wealth as an encumbrance to a man. He would not hear of life being sacrificed to any system of thought or morals. He pointed out that forms and ceremonies were made for man, not man for forms and ceremonies. He took Sabbatarianism* as a type of the things that should be set at nought. The cold philanthropies, the ostentatious public charities, the tedious formalisms so dear to the middle-class mind, he exposed with utter and relentless scorn. To us, what is termed Orthodoxy is merely a facile unintelligent acquiescence, but to them, and in their hands, it was a terrible and paralysing tyranny. Christ swept it aside. He showed that the spirit alone was of value. He took a keen pleasure in pointing out to them that though they were always reading the Law and the Prophets they had not really the smallest idea of what either of them meant. In opposition to their tithing of each separate day into its fixed routine of prescribed duties, as they tithed mint and rue,* he preached the enormous importance of living completely for the moment.

Those whom he saved from their sins are saved simply for beautiful moments in their lives. Mary Magdalen, when she sees Christ, breaks the rich vase of alabaster that one of her seven lovers had given her and spills the odorous spices over his tired, dusty feet, and for that one moment's sake sits for ever with Ruth and Beatrice in the tresses of the snow-white Rose of Paradise.* All that Christ says to us by way of a little warning is that *every* moment should be beautiful, that the soul should *always* be ready for the coming of the Bridegroom, *always* waiting for the voice of the Lover. Philistinism being simply that side of man's nature that is not illumined by the imagination, he sees all the lovely influences of life as modes of Light: the imagination itself is the world-light, τὸ φῶς τοῦ κόσμου:* the world is made by it, and yet the world cannot understand it: that is because the imagination is simply a manifestation of Love, and it is love, and the capacity for it, that distinguishes one human being from another.

But it is when he deals with the Sinner that he is most romantic, in the sense of most real. The world had always loved the Saint as being the nearest possible approach to the perfection of God. Christ, through some divine instinct in him, seems to have always loved the sinner as being the nearest possible approach to the perfection of man. His primary desire was not to reform people, any more than his primary desire was to relieve suffering. To turn an interesting thief into a tedious honest man was not his aim. He would have thought little of the Prisoners' Aid Society and other modern movements of the kind. The conversion of a Publican into a Pharisee* would not have seemed to him a great achievement by any means. But in a manner not yet understood of the world he regarded sin and suffering as being in themselves beautiful, holy things, and modes of perfection. It *sounds* a very dangerous idea. It is so. All great ideas *are* dangerous.* That it was Christ's creed admits of no doubt. That it is the true creed I don't doubt myself.

Of course the sinner must repent. But why? Simply because otherwise he would be unable to realise what he had done. The moment of repentance is the moment of initiation. More than that. It is the means by which one alters one's past. The Greeks thought that impossible. They often say in their gnomic aphorisms 'Even the Gods cannot alter the past'.* Christ showed that the commonest sinner could do it. That it was the one thing he could do. Christ, had he been asked, would have said—I feel quite certain about it—that the moment the prodigal son fell on his knees and wept he really made his having wasted his substance with harlots, and then kept swine and hungered for the husks they ate, beautiful and holy incidents in his life.* It is difficult for most people to grasp the idea. I dare say one has to go to prison to understand it. If so, it may be worth while going to prison.

There is something so unique about Christ. Of course, just as there are false dawns before the dawn itself, and winter-days so full of sudden sunlight that they will cheat the wise crocus into squandering its gold before its time, and make some foolish bird call to its mate to build on barren boughs, so there were Christians before Christ. For that we should be grateful. The unfortunate thing is that there have been none since.* I make one exception, St Francis of Assisi. But then God had given him at his birth the soul of a poet, and he himself when quite young had in mystical marriage taken Poverty as his bride; and with the soul of a poet and the body of a beggar he found the way to perfection not difficult. He understood Christ, and so he became like him. We do not require the *Liber Conformitatum** to teach us that the life of St Francis was the true *Imitatio Christi*: a poem compared to which the book that bears that name is merely prose.* Indeed, that is the charm about Christ, when all is said. He is just like a work of art himself. He does not really teach one anything, but by being brought into his presence one becomes something. And everybody is predestined to his presence. Once at least in his life each man walks with Christ to Emmaus.*

As regards the other subject, the relation of the artistic life to conduct, it will no doubt seem strange to you that I should select it. People point to Reading Gaol, and say 'There is where the artistic life leads a man.' Well, it might lead one to worse places. The more mechanical people, to whom life is a shrewd speculation dependent on a careful calculation of ways and means, always know where they are going, and go there. They start with the desire of being the Parish Beadle, and, in whatever sphere they are placed, they succeed in being the Parish Beadle and no more. A man whose desire is to be something separate from himself, to be a Member of Parliament, or a successful grocer, or a prominent solicitor, or a judge, or something equally tedious, invariably succeeds in being what he wants to be. That is his punishment. Those who want a mask have to wear it.

But with the dynamic forces of life, and those in whom those dynamic forces become incarnate, it is different.

People whose desire is solely for self-realisation never know where they are going. They can't know. In one sense of the word it is, of course, necessary, as the Greek oracle said, to know oneself.* That is the first achievement of knowledge. But to recognise that the soul of a man is unknowable is the ultimate achievement of Wisdom. The final mystery is oneself. When one has weighed the sun in a balance, and measured the steps of the moon, and mapped out the seven heavens star by star, there still remains oneself. Who can calculate the orbit of his own soul? When the son of Kish went out to look for his father's asses, he did not know that a man of God was waiting for him with the very chrism of coronation, and that his own soul was already the Soul of a King.*

I hope to live long enough, and to produce work of such a character, that I shall be able at the end of my days to say, 'Yes: this is just where the artistic life leads a man.' Two of the most perfect lives I have come across in my own experience are the lives of Verlaine and of Prince Kropotkin:* both of them men who passed years in prison: the first, the one Christian poet since Dante, the other a man with the soul of that beautiful white Christ that seems coming out of Russia. And for the last seven or eight months, in spite of a succession of great troubles reaching me from the outside world almost without intermission, I have been placed in direct contact with a new spirit working in this prison through men and things, that has helped me beyond any possibility of expression in words; so that while for the first year of my imprisonment I did nothing else, and can remember doing nothing else, but wring my hands in impotent despair, and say 'What an ending! What an appalling ending!' now I try to say to myself, and sometimes when I am not torturing myself do really and sincerely say, 'What a beginning! What a wonderful beginning!' It may really be so. It may become so. If it does, I shall owe much to this new personality that has altered every man's life in this place.*

Things in themselves are of little importance, have indeed—let us for once thank Metaphysics for something that she has taught us—no real existence. The spirit alone is of importance. Punishment may be inflicted in such a way that it will heal, not make a wound, just as alms may be given in such a manner that the bread changes to a stone in the hands of the giver. What a change there is—not in the regulations, for they are fixed by iron rule, but in the spirit that uses them as its expression—you can realise when I tell you that had I been released last May, as I tried to be, I would have left this place loathing it and every official in it with a bitterness of hatred that would have poisoned my life. I have had a year longer of imprisonment, but Humanity has been in the prison along with us all, and now when I go out I shall always remember great kindnesses that I have received here from almost everybody, and on the day of my release will give my thanks to many people and ask to be remembered by them in turn.

The prison-system is absolutely and entirely wrong. I would give anything to be able to alter it when I go out. I intend to try.* But there is nothing in the world so wrong but that the spirit of Humanity, which is the spirit of Love, the spirit of the Christ who is not in Churches, may make it, if not right, at least possible to be borne without too much bitterness of heart.

I know also that much is waiting for me outside that is very delightful, from what St Francis of Assisi calls '*my brother the wind*' and '*my sister the rain*', lovely things both of them, down to the shop-windows and sunsets of great cities. If I made a list of all that still remains to me, I don't know where I should stop: for, indeed, God made the world just as much for me as for anyone else. Perhaps I may go out with something I had not got before. I need not tell you that to me Reformations in Morals are as meaningless and vulgar as Reformations in Theology. But while to propose to be a better man is a piece of unscientific cant, to have become a *deeper* man is the privilege of those who have suffered. And such I think I have become. You can judge for yourself.

If after I go out a friend of mine gave a feast, and did not invite me to it, I shouldn't mind a bit. I can be perfectly happy by myself. With freedom, books, flowers, and the moon, who could not be happy? Besides, feasts are not for me any more. I have given too many to care about them. That side of life is over for me, very fortunately I dare say. But if, after I go out, a friend of mine had a sorrow, and refused to allow me to share it, I should feel it most bitterly. If he shut the doors of the house of mourning against me I would come back again and again and beg to be admitted, so that I might share in what I was entitled to share in. If he thought me unworthy, unfit to weep with him, I should feel it as the most poignant humiliation, as the most terrible mode in which disgrace could be inflicted on me. But that could not be. I have a right to share in Sorrow, and he who can look at the loveliness of the world, and share its sorrow, and realise something of the wonder of both, is in immediate contact with divine things, and has got as near to God's secret as anyone can get.

Perhaps there may come into my art also, no less than into my life, a still deeper note, one of greater unity of passion, and directness of impulse. Not width but intensity is the true aim of modern Art. We are no longer in Art concerned with the type. It is with the exception we have to do. I cannot put my sufferings into any form they took, I need hardly say. Art only begins where Imitation ends. But something must come into my work, of fuller harmony of words perhaps, of richer cadences, of more curious colour-effects, of simpler architectural-order, of some aesthetic quality at any rate.

When Marsyas was 'torn from the scabbard of his limbs'—*dalla vagina delle membre sue*,* to use one of Dante's most terrible, most Tacitean phrases—he had no more song, the Greeks said. Apollo had been victor. The lyre had vanquished the reed. But perhaps the Greeks were mistaken. I hear in much modern Art the cry of Marsyas.* It is bitter in Baudelaire, sweet and plaintive in Lamartine, mystic in Verlaine. It is in the deferred resolutions of Chopin's music. It is in the discontent that haunts the recurrent faces of Burne-Jones's women. Even Matthew Arnold, whose song of Callicles tells of 'the triumph of the sweet persuasive lyre', and the 'famous final victory', in such a clear note of lyrical beauty—even he, in the troubled undertone of doubt and distress that haunts his verse, has not a little of it.* Neither Goethe nor Wordsworth could heal him, though he followed each in turn, and when he seeks to mourn for 'Thyrsis' or to sing of 'the Scholar Gipsy', it is the reed that he has to take for the rendering of his strain. But whether or not the Phrygian Faun* was silent, I cannot be. Expression is as necessary to me as leaf and blossom are to the black branches of the trees that show themselves above the prison wall and are so restless in the wind. Between my art and the world there is now a wide gulf, but between Art and myself there is none. I hope at least that there is none.

To each of us different fates have been meted out. Freedom, pleasure, amusements, a life of ease have been your lot, and you are not worthy of it. My lot has been one of public infamy, of long imprisonment, of misery, of ruin, of disgrace, and I am not worthy of it either—not yet, at any rate. I remember I used to say that I thought I could bear a real tragedy if it came to me with purple pall and a mask of noble sorrow,* but that the dreadful thing about modernity was that it put Tragedy into the raiment of Comedy, so that the great realities seemed commonplace or grotesque or lacking in style. It is quite true about modernity. It has probably always been true about actual life. It is said that all martyrdoms seemed mean to the looker-on.* The nineteenth century is no exception to the general rule.

Everything about my tragedy has been hideous, mean, repellent, lacking in style. Our very dress makes us grotesques. We are the zanies of sorrow. We are clowns whose hearts are broken. We are specially designed to appeal to the sense of humour. On November 13th 1895 I was brought down here from London. From two o'clock till half-past two on that day I had to stand on the centre platform of Clapham Junction in convict dress and handcuffed, for the world to look at. I had been taken out of the Hospital Ward without a moment's notice being given to me. Of all possible objects I was the most grotesque. When people saw me they laughed. Each train as it came up swelled the audience. Nothing could exceed their amusement. That was of course before they knew who I was. As soon as they had been informed, they laughed still more. For half an hour I stood there in the grey November rain surrounded by a jeering mob. For a year after that was done to me I wept every day at the same hour and for the same space of time. That is not such a tragic thing as possibly it sounds to you. To those who are in prison, tears are a part of every day's experience. A day in prison on which one does not weep is a day on which one's heart is hard, not a day on which one's heart is happy.

Well, now I am really beginning to feel more regret for the people who laughed than for myself. Of course when they saw me I was not on my pedestal. I was in the pillory. But it is a very unimaginative nature that only cares for people on their pedestals. A pedestal may be a very unreal thing. A pillory is a terrific reality. They should have known also how to interpret sorrow better. I have said that behind Sorrow there is always Sorrow. It were still wiser to say that behind sorrow there is always a soul. And to mock at a soul in pain* is a dreadful thing. Unbeautiful are their lives who do it. In the strangely simple economy of the world people only get what they give, and to those who have not enough imagination to penetrate the mere outward of things and feel pity, what pity can be given save that of scorn?

I have told you this account of the mode of my being conveyed here simply that you should realise how hard it has been for me to get anything out of my punishment but bitterness and despair. I have however to do it, and now and then I have moments of submission and acceptance. All the spring may be hidden in a single bud, and the low ground-nest of the lark may hold the joy that is to herald the feet of many rose-red dawns, and so perhaps whatever beauty of life still remains to me is contained in some moment of surrender, abasement and humiliation. I can, at any rate, merely proceed on the lines of my own development, and by accepting all that has happened to me make myself worthy of it.

People used to say of me that I was too individualistic. I must be far more of an individualist than I ever was. I must get far more out of myself than I ever got, and ask far less of the world than I ever asked. Indeed my ruin came, not from too great individualism of life, but from too little. The one disgraceful, unpardonable, and to all time contemptible action of my life was my allowing myself to be forced into appealing to Society for help and protection against your father. To have made such an appeal against anyone would have been from the individualist point of view bad enough, but what excuse can there ever be put forward for having made it against one of such nature and aspect?

Of course once I had put into motion the forces of Society, Society turned on me and said, 'Have you been living all this time in defiance of my laws, and do you now appeal to those laws for protection? You shall have those laws exercised to the full. You shall abide by what you have appealed to.' The result is I am in gaol. And I used to feel bitterly the irony and ignominy of my position when in the course of my three trials, beginning at the Police Court, I used to see your father bustling in and out in the hopes of attracting public attention, as if anyone could fail to note or remember the stableman's gait and dress, the bowed legs, the twitching hands, the hanging lower lip, the bestial and half-witted grin. Even when he was not there, or was out of sight, I used to feel conscious of his presence, and the blank dreary walls of the great Court-room, the very air itself, seemed to me at times to be hung with multitudinous masks of that apelike face. Certainly no man ever fell so ignobly, and by such ignoble instruments, as I did. I say, in *Dorian Gray* somewhere, that 'a man cannot be too careful in the choice of his enemies'.* I little thought that it was by a pariah that I was to be made a pariah myself.

This urging me, forcing me to appeal to Society for help, is one of the things that make me despise you so much, that make me despise myself so much for having yielded to you. Your not appreciating me as an artist was quite excusable. It was temperamental. You couldn't help it. But you might have appreciated me as an Individualist.

For that no culture was required. But you didn't, and so you brought the element of Philistinism into a life that had been a complete protest against it, and from some points of view a complete annihilation of it. The Philistine element in life is not the failure to understand Art. Charming people such as fishermen, shepherds, ploughboys, peasants and the like know nothing about Art, and are the very salt of the earth. He is the Philistine who upholds and aids the heavy, cumbrous, blind mechanical forces of Society, and who does not recognise the dynamic force when he meets it either in a man or a movement.

People thought it dreadful of me to have entertained at dinner the evil things of life, and to have found pleasure in their company. But they, from the point of view through which I, as an artist in life, approached them, were delightfully suggestive and stimulating. It was like feasting with panthers. The danger was half the excitement. I used to feel as the snake-charmer must feel when he lures the cobra to stir from the painted cloth or reed-basket that holds it, and makes it spread its hood at his bidding, and sway to and fro in the air as a plant sways restfully in a stream. They were to me the brightest of gilded snakes. Their poison was part of their perfection. I did not know that when they were to strike at me it was to be at your piping and for your father's pay. I don't feel at all ashamed of having known them. They were intensely interesting. What I do feel ashamed of is the horrible Philistine atmosphere into which you brought me. My business as an artist was with Ariel. You set me to wrestle with Caliban. Instead of making beautiful coloured, musical things such as *Salome*, and the *Florentine Tragedy*, and *La Sainte Courtisane*, I found myself forced to send long lawyer's letters to your father and constrained to appeal to the very things against which I had always protested. Clibborn and Atkins were wonderful in their infamous war against life.* To entertain them was an astounding adventure. Dumas *père*, Cellini, Goya, Edgar Allan Poe, or Baudelaire, would have done just the same. What is loathsome to me is the memory of interminable visits paid by me to the solicitor Humphreys in your company, when in the ghastly glare of a bleak room you and I would sit with serious faces telling serious lies to a bald man, till I really groaned and yawned with *ennui. There* is where I found myself after two years' friendship with you, right in the centre of Philistia, away from everything that was beautiful, or brilliant, or wonderful, or daring. At the end I had to come forward, on your behalf, as the champion of Respectability in conduct, of Puritanism in life, and of Morality in Art. *Voilà où mènent les mauvais chemins!*[*]

And the curious thing to me is that you should have tried to imitate your father in his chief characteristics. I cannot understand why he was to you an exemplar, where he should have been a warning, except that whenever there is hatred between two people there is bond or brotherhood of some kind. I suppose that, by some strange law of the antipathy of similars, you loathed each other, not because in so many points you were so different, but because in some you were so like. In June 1893 when you left Oxford, without a degree and with debts, petty in themselves, but considerable to a man of your father's income, your father wrote you a very vulgar, violent and abusive letter. The letter you sent him in reply was in every way worse, and of course far less excusable, and consequently you were extremely proud of it. I remember quite well your saying to me with your most conceited air that you could beat your father 'at his own trade'. Quite true. But what a trade! What a competition! You used to laugh and sneer at your father for retiring from your cousin's house where he was living in order to write filthy letters to him from a neighbouring hotel. You used to do just the same to me. You constantly lunched with me at some public restaurant, sulked or made a scene during luncheon, and then retired to White's Club and wrote me a letter of the very foulest character. The only difference between you and your father was that after you had dispatched your letter to me by special messenger, you would arrive yourself at my rooms some hours later, not to apologise, but to know if I had ordered dinner at the Savoy, and if not, why not. Sometimes you would actually arrive before the offensive letter had been read.

I remember on one occasion you had asked me to invite to luncheon at the Café Royal two of your friends, one of whom I had never seen in my life. I did so, and at your special request ordered beforehand a specially luxurious luncheon to be prepared. The *chef*, I remember, was sent for, and particular instructions given about the wines. Instead of coming to luncheon you sent me at the Café an abusive letter, timed so as to reach me after we had been waiting half an hour for you. I read the first line, and saw what it was, and putting the letter in my pocket, explained to your friends that you were suddenly taken ill, and that the rest of the letter referred to your symptoms. In point of fact I did not read the letter till I was dressing for dinner at Tite Street that evening. As I was in the middle of its mire, wondering with infinite sadness how you could write letters that were really like the froth and foam on the lips of an epileptic, my servant came in to tell me that you were in the hall and were very anxious to see me for five minutes. I at once sent down and asked you to come up. You arrived, looking I admit very frightened and pale, to beg my advice and assistance, as you had been told that a man from Lumley, the solicitor, had been enquiring for you at Cadogan Place, and you were afraid that your Oxford trouble or some new danger was threatening you. I consoled you, told you, what proved to be the case, that it was merely a tradesman's bill probably, and let you stay to dinner, and pass your evening with me. You never mentioned a single word about your hideous letter, nor did I. I treated it as simply an unhappy symptom of an unhappy temperament. The subject was never alluded to. To write to me a loathsome letter at 2.30, and fly to me for help and sympathy at 7.15 the same afternoon, was a perfectly ordinary occurrence in your life. You went quite beyond your father in such habits, as you did in others. When his revolting letters to you were read in open Court he naturally felt ashamed and pretended to weep. Had your letters to him been read by his own Counsel still more horror and repugnance would have been felt by everyone. Nor was it merely in style that you 'beat him at his own trade', but in mode of attack you distanced him completely. You availed yourself of the public telegram, and the open postcard. I think you might have left such modes of annoyance to people like Alfred Wood whose sole source of income it is.* Don't you? What was a profession to him and his class was a pleasure to you, and a very evil one. Nor have you given up your horrible habit of writing offensive letters, after all that has happened to me through them and for them. You still regard it as one of your accomplishments, and you exercise it on my friends, on those who have been kind to me in prison like Robert Sherard and others. That is disgraceful of you. When Robert Sherard heard from me that I did not wish you to publish any article on me in the *Mercure de France*, with or without letters, you should have been grateful to him for having ascertained my wishes on the point, and for having saved you from, without intending it, inflicting more pain on me than you had done already. You must remember that a patronising and Philistine letter about 'fair play' for a 'man who is down' is all right for an English newspaper. It carries on the old traditions of English journalism in regard to their attitude towards artists. But in France such a tone would have exposed me to ridicule and you to contempt. I could not have allowed any article till I had known its aim, temper, mode of approach and the like. In art good intentions are not of the smallest value. All bad art is the result of good intentions.

Nor is Robert Sherard the only one of my friends to whom you have addressed acrimonious and bitter letters because they sought that my wishes and my feelings should be consulted in matters concerning myself, the publication of articles on me, the dedication of your verses, the surrender of my letters and presents, and such like. You have annoyed or sought to annoy others also.

Does it ever occur to you what an awful position I would have been in if for the last two years, during my appalling sentence, I had been dependent on you as a friend? Do you ever think of that? Do you ever feel any gratitude to those who by kindness without stint, devotion without limit, cheerfulness and joy in giving, have lightened my black burden for me, have visited me again and again, have written to me beautiful and sympathetic letters, have managed my affairs for me, have arranged my future life for me, have stood by me in the teeth of obloquy, taunt, open sneer or insult even? I thank God every day that he gave me friends other than you. I owe everything to them. The very books in my cell are paid for by Robbie out of his pocket-money. From the same source are to come clothes for me, when I am released. I am not ashamed of taking a thing that is given by love and affection. I am proud of it. But do you ever think of what my friends such as More Adey, Robbie, Robert Sherard, Frank Harris, and Arthur Clifton,* have been to me in giving me comfort, help, affection, sympathy and the like? I suppose that has never dawned on you. And yet—if you had any imagination in you—you would know that there is not a single person who has been kind to me in my prison-life, down to the warder who may give me a good-morning or a good-night that is not one of his prescribed duties—down to the common policemen who in their homely rough way strove to comfort me on my journeys to and fro from the Bankruptcy Court under conditions of terrible mental distress—down to the poor thief who, recognising me as we tramped round the yard at Wandsworth, whispered to me in the hoarse prison-voice men get from long and compulsory silence: '*I am sorry for you: it is harder for the likes of you than it is for the likes of us*'—not one of them all, I say, the very mire from whose shoes you should not be proud to be allowed to kneel down and clean.

Have you imagination enough to see what a fearful tragedy it was for me to have come across your family? What a tragedy it would have been for anyone at all, who had a great position, a great name, anything of importance to lose? There is hardly one of the elders of your family—with the exception of Percy, who is really a good fellow—who did not in some way contribute to my ruin.

I have spoken of your mother to you with some bitterness, and I strongly advise you to let her see this letter, for your own sake chiefly. If it is painful to her to read such an indictment against one of her sons, let her remember that *my* mother, who intellectually ranks with Elizabeth Barrett Browning, and historically with Madame Roland,* died broken-hearted because the son of whose genius and art she had been so proud, and whom she had regarded always as a worthy continuer of a distinguished name had been condemned to the treadmill for two years. You will ask me in what way your mother contributed to my destruction. I will tell you. Just as you strove to shift on to me all your immoral responsibilities, so your mother strove to shift on to me all her moral responsibilities with regard to you. Instead of speaking directly to you about your life, as a mother should, she always wrote privately to me with earnest, frightened entreaties not to let you know that she was writing to me. You see the position in which I was placed between you and your mother. It was one as false, as absurd, and as tragic as the one in which I was placed between you and your father. In August 1892, and on the 8th of November in the same year, I had two long interviews with your mother about you. On both occasions I asked her why she did not speak directly to you herself. On both occasions she gave the same answer: '*I am afraid to: he gets so angry when he is spoken to*'. The first time, I knew you so slightly that I did not understand what she meant. The second time, I knew you so well that I understood perfectly. (During the interval you had had an attack of jaundice and been ordered by the doctor to go for a week to Bournemouth, and had induced me to accompany you as you hated being alone.) But the first duty of a mother is not to be afraid of speaking seriously to her son. Had your mother spoken seriously to you about the trouble she saw you were in in July 1892 and made you confide in her it would have been much better, and much happier ultimately for both of you. All the underhand and secret communications with me were wrong. What was the use of your mother sending me endless little notes, marked 'Private' on the envelope, begging me not to ask you so often to dinner, and not to give you any money, each note ending with an earnest postscript 'On no account let Alfred know that I have written to you'? What good could come of such a correspondence? Did you ever wait to be asked to dinner? Never. You took all your meals as a matter of course with me. If I remonstrated, you always had one observation: 'If I don't dine with you, where am I to dine? You don't suppose that I am going to dine at home?' It was unanswerable. And if I absolutely refused to let you dine with me, you always threatened that you would do something foolish, and always did it. What possible result could there be from letters such as your mother used to send me, except that which did occur, a foolish and fatal shifting of the moral responsibility on to my shoulders? Of the various details in which your mother's weakness and lack of courage proved so ruinous to herself, to you, and to me, I don't want to speak any more, but surely, when she heard of your father coming down to my house to make a loathsome scene and create a public scandal, she might then have seen that a serious crisis was impending, and taken some serious steps to try and avoid it? But all she could think of doing was to send down plausible George Wyndham* with his pliant tongue to propose to me—what? That I should 'gradually drop you'!

As if it had been possible for me to gradually drop you! I had tried to end our friendship in every possible way, going so far as actually to leave England and give a false address abroad in the hopes of breaking at one blow a bond that had become irksome, hateful, and ruinous to me. Do you think that I *could* have 'gradually dropped' you? Do you think that would have satisfied your father? You know it would not. What your father wanted, indeed, was not the cessation of our friendship, but a public scandal. That is what he was striving for. His name had not been in the papers for years. He saw the opportunity of appearing before the British public in an entirely new character, that of the affectionate father. His sense of humour was roused. Had I severed my friendship with you it would have been a terrible disappointment to him, and the small notoriety of a second divorce suit, however revolting its details and origin, would have proved but little consolation to him.* For what he was aiming at was popularity, and to pose as a champion of purity, as it is termed, is, in the present condition of the British public, the surest mode of becoming for the nonce a heroic figure. Of this public I have said in one of my plays that if it is Caliban for one half of the year, it is Tartuffe for the other,* and your father, in whom both characters may be said to have become incarnate, was in this way marked out as the proper representative of Puritanism in its aggressive and most characteristic form. No gradual dropping of you would have been of any avail, even had it been practicable. Don't you feel now that the only thing for your mother to have done was to have asked me to come to see her, and had you and your brother present, and said definitely that the friendship must absolutely cease? She would have found in me her warmest seconder, and with Drumlanrig and myself in the room she need not have been afraid of speaking to you. She did not do so. She was afraid of her responsibilities, and tried to shift them on to me. One letter she did certainly write to me. It was a brief one, to ask me not to send the lawyer's letter to your father warning him to desist. She was quite right. It was ridiculous my consulting lawyers and seeking their protection. But she nullified any effect her letter might have produced by her usual postscript: '*On no account let Alfred know that I have written to you.*'

You were entranced at the idea of my sending lawyers' letters to your father, as well as yourself. It was your suggestion. I could not tell you that your mother was strongly against the idea, for she had bound me with the most solemn promises never to tell you about her letters to me, and I foolishly kept my promise to her. Don't you see that it was wrong of her not to speak directly to you? That all the backstairs-interviews with me, and the area-gate correspondence were wrong? Nobody can shift their responsibilities on anyone else. They always return ultimately to the proper owner. Your one idea of life, your one philosophy, if you are to be credited with a philosophy, was that whatever you did was to be paid for by someone else: I don't mean merely in the financial sense—that was simply the practical application of your philosophy to everyday life—but in the broadest, fullest sense of transferred responsibility. You made that your creed. It was very successful as far as it went. You forced me into taking the action because you knew that your father would not attack your life or yourself in any way, and that I would defend both to the utmost, and take on my own shoulders whatever would be thrust on me. You were quite right. Your father and I, each from different motives of course, did exactly as you counted on our doing. But somehow, in spite of everything, you have not really escaped. The 'infant Samuel theory', as for brevity's sake one may term it, is all very well as far as the general world goes. It may be a good deal scorned in London, and a little sneered at in Oxford, but that is merely because there are a few people who know you in each place, and because in each place you left traces of your passage. Outside of a small set in those two cities, the world looks on you as the good young man who was very nearly tempted into wrong-doing by the wicked and immoral artist, but was rescued just in time by his kind and loving father. It sounds all right. And yet, you know you have not escaped. I am not referring to a silly question asked by a silly juryman, which was of course treated with contempt by the Crown and by the Judge.* No one cared about that. I am referring perhaps principally to yourself. In your own eyes, and some day you will have to think of your conduct, you are not, cannot be quite satisfied at the way in which things have turned out. Secretly you must think of yourself with a good deal of shame. A brazen face is a capital thing to show the world, but now and then when you are alone, and have no audience, you have, I suppose, to take the mask off for mere breathing purposes. Else, indeed, you would be stifled.

And in the same manner your mother must at times regret that she tried to shift her grave responsibilities on someone else, who already had enough of a burden to carry. She occupied the position of both parents to you. Did she really fulfil the duties of either? If I bore with your bad temper and your rudeness and your scenes, she might have borne with them too. When last I saw my wife—fourteen months ago now—I told her that she would have to be to Cyril a father as well as a mother. I told her everything about your mother's mode of dealing with you in every detail as I have set it down in this letter, only of course far more fully. I told her the reason of the endless notes with 'Private' on the envelope that used to come to Tite Street from your mother, so constantly that my wife used to laugh and say that we must be collaborating in a society novel or something of that kind. I implored her not to be to Cyril what your mother was to you. I told her that she should bring him up so that if he shed innocent blood he would come and tell her, that she might cleanse his hands for him first, and then teach him how by penance or expiation to cleanse his soul afterwards. I told her that if she was frightened of facing the responsibility of the life of another, though her own child, she should get a guardian to help her. That she has, I am glad to say, done. She has chosen Adrian Hope, a man of high birth and culture and fine character, her own cousin, whom you met once at Tite Street, and with him Cyril and Vyvyan have a good chance of a beautiful future.* Your mother, if she was afraid of talking seriously to you, should have chosen someone amongst her own relatives to whom you might have listened. But she should not have been afraid. She should have had it out with you and faced it. At any rate, look at the result. Is she satisfied and pleased?

I know she puts the blame on me. I hear of it, not from people who know you, but from people who do not know you, and do not desire to know you. I hear of it often. She talks of the influence of an elder over a younger man, for instance. It is one of her favourite attitudes towards the question, and it is always a successful appeal to popular prejudice and ignorance. I need not ask you what influence I had over you. You know I had none. It was one of your frequent boasts that I had none, and the only one indeed that was well-founded. What was there, as a mere matter of fact, in you that I could influence? Your brain? It was undeveloped. Your imagination? It was dead. Your heart? It was not yet born. Of all the people who have ever crossed my life you were the one, and the only one, I was unable in any way to influence in any direction. When I lay ill and helpless in a fever caught from tending on you, I had not sufficient influence over you to induce you to get me even a cup of milk to drink, or to see that I had the ordinary necessaries of a sickroom, or to take the trouble to drive a couple of hundred yards to a bookseller's to get me a book at my own expense. When I was actually engaged in writing, and penning comedies that were to beat Congreve for brilliancy, and Dumas *fils* for philosophy, and I suppose everybody else for every other quality, I had not sufficient influence with you to get you to leave me undisturbed as an artist should be left. Wherever my writing room was, it was to you an ordinary lounge, a place to smoke and drink hock-and-seltzer in, and chatter about absurdities. The 'influence of an elder over a younger man' is an excellent theory till it comes to my ears. Then it becomes grotesque. When it comes to your ears, I suppose you smile—to yourself. You are certainly entitled to do so. I hear also much of what she says about money. She states, and with perfect justice, that she was ceaseless in her entreaties to me not to supply you with money. I admit it. Her letters were endless, and the postscript 'Pray do not let Alfred know that I have written to you' appears in them all. But it was no pleasure to me to have to pay every single thing for you from your morning shave to your midnight hansom. It was a horrible bore. I used to complain to you again and again about it. I used to tell you—you remember, don't you?—how I loathed your regarding me as a '*useful*' person, how no artist wishes to be so regarded or so treated; artists, like art itself, being of their very essence quite useless. You used to get very angry when I said it to you. The truth always made you angry. Truth, indeed, is a thing that is most painful to listen to and most painful to utter. But it did not make you alter your views or your mode of life. Every day I had to pay for every single thing you did all day long. Only a person of absurd good nature or of indescribable folly would have done so. I unfortunately was a complete combination of both. When I used to suggest that your mother should supply you with the money you wanted, you always had a very pretty and graceful answer. You said that the income allowed her by your father—some £1500 a year I believe—was quite inadequate to the wants of a lady of her position, and that you could not go to her for more money than you were getting already. You were quite right about her income being one absolutely unsuitable to a lady of her position and tastes, but you should not have made that an excuse for living in luxury on me: it should on the contrary have been a suggestion to you for economy in your own life. The fact is that you were, and are I suppose still, a typical sentimentalist. For a sentimentalist is simply one who desires to have the luxury of an emotion without paying for it. To propose to spare your mother's pocket was beautiful. To do so at my expense was ugly. You think that one can have one's emotions for nothing. One cannot. Even the finest and the most self-sacrificing emotions have to be paid for.* Strangely enough, that is what makes them fine. The intellectual and emotional life of ordinary people is a very contemptible affair. Just as they borrow their ideas from a sort of circulating library of thought—the *Zeitgeist** of an age that has no soul—and send them back soiled at the end of each week, so they always try to get their emotions on credit, and refuse to pay the bill when it comes in. You should pass out of that conception of life. As soon as you have to pay for an emotion you will know its quality, and be the better for such knowledge. And remember that the sentimentalist is always a cynic at heart. Indeed sentimentality is merely the bank holiday of cynicism. And delightful as cynicism is from its intellectual side, now that it has left the Tub for the Club, it never can be more than the perfect philosophy for a man who has no soul.* It has its social value, and to an artist all modes of expression are interesting, but in itself it is a poor affair, for to the true cynic nothing is ever revealed.

I think that if you look back now to your attitude towards your mother's income, and your attitude towards my income, you will not feel proud of yourself, and perhaps you may some day, if you don't show your mother this letter, explain to her that your living on me was a matter in which my wishes were not consulted for a moment. It was simply a peculiar, and to me personally most distressing, form that your devotion to me took. To make yourself dependent on me for the smallest as well as the largest sums lent you in your own eyes all the charm of childhood, and in the insisting on my paying for every one of your pleasures you thought that you had found the secret of eternal youth. I confess that it pains me when I hear of your mother's remarks about me, and I am sure that on reflection you will agree with me that if she has no word of regret or sorrow for the ruin your race has brought on mine it would be better if she remained silent. Of course there is no reason she should see any portion of this letter that refers to any mental development I have been going through, or to any point of departure I hope to attain to. It would not be interesting to her. But the parts concerned purely with your life I should show her if I were you.

If I were you, in fact, I would not care about being loved on false pretences. There is no reason why a man should show his life to the world. The world does not understand things. But with people whose affection one desires to have it is different. A great friend of mine—a friend of ten years' standing—came to see me some time ago and told me that he did not believe a single word of what was said against me, and wished me to know that he considered me quite innocent, and the victim of a hideous plot concocted by your father. I burst into tears at what he said, and told him that while there was much amongst your father's definite charges that was quite untrue and transferred to me by revolting malice, still that my life had been full of perverse pleasures and strange passions, and that unless he accepted that fact as a fact about me and realised it to the full, I could not possibly be friends with him any more, or ever be in his company. It was a terrible shock to him, but we are friends, and I have not got his friendship on false pretences. I have said to you that to speak the truth is a painful thing. To be forced to tell lies is much worse.

I remember as I was sitting in the dock on the occasion of my last trial listening to Lockwood's* appalling denunciation of me—like a thing out of Tacitus, like a passage in Dante, like one of Savonarola's indictments of the Popes at Rome—and being sickened with horror at what I heard. Suddenly it occurred to me, '*How splendid it would be, if I was saying all this about myself!*' I saw then at once that what is said of a man is nothing. The point is, who says it. A man's very highest moment is, I have no doubt at all, when he kneels in the dust, and beats his breast, and tells all the sins of his life. So with you. You would be much happier if you let your mother know a little at any rate of your life from yourself. I told her a good deal about it in December 1893, but of course I was forced into reticences and generalities. It did not seem to give her any more courage in her relations with you. On the contrary. She avoided looking at the truth more persistently than ever. If you told her yourself it would be different. My words may perhaps be often too bitter to you. But the facts you cannot deny. Things were as I have said they were, and if you have read this letter as carefully as you should have done you have met yourself face to face.

I have now written, and at great length, to you in order that you should realise what you were to me before my imprisonment, during those three years' fatal friendship: what you have been to me during my imprisonment, already within two moons of its completion almost: and what I hope to be to myself and to others when my imprisonment is over. I cannot reconstruct my letter, or rewrite it. You must take it as it stands, blotted in many places with tears, in some with the signs of passion or pain, and make it out as best you can, blots, corrections and all. As for the corrections and *errata*, I have made them in order that my words should be an absolute expression of my thoughts, and err neither through surplusage nor through being inadequate. Language requires to be tuned, like a violin: and just as too many or too few vibrations in the voice of the singer or the trembling of the string will make the note false, so too much or too little in words will spoil the message. As it stands, at any rate, my letter has its definite meaning behind every phrase. There is in it nothing of rhetoric. Wherever there is erasion or substitution, however slight, however elaborate, it is because I am seeking to render my real impression, to find for my mood its exact equivalent. Whatever is first in feeling comes always last in form.

I will admit that it is a severe letter. I have not spared you. Indeed you may say that, after admitting that to weigh you against the smallest of my sorrows, the meanest of my losses, would be really unfair to you, I have actually done so, and made scruple by scruple the most careful assay of your nature. That is true. But you must remember that you put yourself into the scales.

You must remember that, if when matched with one mere moment of my imprisonment the balance in which you lie kicks the beam, Vanity made you choose the balance, and Vanity made you cling to it. *There* was the one great psychological error of our friendship, its entire want of proportion. Your forced your way into a life too large for you, one whose orbit transcended your power of vision no less than your power of cyclic motion, one whose thoughts, passions and actions were of intense import, of wide interest, and fraught, too heavily indeed, with wonderful or awful consequence. Your little life of little whims and moods was admirable in its own little sphere. It was admirable at Oxford, where the worst that could happen to you was a reprimand from the Dean or a lecture from the President, and where the highest excitement was Magdalen becoming head of the river, and the lighting of a bonfire in the quad as a celebration of the august event. It should have continued in its own sphere after you left Oxford. In yourself, you were all right. You were a very complete specimen of a very modern type. It was simply in reference to me that you were wrong. Your reckless extravagance was not a crime. Youth is always extravagant. It was your forcing me to pay for your extravagances that was disgraceful. Your desire to have a friend with whom you could pass your time from morning to night was charming. It was almost idyllic. But the friend you fastened on should not have been a man of letters, an artist, one to whom your continual presence was as utterly destructive of all beautiful work as it was actually paralysing to the creative faculty. There was no harm in your seriously considering that the most perfect way of passing an evening was to have a champagne dinner at the Savoy, a box at a Music-Hall to follow, and a champagne supper at Willis's as a *bonne-bouche** for the end. Heaps of delightful young men in London are of the same opinion. It is not even an eccentricity. It is the qualification for becoming a member of White's. But you had no right to require of me that I should become the purveyor of such pleasures for you. It showed your lack of any real appreciation of my genius. Your quarrel with your father, again, whatever one may think about its character, should obviously have remained a question entirely between the two of you. It should have been carried on in a backyard. Such quarrels, I believe, usually are. Your mistake was in insisting on its being played as a tragi-comedy on a high stage in History, with the whole world as the audience, and myself as the prize for the victor in the contemptible contest. The fact that your father loathed you, and that you loathed your father, was not a matter of any interest to the English public. Such feelings are very common in English domestic life, and should be confined to the place they characterise: the home. Away from the home-circle they are quite out of place. To translate them is an offence. Family-life is not be treated as a red flag to be flaunted in the streets, or a horn to be blown hoarsely on the housetops. You took Domesticity out of its proper sphere, just as you took yourself out of your proper sphere.

And those who quit their proper sphere change their surroundings merely, not their natures. They do not acquire the thoughts or passions appropriate to the sphere they enter. It is not in their power to do so. Emotional forces, as I say somewhere in *Intentions*, are as limited in extent and duration as the forces of physical energy.* The little cup that is made to hold so much can hold so much and no more, though all the purple vats of Burgundy be filled with wine to the brim, and the treaders stand knee-deep in the gathered grapes of the stony vineyards of Spain. There is no error more common than that of thinking that those who are the causes or occasions of great tragedies share in the feelings suitable to the tragic mood: no error more fatal than expecting it of them. The martyr in his 'shirt of flame'* may be looking on the face of God, but to him who is piling the faggots or loosening the logs for the blast the whole scene is no more than the slaying of an ox is to the butcher, or the felling of a tree to the charcoal-burner in the forest, or the fall of a flower to one who is mowing down the grass with a scythe. Great passions are for the great of soul, and great events can be seen only by those who are on a level with them.

I know of nothing in all Drama more incomparable from the point of view of Art, or more suggestive in its subtlety of observation, than Shakespeare's drawing of Rosencrantz and Guildenstern. They are Hamlet's college friends. They have been his companions. They bring with them memories of pleasant days together. At the moment when they come across him in the play he is staggering under the weight of a burden intolerable to one of his temperament. The dead have come armed out of the grave to impose on him a mission at once too great and too mean for him. He is a dreamer, and he is called upon to act. He has the nature of the poet and he is asked to grapple with the common complexities of cause and effect, with life in its practical realisation, of which he knows nothing, not with life in its ideal essence, of which he knows much. He has no conception of what to do, and his folly is to feign folly. Brutus used madness as a cloak to conceal the sword of his purpose, the dagger of his will,* but to Hamlet madness is a mere mask for the hiding of weakness. In the making of mows and jests he sees a chance of delay. He keeps playing with action, as an artist plays with a theory. He makes himself the spy of his proper actions, and listening to his own words knows them to be but 'words, words, words'. Instead of trying to be the hero of his own history, he seeks to be the spectator of his own tragedy. He disbelieves in everything, including himself, and yet his doubt helps him not, as it comes not from scepticism but from a divided will.

Of all this, Guildenstern and Rosencrantz realise nothing. They bow and smirk and smile, and what the one says the other echoes with sicklier iteration. When at last, by means of the play within the play and the puppets in their dalliance, Hamlet 'catches the conscience' of the King, and drives the wretched man in terror from his throne, Guildenstern and Rosencrantz see no more in his conduct than a rather painful breach of court-etiquette. That is as far as they can attain to in 'the contemplation of the spectacle of life with appropriate emotions'.* They are close to his very secret and know nothing of it. Nor would there be any use in telling them. They are the little cups than can hold so much and no more. Towards the close it is suggested that, caught in a cunning springe set for another, they have met, or may meet with a violent and sudden death. But a tragic ending of this kind, though touched by Hamlet's humour with something of the surprise and justice of comedy, is really not for such as they. They never die. Horatio who, in order to 'report Hamlet and his cause aright to the unsatisfied',

> Absents him from felicity a while
> And in this harsh world draws his breath in pain,

dies, though not before an audience, and leaves no brother. But Guildenstern and Rosencrantz are as immortal as Angelo and Tartuffe,* and should rank with them. They are what modern life has contributed to the antique ideal of friendship. He who writes a new *De Amicitia* must find a niche for them and praise them in Tusculan prose.* They are types fixed for all time. To censure them would show a lack of appreciation. They are merely out of their sphere: that is all. In sublimity of soul there is no contagion. High thoughts and high emotions are by their very existence isolated. What Ophelia herself could not understand was not to be realised by 'Guildenstern and gentle Rosencrantz', by 'Rosencrantz and gentle Guildenstern'. Of course I do not propose to compare you. There is a wide difference between you. What with them was chance, with you was choice. Deliberately and by me uninvited you thrust yourself into my sphere, usurped there a place for which you had neither right nor qualifications, and having by curious persistence, and by the rendering of your very presence a part of each separate day, succeeded in absorbing my entire life, could do no better with that life than break it in pieces. Strange as it may sound to you, it was but natural that you should do so. If one gives to a child a toy too wonderful for its little mind, or too beautiful for its but half-awakened eyes, it breaks the toy, if it is wilful; if it is listless it lets it fall and goes its way to its own companions. So it was with you. Having got hold of my life, you did not know what to do with it. You couldn't have known. It was too wonderful a thing to be in your grasp. You should have let it slip from your hands and gone back to your own companions at their play. But unfortunately you were wilful, and so you broke it. That, when everything is said, is perhaps the ultimate secret of all that has happened. For secrets are always smaller than their manifestations. By the displacement of an atom a world may be shaken. And that I may not spare myself any more than you I will add this: that dangerous to me as my meeting with you was, it was rendered fatal to me by the particular moment in which we met. For you were at that time of life when all that one does is no more than the sowing of the seed, and I was at that time of life when all that one does is no less than the reaping of the harvest.

There are some few things more about which I must write to you. The first is about my Bankruptcy. I heard some days ago, with great disappointment I admit, that it is too late now for your family to pay your father off, that it would be illegal, and that I must remain in my present painful position for some considerable time to come. It is bitter to me because I am assured on legal authority that I cannot even publish a book without the permission of the Receiver to whom all the accounts must be submitted. I cannot enter into a contract with the manager of a theatre, or produce a play without the receipts passing to your father and my few other creditors. I think that even you will admit now that the scheme of 'scoring off' your father by allowing him to make me a bankrupt has not really been the brilliant all-round success you imagined it was going to turn out.

It has not been so to me at any rate, and my feelings of pain and humiliation at my pauperism should have been consulted rather than your own sense of humour, however caustic or unexpected. In point of actual fact, in permitting my Bankruptcy, as in urging me on to the original trial, you really were playing right into your father's hands, and doing just what he wanted. Alone, and unassisted, he would from the very outset have been powerless. In you—though you did not mean to hold such a horrible office—he has always found his chief ally.

I am told by More Adey in his letter that last summer you really did express on more than one occasion your desire to repay me 'a little of what I spent' on you. As I said to him in my answer,* unfortunately I spent on you my art, my life, my name, my place in history, and if your family had all the marvellous things in the world at their command, or what the world holds as marvellous, genius, beauty, wealth, high position and the like, and laid them all at my feet, it would not repay me for one tithe of the smallest things that have been taken from me, or one tear of the least tears that I have shed. However, of course everything one does has to be paid for. Even to the Bankrupt it is so. You seem to be under the impression that Bankruptcy is a convenient means by which a man can avoid paying his debts, a 'score off his creditors' in fact. It is quite the other way. It is the method by which a man's creditors 'score off' him, if we are to continue your favourite phrase, and by which the Law by the confiscation of all his property forces him to pay every one of his debts, and if he fails to do so leaves him as penniless as the commonest mendicant who stands in an archway, or creeps down a road, holding out his hand for the alms for which, in England at any rate, he is afraid to ask. The Law has taken from me not merely all that I have, my books, furniture, pictures, my copyright in my published works, my copyright in my plays, everything in fact from *The Happy Prince* and *Lady Windermere's Fan* down to the stair-carpets and door-scraper of my house, but also all that I am ever going to have. My interest in my marriage-settlement, for instance, was sold. Fortunately

I was able to buy it in through my friends. Otherwise, in case my wife died, my two children during my lifetime would be as penniless as myself. My interest in our Irish estate, entailed on me by my own father, will I suppose have to go next. I feel very bitterly about its being sold, but I must submit.

Your father's seven hundred pence—or pounds is it?—stand in the way, and must be refunded. Even when I am stripped of all I have, and am ever to have, and am granted a discharge as a hopeless Insolvent, I have still got to pay my debts. The Savoy dinners—the clear turtle-soup, the luscious ortolans wrapped in their crinkled Sicilian vine-leaves, the heavy amber-coloured, indeed almost amber-scented champagne—Dagonet 1880, I think, was your favourite wine?—all have still to be paid for. The suppers at Willis's, the special *cuvée* of Perrier–Jouet reserved always for us, the wonderful *pâtés* procured directly from Strasburg, the marvellous *fine champagne* served always at the bottom of great bell-shaped glasses that its bouquet might be the better savoured by the true epicures of what was really exquisite in life—these cannot be left unpaid, as bad debts of a dishonest *client*. Even the dainty sleeve-links—four heart-shaped moonstones of silver mist, girdled by alternate ruby and diamond for their setting—that I designed, and had made at Henry Lewis's as a special little present to you, to celebrate the success of my second comedy—these even—though I believe you sold them for a song a few months afterwards—have to be paid for. I cannot leave the jeweller out of pocket for the presents I gave you, no matter what you did with them. So, even if I get my discharge, you see I have still my debts to pay.

And what is true of a bankrupt is true of everyone else in life. For every single thing that is done someone has to pay.* Even you yourself—with all your desire for absolute freedom from all duties, your insistence on having everything supplied to you by others, your attempts to reject any claim on your affection, or regard, or gratitude—even you will have some day to reflect seriously on what you have done, and try, however unavailingly, to make some attempt at atonement. The fact that you will not be able really to do so will be part of your punishment. You can't wash your hands of all responsibility, and propose with a shrug or a smile to pass on to a new friend and a freshly spread feast. You can't treat all that you have brought upon me as a sentimental reminiscence to be served up occasionally with the cigarettes and *liqueurs*, a picturesque background to a modern life of pleasure like an old tapestry hung in a common inn. It may for the moment have the charm of a new sauce or a fresh vintage, but the scraps of a banquet grow stale, and the dregs of a bottle are bitter. Either today, or tomorrow, or some day you have got to realise it. Otherwise you may die without having done so, and then what a mean, starved, unimaginative life you would have had. In my letter to More I have suggested one point of view from which you had better approach the subject as soon as possible. He will tell you what it is. To understand it you will have to cultivate your imagination. Remember that imagination is the quality that enables one to see things and people in their real as in their ideal relations. If you cannot realise it by yourself, talk to others on the subject. I have had to look at my past face to face. Look at your past face to face. Sit down quietly and consider it. The supreme vice is shallowness. Whatever is realised is right. Talk to your brother about it. Indeed the proper person to talk to *is* Percy. Let him read this letter, and know all the circumstances of our friendship. When things are clearly put before him, no judgment is better. Had we told him the truth, what a lot would have been saved to me of suffering and disgrace! You remember I proposed to do so, the night you arrived in London from Algiers. You absolutely refused. So when he came in after dinner we had to play the comedy of your father being an insane man subject to absurd and unaccountable delusions. It was a capital comedy while it lasted, none the less so because Percy took it all quite seriously. Unfortunately it ended in a very revolting manner. The subject on which I write now is one of its results, and if it be a trouble to you, pray do not forget that it is the deepest of my humiliations, and one I must go through. I have no option. You have none either.

The second thing about which I have to speak to you is with regard to the conditions, circumstances, and place of our meeting when my term of imprisonment is over. From extracts from your letter to Robbie written in the early summer of last year I understand that you have sealed up in two packages my letters and my presents to you—such at least as remain of either—and are anxious to hand them personally to me. It is, of course, necessary that they should be given up. You did not understand why I wrote beautiful letters to you, any more than you understood why I gave you beautiful presents. You failed to see that the former were not meant to be published, any more than the latter were meant to be pawned. Besides, they belong to a side of life that is long over, to a friendship that somehow you were unable to appreciate at its proper value. You must look back with wonder now to the days when you had my entire life in your hands. I too look back to them with wonder, and with other, with far different, emotions.

I am to be released, if all goes well with me, towards the end of May, and hope to go at once to some little seaside village abroad with Robbie and More Adey. The sea, as Euripides says in one of his plays about Iphigenia, washes away the stains and wounds of the world. Θάλασσα κλύζει πάντα τἀνθρώπων κακά.*

I hope to be at least a month with my friends, and to gain, in their healthful and affectionate company, peace, and balance, and a less troubled heart, and a sweeter mood. I have a strange longing for the great simple primeval things, such as the Sea, to me no less of a mother than the Earth. It seems to me that we all look at Nature too much, and live with her too little. I discern great sanity in the Greek attitude. They never chattered about sunsets, or discussed whether the shadows on the grass were really mauve or not. But they saw that the sea was for the swimmer, and the sand for the feet of the runner. They loved the trees for the shadow that they cast, and the forest for its silence at noon. The vineyard-dresser wreathed his hair with ivy that he might keep off the rays of the sun as he stooped over the young shoots, and for the artist and the athlete, the two types that Greece gave us, they plaited into garlands the leaves of the bitter laurel and of the wild parsley which else had been of no service to man.

We call ourselves a utilitarian age, and we do not know the uses of any single thing. We have forgotten that Water can cleanse, and Fire purify, and that the Earth is mother to us all. As a consequence our Art is of the Moon and plays with shadows, while Greek art is of the Sun and deals directly with things. I feel sure that in elemental forces there is purification, and I want to go back to them and live in their presence. Of course, to one so modern as I am, *enfant de mon siècle,* merely to look at the world will be always lovely. I tremble with pleasure when I think that on the very day of my leaving prison both the laburnum and the lilac will be blooming in the gardens, and that I shall see the wind stir into restless beauty the swaying gold of the one, and make the other toss the pale purple of its plumes so that all the air shall be Arabia for me. Linnaeus* fell on his knees and wept for joy when he saw for the first time the long heath of some English upland made yellow with the tawny aromatic blossoms of the common furze, and I know that for me, to whom flowers are part of desire, there are tears waiting in the petals of some rose. It has always been so with me from my boyhood. There is not a single colour hidden away in the chalice of a flower, or the curve of a shell, to which, by some subtle sympathy with the very soul of things, my nature does not answer. Like Gautier I have always been one of those *pour qui le monde visible existe.**

Still, I am conscious now that behind all this Beauty, satisfying though it be, there is some Spirit hidden of which the painted forms and shapes are but modes of manifestation, and it is with this Spirit that I desire to become in harmony. I have grown tired of the articulate utterances of men and things. The Mystical in Art, the Mystical in Life, the Mystical in Nature—this is what I am looking for, and in the great symphonies of Music, in the initiation of Sorrow, in the depths of the Sea I may find it. It is absolutely necessary for me to find it somewhere.

All trials are trials for one's life, just as all sentences are sentences of death, and three times have I been tried. The first time I left the box to be arrested, the second time to be led back to the House of Detention, the third time to pass into a prison for two years. Society, as we have constituted it, will have no place for me, has none to offer; but Nature, whose sweet rains fall on unjust and just alike, will have clefts in the rocks where I may hide, and secret valleys in whose silence I may weep undisturbed. She will hang the night with stars so that I may walk abroad in the darkness without stumbling, and send the wind over my footprints so that none may track me to my hurt: she will cleanse me in great waters, and with bitter herbs make me whole.

At the end of a month, when the June roses are in all their wanton opulence, I will, if I feel able, arrange through Robbie to meet you in some quiet foreign town like Bruges, whose grey houses and green canals and cool still ways had a charm for me, years ago. For the moment you will have to change your name. The little title of which you were so vain—and indeed it made your name sound like the name of a flower—you will have to surrender, if you wish to see *me*; just as *my* name, once so musical in the mouth of Fame, will have to be abandoned by me, in turn. How narrow, and mean, and inadequate to its burdens is this century of ours! It can give to Success its palace of porphyry, but for Sorrow and Shame it does not keep even a wattled house in which they may dwell: all it can do for *me* is to bid me alter my name into some other name, where even mediaevalism would have given me the cowl of the monk or the face-cloth of the leper behind which I might be at peace.

I hope that our meeting will be what a meeting between you and me should be, after everything that has occurred. In old days there was always a wide chasm between us, the chasm of achieved Art and acquired culture: there is a still wider chasm between us now, the chasm of Sorrow: but to Humility there is nothing that is impossible, and to Love all things are easy.

As regards your letter to me in answer to this, it may be as long or as short as you choose. Address the envelope to 'The

Governor, HM Prison, Reading'. Inside, in another, and an open envelope, place your own letter to me: if your paper is very thin do not write on both sides, as it makes it hard for others to read. I have written to you with perfect freedom. You can write to me with the same. What I must know from you is why you have never made any attempt to write to me, since the August of the year before last, more especially after, in the May of last year, eleven months ago now, you knew, and admitted to others that you knew, how you had made me suffer, and how I realised it. I waited month after month to hear from you. Even if I had not been waiting but had shut the doors against you, you should have remembered that no one can possibly shut the doors against Love for ever. The unjust judge in the Gospels rises up at length to give a just decision because Justice comes knocking daily at his door;* and at night-time the friend, in whose heart there is no real friendship, yields at length to his friend 'because of his importunity'.* There is no prison in any world into which Love cannot force an entrance. If you did not understand that, you did not understand anything about Love at all. Then, let me know all about your article on me for the *Mercure de France*. I know something of it. You had better quote from it. It is set up in type. Also, let me know the exact terms of your Dedication of your poems. If it is in prose, quote the prose; if in verse, quote the verse. I have no doubt that there will be beauty in it. Write to me with full frankness about yourself: about your life: your friends: your occupations: your books. Tell me about your volume and its reception. Whatever you have to say for yourself, say it without fear. Don't write what you don't mean: that is all. If anything in your letter is false or counterfeit I shall detect it by the ring at once. It is not for nothing, or to no purpose, that in my lifelong cult of literature I have made myself

> Miser of sound and syllable, no less
> Than Midas of his coinage.*

Remember also that I have yet to know you. Perhaps we have yet to know each other.

For yourself, I have but this last thing to say. Do not be afraid of the past. If people tell you that it is irrevocable, do not believe them. The past, the present and the future are but one moment in the sight of God, in whose sight we should try to live. Time and space, succession and extension, are merely accidental conditions of Thought. The Imagination can transcend them, and move in a free sphere of ideal existences. Things, also, are in their essence what we choose to make them. A thing *is*, according to the mode in which one looks at it. 'Where others', says Blake, 'see but the Dawn coming over the hill, I see the sons of God shouting for joy'.[*] What seemed to the world and to myself my future I lost irretrievably when I let myself be taunted into taking the action against your father: had, I dare say, lost it really long before that. What lies before me is my past. I have got to make myself look on that with different eyes, to make the world look on it with different eyes, to make God look on it with different eyes. This I cannot do by ignoring it, or slighting it, or praising it, or denying it. It is only to be done by fully accepting it as an inevitable part of the evolution of my life and character: by bowing my head to everything that I have suffered. How far I am away from the true temper of soul, this letter in its changing, uncertain moods, its scorn and bitterness, its aspirations and its failure to realise those aspirations, shows you quite clearly. But do not forget in what a terrible school I am sitting at my task. And incomplete, imperfect, as I am, yet from me you may have still much to gain. You came to me to learn the Pleasure of Life and the Pleasure of Art. Perhaps I am chosen to teach you something much more wonderful, the meaning of Sorrow, and its beauty. Your affectionate friend

OSCAR WILDE

Wilde's first post-prison letter to the
Daily Chronicle

To the Editor of the Daily Chronicle

27 May [1897]   [*Dieppe*]

Sir, I learn with great regret, through the columns of your paper, that the warder Martin, of Reading Prison, has been dismissed by the Prison Commissioners for having given some sweet biscuits to a little hungry child. I saw the three children myself on the Monday preceding my release. They had just been convicted, and were standing in a row in the central hall in their prison dress, carrying their sheets under their arms previous to their being sent to the cells allotted to them. I happened to be passing along one of the galleries on my way to the reception room, where I was to have an interview with a friend. They were quite small children, the youngest—the one to whom the warder gave the biscuits—being a tiny little chap, for whom they had evidently been unable to find clothes small enough to fit. I had, of course, seen many children in prison during the two years during which I was myself confined. Wandsworth Prison especially contained always a large number of children. But the little child I saw on the afternoon of Monday the 17th, at Reading, was tinier than any one of them. I need not say how utterly distressed I was to see these children at Reading, for I knew the treatment in store for them. The cruelty that is practised by day and night on children in English prisons is incredible, except to those that have witnessed it and are aware of the brutality of the system.

People nowadays do not understand what cruelty is. They regard it as a sort of terrible mediaeval passion, and connect it with the race of men like Eccelino da Romano,[*] and others, to whom the deliberate infliction of pain gave a real madness of pleasure. But men of the stamp of Eccelino are merely abnormal types of perverted individualism. Ordinary cruelty is simply stupidity. It is the entire want of imagination. It is the result in our days of stereotyped systems of hard-and-fast rules, and of stupidity. Wherever there is centralisation there is stupidity. What is inhuman in modern life is officialism. Authority is as destructive to those who exercise it as it is to those on whom it is exercised. It is the Prison Board, and the system that it carries out, that is the primary source of the cruelty that is exercised on a child in prison. The people who uphold the system have excellent intentions. Those who carry it out are humane in intention also. Responsibility is shifted on to the disciplinary regulations. It is supposed that because a thing is the rule it is right.

The present treatment of children is terrible, primarily from people not understanding the peculiar psychology of a child's nature. A child can understand a punishment inflicted by an individual, such as a parent or guardian, and bear it with a certain amount of acquiescence. What it cannot understand is a punishment inflicted by society. It cannot realise what society is. With grown people it is, of course, the reverse. Those of us who are either in prison or have been sent there, can understand, and do understand, what that collective force called society means, and whatever we may think of its methods or claims, we can force ourselves to accept it. Punishment inflicted on us by an individual, on the other hand, is a thing that no grown person endures, or is expected to endure.

The child consequently, being taken away from its parents by people whom it has never seen, and of whom it knows nothing, and finding itself in a lonely and unfamiliar cell, waited on by strange faces, and ordered about and punished by the representatives of a system that it cannot understand, becomes an immediate prey to the first and most prominent emotion produced by modern prison life—the emotion of terror. The terror of a child in prison is quite limitless. I remember once in Reading, as I was going out to exercise, seeing in the dimly lit cell right opposite my own a small boy. Two warders—not unkindly men—were talking to him, with some sternness apparently, or perhaps giving him some useful advice about his conduct. One was in the cell with him, the other was standing outside. The child's face was like a white wedge of sheer terror. There was in his eyes the terror of a hunted animal. The next morning I heard him at breakfast-time crying, and calling to be let out. His cry was for his parents. From time to time I could hear the deep voice of the warder on duty telling him to keep quiet. Yet he was not even convicted of whatever little offence he had been charged with. He was simply on remand. That I knew by his wearing his own clothes, which seemed neat enough. He was, however, wearing prison socks and shoes. This showed that he was a very poor boy, whose own shoes, if he had any, were in a bad state. Justices and magistrates, an entirely ignorant class as a rule, often remand children for a week, and then perhaps remit whatever sentence they are entitled to pass. They call this 'not sending a child to prison'. It is, of course, a stupid view on their part. To a little child, whether he is in prison on remand or after conviction is not a subtlety of social position he can comprehend. To him the horrible thing is to be there at all. In the eyes of humanity it should be a horrible thing for him to be there at all.

This terror that seizes and dominates the child, as it seizes the grown man also, is of course intensified beyond power of expression by the solitary cellular system of our prisons. Every child is confined to its cell for twenty-three hours out of the twenty-four. This is the appalling thing. To shut up a child in a dimly lit cell, for twenty-three hours out of the twenty-four, is an example of the cruelty of stupidity. If an individual, parent or guardian, did this to a child, he would be severely punished. The Society for the Prevention of Cruelty to Children would take the matter up at once. There would be on all hands the utmost detestation of whomsoever had been guilty of such cruelty. A heavy sentence would, undoubtedly, follow conviction. But our own actual society does worse itself, and to the child to be so treated by a strange abstract force, of whose claims it has no cognisance, is much worse than it would be to receive the same treatment from its father or mother, or someone it knew. The inhuman treatment of a child is always inhuman, by whomsoever it is inflicted. But inhuman treatment by society is to the child the more terrible because there is no appeal. A parent or guardian can be moved, and let out a child from the dark lonely room in which it is confined. But a warder cannot. Most warders are very fond of children. But the system prohibits them from rendering the child any assistance. Should they do so, as Warder Martin did, they are dismissed.

The second thing from which a child suffers in prison is hunger. The food that is given to it consists of a piece of usually badly-baked prison bread and a tin of water for breakfast at half-past seven. At twelve o'clock it gets dinner, composed of a tin of coarse Indian meal stirabout, and at half-past five it gets a piece of dry bread and a tin of water for its supper. This diet in the case of a strong grown man is always productive of illness of some kind, chiefly, of course, diarrhoea, with its attendant weakness. In fact in a big prison astringent medicines are served out regularly by the warders as a matter of course. In the case of a child, the child is, as a rule, incapable of eating the food at all. Anyone who knows anything about children knows how easily a child's digestion is upset by a fit of crying, or trouble and mental distress of any kind. A child who has been crying all day long, and perhaps half the night, in a lonely dimly-lit cell, and is preyed upon by terror, simply cannot eat food of this coarse, horrible kind. In the case of the little child to whom Warder Martin gave the biscuits, the child was crying with hunger on Tuesday morning, and utterly unable to eat the bread and water served to it for its breakfast. Martin went out after the breakfasts had been served, and bought the few sweet biscuits for the child rather than see it starving. It was a beautiful action on his part, and was so recognised by the child, who, utterly unconscious of the regulation of the Prison Board, told one of the senior warders how kind this junior warder had been to him. The result was, of course, a report and a dismissal.

I know Martin extremely well, and I was under his charge for the last seven weeks of my imprisonment. On his appointment at Reading he had charge of Gallery C, in which I was confined, so I saw him constantly. I was struck by the singular kindness and humanity of the way in which he spoke to me and to the other prisoners. Kind words are much in prison, and a pleasant 'Good-morning' or 'Good-evening' will make one as happy as one can be in prison. He was always gentle and considerate. I happen to know another case in which he showed great kindness to one of the prisoners, and I have no hesitation in mentioning it. One of the most horrible things in prison is the badness of the sanitary arrangements. No prisoner is allowed under any circumstances to leave his cell after half-past five p.m. If, consequently, he is suffering from diarrhoea, he has to use his cell as a latrine, and pass the night in a most fetid and unwholesome atmosphere. Some days before my release Martin was going the rounds at half-past seven with one of the senior warders for the purpose of collecting the oakum* and tools of the prisoners. A man just convicted, and suffering from violent diarrhoea in consequence of the food, as is always the case, asked the senior warder to allow him to empty the slops in his cell on account of the horrible odour of the cell and the possibility of illness again in the night. The senior warder refused absolutely; it was against the rules. The man had to pass the night in this dreadful condition. Martin, however, rather than see this wretched man in such a loathsome predicament, said he would empty the man's slops himself, and did so. A warder emptying a prisoner's slops is, of course, against the rules, but Martin did this act of kindness to the man out of the simple humanity of his nature, and the man was naturally most grateful.

As regards the children, a great deal has been talked and written lately about the contaminating influence of prison on young children. What is said is quite true. A child is utterly contaminated by prison life. But the contaminating influence is not that of the prisoners. It is that of the whole prison system—of the governor, the chaplain, the warders, the lonely cell, the isolation, the revolting food, the rules of the Prison Commissioners, the mode of discipline, as it is termed, of the life. Every care is taken to isolate a child from the sight even of all prisoners over sixteen years of age. Children sit behind a curtain in chapel, and are sent to take exercise in small sunless yards—sometimes a stone-yard, sometimes a yard at the back of the mills—rather than they should see the elder prisoners at exercise. But the only really humanising influence in prison is the influence of the prisoners. Their cheerfulness under terrible circumstances, their sympathy for each other, their humility, their gentleness, their pleasant smiles of greeting when they meet each other, their complete acquiescence in their punishments, are all quite wonderful, and I myself learned many sound lessons from them. I am not proposing that the children should not sit behind a curtain in chapel, or that they should take exercise in a corner of the common yard. I am merely pointing out that the bad influence on children is not, and could never be, that of the prisoners, but is, and will always remain, that of the prison system itself. There is not a single man in Reading Gaol that would not gladly have done the three children's punishment for them. When I saw them last it was on the Tuesday following their conviction. I was taking exercise at half-past eleven with about twelve other men, as the three children passed near us, in charge of a warder, from the damp, dreary stone-yard in which they had been at their exercise. I saw the greatest pity and sympathy in the eyes of my companions as they looked at them. Prisoners are, as a class, extremely kind and sympathetic to each other. Suffering and the community of suffering makes people kind, and day after day as I tramped the yard I used to feel with pleasure and comfort what Carlyle calls somewhere 'the silent rhythmic charm of human companionship'.* In this, as in all other things, philanthropists and people of that kind are astray. It is not the prisoners who need reformation. It is the prisons.

Of course no child under fourteen years of age should be sent to prison at all. It is an absurdity, and, like many absurdities, of absolutely tragic results. If, however, they are to be sent to prison, during the daytime they should be in a workshop or schoolroom with a warder. At night they should sleep in a dormitory, with a night-warder to look after them. They should be allowed exercise for at least three hours a day. The dark, badly ventilated, ill-smelling prison cells are dreadful for a child, dreadful indeed for anyone. One is always breathing bad air in prison. The food given to children should consist of tea and bread-and-butter and soup. Prison soup is very good and wholesome. A resolution of the House of Commons could settle the treatment of children in half an hour. I hope you will use your influence to have this done. The way that children are treated at present is really an outrage on humanity and common sense. It comes from stupidity.

Let me draw attention now to another terrible thing that goes on in English prisons, indeed in prisons all over the world where the system of silence and cellular confinement is practised. I refer to the large number of men who become insane or weak-minded in prison. In convict prisons this is, of course, quite common; but in ordinary gaols also, such as that I was confined in, it is to be found.

About three months ago I noticed amongst the prisoners who took exercise with me a young man who seemed to me to be silly or half-witted. Every prison, of course, has its half-witted clients, who return again and again, and may be said to live in the prison. But this young man struck me as being more than usually half-witted on account of his silly grin and idiotic laughter to himself, and the peculiar restlessness of his eternally twitching hands. He was noticed by all the other prisoners on account of the strangeness of his conduct. From time to time he did not appear at exercise, which showed me that he was being punished by confinement to his cell. Finally, I discovered that he was under observation, and being watched night and day by warders. When he did appear at exercise he always seemed hysterical, and used to walk round crying or laughing. At chapel he had to sit right under the observation of two warders, who carefully watched him all the time. Sometimes he would bury his head in his hands, an offence against the chapel regulations, and his head would be immediately struck by a warder so that he should keep his eyes fixed permanently in the direction of the Communion-table. Sometimes he would cry—not making any disturbance—but with tears streaming down his face and an hysterical throbbing in the throat. Sometimes he would grin idiot-like to himself and make faces. He was on more than one occasion sent out of chapel to his cell, and of course he was continually punished. As the bench on which I used to sit in chapel was directly behind the bench at the end of which this unfortunate man was placed I had full opportunity of observing him. I also saw him, of course, at exercise continually, and I saw that he was becoming insane, and was being treated as if he was shamming.

On Saturday week last I was in my cell at about one o'clock occupied in cleaning and polishing the tins I had been using for dinner. Suddenly I was startled by the prison silence being broken by the most horrible and revolting shrieks, or rather howls, for at first I thought some animal like a bull or a cow was being unskilfully slaughtered outside the prison walls. I soon realised, however, that the howls proceeded from the basement of the prison, and I knew that some wretched man was being flogged. I need not say how hideous and terrible it was for me, and I began to wonder who it was who was being punished in this revolting manner. Suddenly it dawned upon me that they might be flogging this unfortunate lunatic. My feelings on the subject need not be chronicled; they have nothing to do with the question.

The next day, Sunday 16th, I saw the poor fellow at exercise, his weak, ugly, wretched face bloated by tears and hysteria almost beyond recognition. He walked in the centre ring along with the old men, the beggars, and the lame people, so that I was able to observe him the whole time. It was my last Sunday in prison, a perfectly lovely day, the finest day we had had the whole year, and there, in the beautiful sunlight, walked this poor creature—made once in the image of God—grinning like an ape, and making with his hands the most fantastic gestures, as though he was playing in the air on some invisible stringed instrument, or arranging and dealing counters in some curious game. All the while these hysterical tears, without which none of us ever saw him, were making soiled runnels on his white swollen face. The hideous and deliberate grace of his gestures made him like an antic. He was a living grotesque. The other prisoners all watched him, and not one of them smiled. Everybody knew what had happened to him, and that he was being driven insane—was insane already. After half an hour he was ordered in by the warder, and I suppose punished. At least he was not at exercise on Monday, though I think I caught sight of him at the corner of the stone-yard, walking in charge of a warder.

On the Tuesday—my last day in prison—I saw him at exercise. He was worse than before, and again was sent in. Since then I know nothing of him, but I found out from one of the prisoners who walked with me at exercise that he had had twenty-four lashes in the cookhouse on Saturday afternoon, by order of the visiting justices on the report of the doctor. The howls that had horrified us all were his.

This man is undoubtedly becoming insane. Prison doctors have no knowledge of mental disease of any kind. They are as a class ignorant men. The pathology of the mind is unknown to them. When a man grows insane, they treat him as shamming. They have him punished again and again. Naturally the man becomes worse. When ordinary punishments are exhausted, the doctor reports the case to the justices. The result is flogging. Of course the flogging is not done with a cat-of-nine-tails. It is what is called birching. The instrument is a rod; but the result on the wretched half-witted man may be imagined.

His number is, or was, A.2.II. I also managed to find out his name. It is Prince. Something should be done at once for him. He is a soldier, and his sentence is one of court-martial. The term is six months. Three have yet to run. May I ask you to use your influence to have this case examined into, and to see that the lunatic prisoner is properly treated?

No report of the Medical Commissioners is of any avail. It is not to be trusted. The medical inspectors do not seem to understand the difference between idiocy and lunacy—between the entire absence of a function or organ and the diseases of a function or organ. This man A.2.II will, I have no doubt, be able to tell his name, the nature of his offence, the day of the month, the date of the beginning and expiration of his sentence, and answer any ordinary simple question; but that his mind is diseased admits of no doubt. At present it is a horrible duel between himself and the doctor. The doctor is fighting for a theory. The man is fighting for his life. I am anxious that the man should win. But let the whole case be examined into by experts who understand brain-disease, and by people of humane feelings who have still some common sense and some pity. There is no reason that the sentimentalist should be asked to interfere. He always does harm.

The case is a special instance of the cruelty inseparable from a stupid system, for the present Governor of Reading is a man of gentle and humane character, greatly liked and respected by all the prisoners.* He was appointed in July last, and though he cannot alter the rules of the prison system he has altered the spirit in which they used to be carried out under his predecessor. He is very popular with the prisoners and with the warders. Indeed he has quite altered the whole tone of the prison life. Upon the other hand, the system is of course beyond his reach so far as altering its rules is concerned. I have no doubt that he sees daily much of what he knows to be unjust, stupid, and cruel. But his hands are tied. Of course I have no knowledge of his real views of the case of A. 2. II, nor, indeed, of his views on our present system. I merely judge him by the complete change he brought about in Reading Prison. Under his predecessor the system was carried out with the greatest harshness and stupidity.

I remain, sir, your obedient servant   OSCAR WILDE

The Ballad of Reading Gaol*

In Memoriam
C. T. W.
Sometime Trooper of the Royal Horse Guards.
Obiit HM Prison, Reading, Berkshire,
July 7th, 1896.*

I

HE did not wear his scarlet coat,*   1
  For blood and wine are red,
And blood and wine were on his hands
  When they found him with the dead,
The poor dead woman whom he loved,
  And murdered in her bed.

He walked amongst the Trial Men
  In a suit of shabby gray;
A cricket cap was on his head,
  And his step seemed light and gay;   10
But I never saw a man who looked
  So wistfully at the day.

I never saw a man who looked
  With such a wistful eye
Upon that little tent of blue
  Which prisoners call the sky,
And at every drifting cloud that went
  With sails of silver by.

I walked, with other souls in pain,
  Within another ring,   20
And was wondering if the man had done
  A great or little thing,
When a voice behind me whispered low,
  That fellow's got to swing.

Dear Christ! the very prison walls
  Suddenly seemed to reel,
And the sky above my head became
  Like a casque of scorching steel;
And, though I was a soul in pain,
  My pain I could not feel.

I only knew what hunted thought
  Quickened his step, and why
He looked upon the garish day
  With such a wistful eye;
The man had killed the thing he loved,
  And so he had to die.

*

Yet each man kills the thing he loves,*
  By each let this be heard,
Some do it with a bitter look,
  Some with a flattering word,
The coward does it with a kiss,*
  The brave man with a sword!

Some kill their love when they are young,
  And some when they are old;
Some strangle with the hands of Lust,
  Some with the hands of Gold:
The kindest use a knife, because
  The dead so soon grow cold.

Some love too little, some too long,
  Some sell, and others buy;
Some do the deed with many tears,
  And some without a sigh:
For each man kills the thing he loves,
  Yet each man does not die.

*

He does not die a death of shame
  On a day of dark disgrace,
Nor have a noose about his neck,
  Nor a cloth upon his face,
Nor drop feet foremost through the floor
  Into an empty space.   60

He does not sit with silent men*
  Who watch him night and day;
Who watch him when he tries to weep,
  And when he tries to pray;
Who watch him lest himself should rob
  The prison of its prey.

He does not wake at dawn to see
  Dread figures throng his room,
The shivering Chaplain robed in white,
  The Sheriff stern with gloom,   70
And the Governor all in shiny black,
  With the yellow face of Doom.

He does not rise in piteous haste
  To put on convict-clothes,
While some coarse-mouthed Doctor gloats,
    and notes
  Each new and nerve-twitched pose,
Fingering a watch whose little ticks
  Are like horrible hammer-blows.

He does not know that sickening thirst
  That sands one's throat, before   80
The hangman with his gardener's gloves
  Slips through the padded door,
And binds one with three leathern thongs,*
  That the throat may thirst no more.

He does not bend his head to hear
  The Burial Office read,
Nor, while the terror of his soul
  Tells him he is not dead,
Cross his own coffin, as he moves
  Into the hideous shed.*   90

He does not stare upon the air
    Through a little roof of glass:
He does not pray with lips of clay
    For his agony to pass;
Nor feel upon his shuddering cheek
    The kiss of Caiaphas.*

II

SIX weeks our guardsman walked the yard,
    In the suit of shabby gray:
His cricket cap was on his head,
    And his step seemed light and gay,
But I never saw a man who looked
    So wistfully at the day.

I never saw a man who looked
    With such a wistful eye
Upon that little tent of blue
    Which prisoners call the sky,
And at every wandering cloud that trailed
    Its ravelled fleeces by.

He did not wring his hands, as do
    Those witless men who dare
To try to rear the changeling Hope
    In the cave of black Despair:
He only looked upon the sun,
    And drank the morning air.

He did not wring his hands nor weep,
    Nor did he peek* or pine,
But he drank the air as though it held
    Some healthful anodyne;
With open mouth he drank the sun
    As though it had been wine!*

And I and all the souls in pain,
    Who tramped the other ring,
Forgot if we ourselves had done
    A great or little thing,
And watched with gaze of dull amaze
    The man who had to swing.

And strange it was to see him pass
　　With a step so light and gay,
And strange it was to see him look
　　So wistfully at the day,　　　　　　130
And strange it was to think that he
　　Had such a debt to pay.

*

For oak and elm have pleasant leaves
　　That in the spring-time shoot:
But grim to see is the gallows-tree,
　　With its adder-bitten root,
And, green or dry, a man must die
　　Before it bears its fruit!*

The loftiest place is that seat of grace
　　For which all worldlings try:
But who would stand in hempen band　　140
　　Upon a scaffold high,
And through a murderer's collar take
　　His last look at the sky?

It is sweet to dance to violins
　　When Love and Life are fair:
To dance to flutes, to dance to lutes
　　Is delicate and rare:
But it is not sweet with nimble feet
　　To dance upon the air!　　　　　　150

So with curious eyes and sick surmise
　　We watched him day by day,
And wondered if each one of us
　　Would end the self-same way,
For none can tell to what red Hell
　　His sightless soul may stray.

*

At last the dead man walked no more
   Amongst the Trial Men,
And I knew that he was standing up
160   In the black dock's dreadful pen,
And that never would I see his face
   In God's sweet world again.

Like two doomed ships that pass in storm
   We had crossed each other's way:
But we made no sign, we said no word,
   We had no word to say;
For we did not meet in the holy night,*
   But in the shameful day.

A prison wall was round us both,
170   Two outcast men we were:
The world had thrust us from its heart,
   And God from out His care:
And the iron gin* that waits for Sin
   Had caught us in its snare.

III

IN Debtors' Yard the stones are hard,
   And the dripping wall is high,
So it was there he took the air
   Beneath the leaden sky,
And by each side a Warder walked,
180   For fear the man might die.

Or else he sat with those who watched
   His anguish night and day;
Who watched him when he rose to weep,
   And when he crouched to pray;
Who watched him lest himself should rob
   Their scaffold of its prey.

The Governor was strong upon
  The Regulations Act:
The Doctor said that Death was but
  A scientific fact: 190
And twice a day the Chaplain called,
  And left a little tract.

And twice a day he smoked his pipe,
  And drank his quart of beer:
His soul was resolute, and held
  No hiding-place for fear;
He often said that he was glad
  The hangman's hands were near.

But why he said so strange a thing
  No Warder dared to ask: 200
For he to whom a watcher's doom
  Is given as his task,
Must set a lock upon his lips,
  And make his face a mask.

Or else he might be moved, and try
  To comfort or console:
And what should Human Pity do
  Pent up in Murderers' Hole?
What word of grace in such a place
  Could help a brother's soul?   210

*

With slouch and swing around the ring
  We trod the Fools' Parade!
We did not care: we knew we were
  The Devil's Own Brigade:
And shaven head and feet of lead
  Make a merry masquerade.

We tore the tarry rope* to shreds
  With blunt and bleeding nails;
We rubbed the doors, and scrubbed the floors,
  And cleaned the shining rails: 220
And, rank by rank, we soaped the plank,
  And clattered with the pails.

We sewed the sacks, we broke the stones,*
    We turned the dusty drill:*
We banged the tins, and bawled the hymns,
    And sweated on the mill:*
But in the heart of every man
    Terror was lying still.

So still it lay that every day
230   Crawled like a weed-clogged wave:
And we forgot the bitter lot
    That waits for fool and knave,
Till once, as we tramped in from work,
    We passed an open grave.

With yawning mouth the yellow hole
    Gaped for a living thing;
The very mud cried out for blood*
    To the thirsty asphalte ring:
And we knew that ere one dawn grew fair
240   Some prisoner had to swing.

Right in we went, with soul intent
    On Death and Dread and Doom:
The hangman, with his little bag,
    Went shuffling through the gloom:
And each man trembled as he crept
    Into his numbered tomb.*

*

That night the empty corridors
    Were full of forms of Fear,
And up and down the iron town
250   Stole feet we could not hear,
And through the bars that hide the stars
    White faces seemed to peer.

He lay as one who lies and dreams
    In a pleasant meadow-land,
The watchers watched him as he slept,
    And could not understand
How one could sleep so sweet a sleep
    With a hangman close at hand.

But there is no sleep when men must weep
    Who never yet have wept: 260
So we—the fool, the fraud, the knave—
    That endless vigil kept,
And through each brain on hands of pain
    Another's terror crept.

*

Alas! it is a fearful thing
    To feel another's guilt!
For, right within, the sword of Sin
    Pierced to its poisoned hilt,
And as molten lead were the tears we shed
    For the blood we had not spilt.   270

The Warders with their shoes of felt
    Crept by each padlocked door,
And peeped and saw, with eyes of awe,
    Gray figures on the floor,
And wondered why men knelt to pray
    Who never prayed before.

All through the night we knelt and prayed,
    Mad mourners of a corse!
The troubled plumes of midnight were
    The plumes upon a hearse:*   280
And bitter wine upon a sponge*
    Was the savour of Remorse.

*

The gray cock crew, the red cock crew,*
    But never came the day:
And crooked shapes of Terror crouched,
    In the corners where we lay:
And each evil sprite that walks by night
    Before us seemed to play.

They glided past, they glided fast,*
290   Like travellers through a mist:
They mocked the moon in a rigadoon*
    Of delicate turn and twist,
And with formal pace and loathsome grace
    The phantoms kept their tryst.

With mop and mow,* we saw them go,
    Slim shadows hand in hand:
About, about, in ghostly rout
    They trod a saraband:
And the damned grotesques made arabesques,
300   Like the wind upon the sand!

With the pirouettes of marionettes,
    They tripped on pointed tread:
But with flutes of Fear they filled the ear,
    As their grisly masque they led,
And loud they sang, and long they sang,
    For they sang to wake the dead.

'Oho!' they cried, 'The world is wide,
    But fettered limbs go lame!
And once, or twice, to throw the dice
310   Is a gentlemanly game,
But he does not win who plays with Sin
    In the secret House of Shame.'

*

No things of air these antics* were,
    That frolicked with such glee:
To men whose lives were held in gyves,*
    And whose feet might not go free,
Ah! wounds of Christ! they were living things,
    Most terrible to see.

Around, around, they waltzed and wound;
    Some wheeled in smirking pairs;   320
With the mincing step of a demirep*
    Some sidled up the stairs:
And with subtle sneer, and fawning leer,
    Each helped us at our prayers.

*

The morning wind began to moan,
    But still the night went on:
Through its giant loom the web of gloom
    Crept till each thread was spun:
And, as we prayed, we grew afraid
    Of the Justice of the Sun.   330

The moaning wind went wandering round
    The weeping prison-wall:
Till like a wheel of turning steel
    We felt the minutes crawl:
O moaning wind! what had we done
    To have such a seneschal?*

At last I saw the shadowed bars,
    Like a lattice wrought in lead,
Move right across the whitewashed wall
    That faced my three-plank bed,   340
And I knew that somewhere in the world
    God's dreadful dawn was red.

*

At six o'clock we cleaned our cells,
    At seven all was still,
But the sough and swing of a mighty wing*
    The prison seemed to fill,
For the Lord of Death with icy breath
    Had entered in to kill.

He did not pass in purple pomp,
350   Nor ride a moon-white steed.
Three yards of cord and a sliding board
    Are all the gallows' need:
So with rope of shame the Herald came
    To do the secret deed.

*

We were as men who through a fen
    Of filthy darkness grope:
We did not dare to breathe a prayer,
    Or to give our anguish scope:
Something was dead in each of us,
360   And what was dead was Hope.

For Man's grim Justice goes its way,
    And will not swerve aside:
It slays the weak, it slays the strong,
    It has a deadly stride:
With iron heel it slays the strong,
    The monstrous parricide!

*

We waited for the stroke of eight:*
    Each tongue was thick with thirst:
For the stroke of eight is the stroke of Fate
370   That makes a man accursed,
And Fate will use a running noose*
    For the best man and the worst.

We had no other thing to do,
    Save to wait for the sign* to come:
So, like things of stone in a valley lone,
    Quiet we sat and dumb:
But each man's heart beat thick and quick,
    Like a madman on a drum!

*

With sudden shock the prison-clock
  Smote on the shivering air,
And from all the gaol rose up a wail
  Of impotent despair,
Like the sound that frightened marshes hear
  From some leper in his lair.

And as one sees most fearful things
  In the crystal of a dream,
We saw the greasy hempen rope
  Hooked to the blackened beam,
And heard the prayer the hangman's snare
  Strangled into a scream.

And all the woe that moved him so
  That he gave that bitter cry,*
And the wild regrets, and the bloody sweats,*
  None knew so well as I:
For he who lives more lives than one
  More deaths than one must die.

IV

THERE is no chapel on the day
  On which they hang a man:
The Chaplain's heart is far too sick,
  Or his face is far too wan,
Or there is that written in his eyes
  Which none should look upon.

So they kept us close till nigh on noon,
  And then they rang the bell,
And the Warders with their jingling keys
  Opened each listening cell,
And down the iron stair we tramped,
  Each from his separate Hell.

380

390

400

Out into God's sweet air we went,
 But not in wonted way,
For this man's face was white with fear,
 And that man's face was gray,
And I never saw sad men who looked
 So wistfully at the day.

I never saw sad men who looked
 With such a wistful eye
Upon that little tent of blue
 We prisoners called the sky,
And at every careless cloud that passed
 In happy freedom by.

But there were those amongst us all
 Who walked with downcast head,
And knew that, had each got his due,
 They should have died instead:
He had but killed a thing that lived,
 Whilst they had killed the dead.

For he who sins a second time
 Wakes a dead soul to pain,
And draws it from its spotted shroud,
 And makes it bleed again,
And makes it bleed great gouts of blood,
 And makes it bleed in vain!

*

Like ape or clown, in monstrous garb
 With crooked arrows starred,
Silently we went round and round,
 The slippery asphalte yard;
Silently we went round and round,
 And no man spoke a word.

Silently we went round and round,
 And through each hollow mind
The Memory of dreadful things
 Rushed like a dreadful wind,
And Horror stalked before each man,
 And Terror crept behind.

*

The Warders strutted up and down,
    And kept their herd of brutes,
Their uniforms were spick and span,
    And they wore their Sunday suits,
But we knew the work they had been at,
    By the quicklime* on their boots.   450

For where a grave had opened wide,
    There was no grave at all:
Only a stretch of mud and sand
    By the hideous prison-wall,
And a little heap of burning lime,
    That the man should have his pall.

For he has a pall, this wretched man,
    Such as few men can claim:
Deep down below a prison-yard,
    Naked for greater shame,   460
He lies, with fetters on each foot,
    Wrapt in a sheet of flame!

And all the while the burning lime
    Eats flesh and bone away,
It eats the brittle bone by night,
    And the soft flesh by day,
It eats the flesh and bone by turns,
    But it eats the heart alway.

*

For three long years they will not sow
    Or root or seedling there: 470
For three long years the unblessed spot
    Will sterile be and bare,
And look upon the wondering sky
    With unreproachful stare.

They think a murderer's heart would taint
    Each simple seed they sow.
It is not true! God's kindly earth
    Is kindlier than men know,
And the red rose would but blow more red,
480   The white rose whiter blow.

Out of his mouth a red, red rose!
    Out of his heart a white!
For who can say by what strange way,
    Christ brings His will to light,
Since the barren staff the pilgrim bore
    Bloomed in the great Pope's sight?*

                    ✳

But neither milk-white rose nor red
    May bloom in prison air;
The shard, the pebble, and the flint,
490   Are what they give us there:
For flowers have been known to heal
    A common man's despair.

So never will wine-red rose or white,
    Petal by petal, fall
On that stretch of mud and sand that lies
    By the hideous prison-wall,
To tell the men who tramp the yard
    That God's Son died for all.

                    ✳

Yet though the hideous prison-wall
500   Still hems him round and round,
And a spirit may not walk by night
    That is with fetters bound,
And a spirit may but weep that lies
    In such unholy ground,

He is at peace—this wretched man—
    At peace, or will be soon:
There is no thing to make him mad,
    Nor does Terror walk at noon,
For the lampless Earth in which he lies
    Has neither Sun nor Moon.   510

*

They hanged him as a beast is hanged:
    They did not even toll
A requiem that might have brought
    Rest to his startled soul,
But hurriedly they took him out,
    And hid him in a hole.

They stripped him of his canvas clothes,
    And gave him to the flies:
They mocked the swollen purple throat,
    And the stark and staring eyes: 520
And with laughter loud they heaped the shroud
    In which their convict lies.

The Chaplain would not kneel to pray
    By his dishonoured grave:
Nor mark it with that blessed Cross
    That Christ for sinners gave,
Because the man was one of those
    Whom Christ came down to save.

Yet all is well; he has but passed
    To Life's appointed bourne:*   530
And alien tears will fill for him
    Pity's long-broken urn,
For his mourners will be outcast men,
    And outcasts always mourn.

V

I KNOW not whether Laws be right,
   Or whether Laws be wrong;
All that we know who lie in gaol
   Is that the wall is strong;
And that each day is like a year,
540   A year whose days are long.

But this I know, that every Law
   That men have made for Man,
Since first Man took his brother's life,
   And the sad world began,
But straws the wheat and saves the chaff
   With a most evil fan.*

This too I know—and wise it were
   If each could know the same—
That every prison that men build
550   Is built with bricks of shame,
And bound with bars lest Christ should see
   How men their brothers maim.

With bars they blur the gracious moon,
   And blind the goodly sun:
And they do well to hide their Hell,
   For in it things are done
That Son of God nor son of Man
   Ever should look upon!

*

The vilest deeds like poison weeds
   Bloom well in prison-air:
It is only what is good in Man   560
   That wastes and withers there:
Pale Anguish keeps the heavy gate,
   And the Warder is Despair.

For they starve the little frightened child*
  Till it weeps both night and day:
And they scourge the weak, and flog the fool,
  And gibe the old and gray,
And some grow mad, and all grow bad,
  And none a word may say.   570

Each narrow cell in which we dwell
  Is a foul and dark latrine,
And the fetid breath of living Death
  Chokes up each grated screen,
And all, but Lust, is turned to dust
  In Humanity's machine.

The brackish water that we drink
  Creeps with a loathsome slime,
And the bitter bread they weigh in scales
  Is full of chalk and lime,*   580
And Sleep will not lie down, but walks
  Wild-eyed, and cries to Time.

                    *

But though lean Hunger and green Thirst
  Like asp with adder fight,
We have little care of prison fare,
  For what chills and kills outright
Is that every stone one lifts by day
  Becomes one's heart by night.

With midnight always in one's heart,
  And twilight in one's cell,   590
We turn the crank, or tear the rope,
  Each in his separate Hell,
And the silence is more awful far
  Than the sound of a brazen bell.

And never a human voice comes near
   To speak a gentle word:
And the eye that watches through the door
   Is pitiless and hard:
And by all forgot, we rot and rot,
600   With soul and body marred.

And thus we rust Life's iron chain
   Degraded and alone:
And some men curse, and some men weep,
   And some men make no moan:
But God's eternal Laws are kind
   And break the heart of stone.

*

And every human heart that breaks,
   In prison-cell or yard,
Is as that broken box that gave
610   Its treasure to the Lord,
And filled the unclean leper's house
   With the scent of costliest nard.*

Ah! happy they whose hearts can break
   And peace of pardon win!
How else may man make straight his plan
   And cleanse his soul from Sin?
How else but through a broken heart
   May Lord Christ enter in?

*

And he of the swollen purple throat,
620   And the stark and staring eyes,
Waits for the holy hands that took
   The Thief to Paradise;*
And a broken and a contrite heart
   The Lord will not despise.*

The man in red who reads the Law*
  Gave him three weeks of life,
Three little weeks in which to heal
  His soul of his soul's strife,
And cleanse from every blot of blood
  The hand that held the knife.   630

And with tears of blood he cleansed the hand,
  The hand that held the steel:
For only blood can wipe out blood,
  And only tears can heal:
And the crimson stain that was of Cain*
  Became Christ's snow-white seal.*

VI

IN Reading gaol by Reading town
  There is a pit of shame,
And in it lies a wretched man
  Eaten by teeth of flame,   640
In a burning winding-sheet he lies,
  And his grave has got no name.

And there, till Christ call forth the dead,
  In silence let him lie:
No need to waste the foolish tear,
  Or heave the windy sigh:
The man had killed the thing he loved,
  And so he had to die.

And all men kill the thing they love,
  By all let this be heard,   650
Some do it with a bitter look,
  Some with a flattering word,
The coward does it with a kiss,
  The brave man with a sword!

Wilde's second post-prison letter to the *Daily Chronicle*

To the Editor of the Daily Chronicle

*23 March [1898]**   [*Paris*]

Sir, I understand that the Home Secretary's Prison Reform
Bill is to be read this week for the first or second time, and
as your journal has been the one paper in England that has
taken a real and vital interest in this important question,
I hope that you will allow me, as one who has had long
personal experience of life in an English gaol, to point out
what reforms in our present stupid and barbarous system
are urgently necessary.

From a leading article that appeared in your columns
about a week ago, I learn that the chief reform proposed is
an increase in the number of inspectors and official visitors,
that are to have access to our English prisons.

Such a reform as this is entirely useless. The reason is
extremely simple. The inspectors and justices of the peace
that visit prisons come there for the purpose of seeing that
the prison regulations are duly carried out. They come for
no other purpose, nor have they any power, even if they
had the desire, to alter a single clause in the regulations.
No prisoner has ever had the smallest relief, or attention,
or care from any of the official visitors. The visitors arrive not to help the prisoners, but to see that the rules
are carried out. Their object in coming is to ensure the
enforcement of a foolish and inhuman code. And, as they
must have some occupation, they take very good care to do
it. A prisoner who has been allowed the smallest privilege
dreads the arrival of the inspectors. And on the day of any
prison inspection the prison officials are more than usually
brutal to the prisoners. Their object is, of course, to show
the splendid discipline they maintain.

The necessary reforms are very simple. They concern
the needs of the body and the needs of the mind of each

unfortunate prisoner. With regard to the first, there are three permanent punishments authorised by law in English prisons:

1. Hunger.
2. Insomnia.
3. Disease.

The food supplied to prisoners is entirely inadequate. Most of it is revolting in character. All of it is insufficient. Every prisoner suffers day and night from hunger. A certain amount of food is carefully weighed out ounce by ounce for each prisoner. It is just enough to sustain, not life exactly, but existence. But one is always racked by the pain and sickness of hunger.

The result of the food—which in most cases consists of weak gruel, badly-baked bread, suet, and water—is disease in the form of incessant diarrhoea. This malady, which ultimately with most prisoners becomes a permanent disease, is a recognised institution in every prison. At Wandsworth Prison, for instance—where I was confined for two months, till I had to be carried into hospital, where I remained for another two months—the warders go round twice or three times a day with astringent medicines, which they serve out to the prisoners as a matter of course. After about a week of such treatment it is unnecessary to say the medicine produces no effect at all. The wretched prisoner is then left a prey to the most weakening, depressing, and humiliating malady that can be conceived; and if, as often happens, he fails, from physical weakness, to complete his required revolutions at the crank or the mill* he is reported for idleness, and punished with the greatest severity and brutality. Nor is this all.

Nothing can be worse than the sanitary arrangements of English prisons. In old days each cell was provided with a form of latrine. These latrines have now been suppressed. They exist no longer. A small tin vessel is supplied to each prisoner instead. Three times a day a prisoner is allowed to empty his slops. But he is not allowed to have access to the prison lavatories, except during the one hour when he is at exercise. And after five o'clock in the evening he is not allowed to leave his cell under any pretence, or for any reason. A man suffering from diarrhoea is consequently placed in a position so loathsome that it is unnecessary to dwell on it, that it would be unseemly to dwell on it. The misery and tortures that prisoners go through in consequence of the revolting sanitary arrangements are quite indescribable. And the foul air of the prison cells, increased by a system of ventilation that is utterly ineffective, is so sickening and unwholesome that it is no uncommon thing for warders, when they come in the morning out of the fresh air and open and inspect each cell, to be violently sick. I have seen this myself on more than three occasions, and several of the warders have mentioned it to me as one of the disgusting things that their office entails on them.

The food supplied to prisoners should be adequate and wholesome. It should not be of such a character as to produce the incessant diarrhoea that, at first a malady, becomes a permanent disease.

The sanitary arrangements in English prisons should be entirely altered. Every prisoner should be allowed to have access to the lavatories when necessary, and to empty his slops when necessary. The present system of ventilation in each cell is utterly useless. The air comes through choked-up gratings, and through a small ventilator in the tiny barred window, which is far too small, and too badly constructed, to admit any adequate amount of fresh air. One is only allowed out of one's cell for one hour out of the twenty-four that compose the long day, and so for twenty-three hours one is breathing the foulest possible air.

With regard to the punishment of insomnia, it only exists in Chinese and English prisons. In China it is inflicted by placing the prisoner in a small bamboo cage; in England by means of the plank bed. The object of the plank bed is to produce insomnia. There is no other object in it, and it invariably succeeds. And even when one is subsequently allowed a hard mattress, as happens in the course of imprisonment, one still suffers from insomnia. For sleep, like all wholesome things, is a habit. Every prisoner who has been on a plank bed suffers from insomnia. It is a revolting and ignorant punishment.

With regard to the needs of the mind, I beg that you will allow me to say something.

The present prison system seems almost to have for its aim the wrecking and the destruction of the mental faculties. The production of insanity is, if not its object, certainly its result. That is a well ascertained fact. Its causes are obvious. Deprived of books, of all human intercourse, isolated from every humane and humanising influence, condemned to eternal silence, robbed of all intercourse with the external world, treated like an unintelligent animal, brutalised below the level of any of the brute-creation, the wretched man who is confined in an English prison can hardly escape becoming insane. I do not wish to dwell on these horrors; still less to excite any momentary sentimental interest in these matters. So I will merely, with your permission, point out what should be done.

Every prisoner should have an adequate supply of good books. At present, during the first three months of imprisonment, one is allowed no books at all, except a Bible, prayer-book, and hymn-book. After that, one is allowed one book a week. That is not merely inadequate, but the books that compose an ordinary prison library are perfectly useless. They consist chiefly of third-rate, badly-written, religious books, so-called, written apparently for children, and utterly unsuitable for children or for anyone else. Prisoners should be encouraged to read, and should have whatever books they want, and the books should be well chosen. At present the selection of books is made by the prison chaplain.

Under the present system a prisoner is only allowed to see his friends four times a year, for twenty minutes each time. This is quite wrong. A prisoner should be allowed to see his friends once a month, and for a reasonable time. The mode at present in vogue of exhibiting a prisoner to his friends should be altered. Under the present system the prisoner is either locked up in a large iron cage or in a large wooden box, with a small aperture, covered with wire netting, through which he is allowed to peer. His friends are placed in a similar cage, some three or four feet distant, and two warders stand between, to listen to, and, if they wish, stop or interrupt the conversation such as it may be. I propose that a prisoner should be allowed to see his relatives or friends in a room. The present regulations are inexpressibly revolting and harassing. A visit from our relatives or friends is to every prisoner an intensification of humiliation and mental distress. Many prisoners, rather than support such an ordeal, refuse to see their friends at all. And I cannot say I am surprised. When one sees one's solicitor, one sees him in a room with a glass door, on the other side of which stands the warder. When a man sees his wife and children, or his parents, or his friends, he should be allowed the same privilege. To be exhibited, like an ape in a cage, to people who are fond of one, and of whom one is fond, is a needless and horrible degradation.

Every prisoner should be allowed to write and receive a letter at least once a month. At present one is allowed to write only four times a year. This is quite inadequate. One of the tragedies of prison life is that it turns a man's heart to stone. The feelings of natural affection, like all other feelings, require to be fed. They die easily of inanition. A brief letter, four times a year, is not enough to keep alive the gentler and more humane affections by which ultimately the nature is kept sensitive to any fine or beautiful influences that may heal a wrecked and ruined life.

The habit of mutilating and expurgating prisoners' letters should be stopped. At present, if a prisoner in a letter makes any complaint of the prison system, that portion of his letter is cut out with a pair of scissors. If, upon the other hand, he makes any complaint when he speaks to his friends through the bars of the cage, or the aperture of the wooden box, he is brutalised by the warders, and reported for punishment every week till his next visit comes round, by which time he is expected to have learned, not wisdom, but cunning, and one always learns that. It is one of the few things that one does learn in prison. Fortunately, the other things are, in some instances, of higher import.

If I may trespass on your space for a little longer, may I say this? You suggested in your leading article that no prison chaplain should be allowed to have any care or employment outside the prison itself. But this is a matter of no moment. The prison chaplains are entirely useless. They are, as a class, well-meaning, but foolish, indeed silly, men. They are of no help to any prisoner. Once every six weeks or so a key turns in the lock of one's cell door, and the chaplain enters. One stands, of course, at attention. He asks one whether one has been reading the Bible. One answers 'Yes' or 'No', as the case may be. He then quotes a few texts, and goes out and locks the door. Sometimes he leaves a tract.*

The officials who should not be allowed to hold any employment outside the prison, or to have any private practice, are the prison doctors. At present the prison doctors have usually, if not always, a large private practice, and hold appointments in other institutions. The consequence is that the health of the prisoners is entirely neglected, and the sanitary condition of the prison entirely overlooked. As a class I regard, and have always from my earliest youth regarded, doctors as by far the most humane profession in the community. But I must make an exception for prison doctors. They are, as far as I came across them, and from what I saw of them in hospital and elsewhere, brutal in manner, coarse in temperament, and utterly indifferent to the health of the prisoners or their comfort. If prison doctors were prohibited from private practice they would be compelled to take some interest in the health and sanitary condition of the people under their charge.

I have tried to indicate in my letter a few of the reforms necessary to our English prison system. They are simple, practical, and humane. They are, of course, only a beginning. But it is time that a beginning should be made, and it can only be started by a strong pressure of public opinion formularised in your powerful paper, and fostered by it.

But to make even these reforms effectual, much has to be done. And the first, and perhaps the most difficult task is to humanise the governors of prisons, to civilise the warders and to Christianise the chaplains. Yours, etc.

THE AUTHOR OF 'THE BALLAD OF READING GAOL'

EXPLANATORY NOTES

ABBREVIATIONS

Wilde's works. The following are cited from *Writings of Oscar Wilde* (1989): WOW:

DG	*The Picture of Dorian Gray*
DL	*The Decay of Lying*
CA I	*The Critic as Artist Part I*
CA II	*The Critic as Artist Part II*
LWF	*Lady Windermere's Fan*
IH	*An Ideal Husband*
IBE	*The Importance of Being Earnest*
BRG	*The Ballad of Reading Gaol*

Other works are cited as follows:

CSF	*The Complete Shorter Fiction*
SM	*The Soul of Man*
WNI	*A Woman of No Importance*
Rev	*Reviews* (1908)
Misc	*Miscellanies* (1908)
L and SL	*The Letters of Oscar Wilde* (1962) and *Selected Letters of Oscar Wilde* (1979), both ed. Rupert Hart-Davis. As *L* is long out of print and *SL* is available, references are made wherever possible to *SL*, and only where necessary to *L*. Where notes to *De Profundis* are taken from this text, they are identified by RH-D. All references are to pages.
ML	*More Letters of Oscar Wilde,* ed. Rupert Hart-Davis (1985)

Emerson. Where possible, reference is made to the ongoing edition of his work, *The Collected Works of Ralph Waldo Emerson,* ed. variously by Robert E. Spiller, Alfred R. Ferguson, Joseph Slater, Jean Ferguson Carr, Wallace E. Williams, and Douglas Emory Wilson. Four volumes have been published to date:

CWRWE I	Volume I: Nature, Addresses, and Lectures
CWRWE II	Volume II: Essays: First Series
CWRWE III	Volume III: Essays: Second Series
CWRWE IV	Volume IV: Representative Men

Other works of Emerson are referred to by essay and/or volume title. The essay most frequently quoted, 'Self-Reliance' (*CWRWE II*) is referred to as SR.

All biblical quotations are from the Authorized Version.

The Soul of Man

1: *for others*: an important initial paradox: living (or dying) for others is one of the central tenets of Christianity, which Wilde resists. See also *CA II* 279, duty to one's neighbour, and *Rev* 531, 'the intolerable sense of obligation'. Wilde is aided here by the work of the Taoist philosopher Chuang Tzŭ of the fourth century BC, whose newly translated work he had recently reviewed at length and with enjoyment (*Rev* 528–38), and whom he quotes (13 n.). Chuang Tzŭ's creed of self-culture and self-development is very relevant to this essay. For a fuller discussion of his influence on Wilde, see Isobel Murray, 'Oscar Wilde's Absorption of "Influences": The Case History of Chuang Tzŭ', *Durham University Journal* 64/1 (Dec. 1971), 1–13. But a more pervasive influence here is the American Transcendentalist Ralph Waldo Emerson (1803–82): see Introduction.

Darwin: 1809–82, author of *The Origin of Species* (1859) and *The Descent of Man* (1871); much praised by Wilde in *CA II* 295–6.

Renan: 1823–92, French philologist and historian famous for his 1863 *Life of Jesus*, expressing his loss of faith in traditional supernatural aspects of Christianity. See also p. 113, and *CA II* 283, 296.

Plato puts it: *Republic*, Book 6 section 496.

in him: cf. Emerson in 'The American Scholar': 'In a century, in a millennium, one or two men: that is to say—one or two approximations to the right state of every man' (*CWRWE I* 65; see also pp. 127–8).

of criticism: revised in *Intentions* as *The Critic as Artist*: see *CA II* 280 and *passim*.

the poor: see note on the People's Palace in *WOW* 594, and Lord Henry Wotton's comments on amusing the slaves at *DG* 78.

2: *The proper ... impossible*: in *The Fortnightly Review* version of this essay (Feb. 1891), certain sentences were given in italics, to indicate their centrality. This form was rejected for the volume reprint, but for interest will be shown in the notes here, as 'originally italicized'.

most good: cf. *IH* 421, *CA I* 257, *CA II* 278–81.

demoralizes: cf. Engels's attack on philanthropy in the 1887 preface to *The Condition of the Working-Class in England*.

of sins: cf. 1 Pet. 4: 8: 'And above all things have fervent charity among yourselves: for charity shall cover the multitude of sins.' Cf. *CA I* 257.

frost comes: a new paper, *The Star*, said in 1888: 'One fall of snow, a single fog reduces London to chaos.'

Socialism ... Individualism: originally italicized. *Individualism*: Wilde consciously uses a resonant and deeply ambiguous term: some capitalists proudly used it as almost a synonym for Capitalism in one sense: some Socialists used it as almost synonymous with Anarchism when they were defending authoritarian state socialism in another: as Wilde uses it it becomes almost synonymous with Emerson's 'self-reliance'.

4: *has duties*: cf. *IBE* 493.

but ... grateful: originally italicized.

man's table: Mark 7: 26–9.

original virtue: in Christian teaching, disobedience was the original sin. Cf. *CA II* 257: 'What is termed Sin is an essential element of progress.'

5: *pottage*: cf. Gen. 25.

Abolitionists: in Boston in 1882, Wilde had met the most celebrated of these, Wendell Phillips, now 71.

to starve: cf. William Morris's lecture 'Art and Socialism': 'the freedom left the most of men free—to take at a wretched wage what slave's work lay nearest to them, or starve.'

6: *industrial-barrack system*: different socialist programmes advocated more or less authoritarian and disciplined approaches to life: see, e.g., Edward Bellamy's novel *Looking Backward* (1888), with its adaptation of national military service to the labour problem.

It is ... is fine: originally italicized.

7: *is to be*: cf. *WOW* xviii–xix. This whole paragraph is very close to Emerson's SR. Emerson opposes reliance on property to self-reliance: men 'measure their esteem of each other, by what each has, and not by what each is'. The essay ends with this message: 'Do not believe it. Nothing can bring you peace but yourself. Nothing can bring you peace but the triumph of principles' (49, 51).

The true . . . man is: originally italicized.

8: *except himself*: Emerson in 'Compensation' says: 'It is impossible for a man to be cheated by anyone but himself', and quotes St Bernard: 'Nothing can work me damage except myself, the harm that I sustain, I carry about with me, and never am a real sufferer but by my own fault' (*CWR WE I* 69, 71).

Mommsen: in Volume 5 of his *History of Rome* (trans. 1868), Theodor Mommsen calls Julius Caesar 'the entire and perfect man'.

Renan: in *Marc-Aurèle et la fin du monde antique* (1882), Renan says that the emperor 'will remain inimitable by his greatness of soul, his unsurpassable nobility of character and the perfection of his goodness'.

Most . . . friction: originally italicized.

9: *authority*: Emerson's SR rejects the past—'dead institutions' (30), 'corpse of your memory' (33); law—'No law can be sacred to me but that of my nature' (30); authority—'But keep thy state; come not into their confusion' (41).

antique world: cf. below p. 126 and n.

Be thyself: cf. SR 28: 'Trust thyself: every heart vibrates to that iron string', and 'The Divinity School Address': 'the great stoical doctrine, Obey thyself (*CWR WE I*, 82).

When . . . their personalities: originally italicized.

10: *every step*: Wilde paraphrases Jesus in Emersonian terms: SR ends with an attack on the harmful effects of property: 'And so the reliance on Property, including the reliance on governments which protect it, is the want of self-reliance . . . But a cultivated man becomes ashamed of his property, out of respect for his nature', etc. (49 f.) Cf. *CWR WE I* 80–3.

There is . . . poor: originally italicized.

to Jesus: cf. Wilde's account with Matt. 19: 16–24.

11: *other things*: Matt. 6: 19–34.

their coat: Matt. 5: 40.

12: *a saint*: Wilde's reference is clearly to Mary Magdalene, of whom Christ said: 'Her sins are forgiven her because she loved much': see the early sonnet 'On the Recent Massacre of the Christians in Bulgaria'—'Her/Whose love of thee for all her sin atones.' Christian tradition has sometimes conflated some of the NT Marys, but Wilde here individually confuses Mary Magdalene, out of whom Christ is said to have cast 'seven devils' (Luke 8: 2) with the woman taken in adultery to whose accusers he said: 'He that is without sin among you, let him first cast a stone at her' (John 8: 3–11). In prison, with his Greek NT to hand, Wilde still mentions these women together, but has unscrambled them (pp. 122–3).

my brothers: see Matt. 12: 47–50. See also Emerson's SR, 30: 'I shun father and mother and wife and brother, when my genius calls me.'

bury his father: Matt. 8: 21–2.

is wrong: Emerson in SR: 'Imitation is suicide' (27); 'Insist on yourself; never imitate', etc. (47).

Father Damien: Belgian priest (1841–89) who devoted his life to caring for lepers and himself died of leprosy; defended and celebrated by Robert Louis Stevenson in 1890.

Wagner: Richard Wagner (1813–83), controversial German composer on the grand scale, originator of the *Ring* cycle, dramatizing the Norse *Nibelungenlied*.

13: *once said*: Chuang Tzŭ: see above 1n. *for others*, and n. to p. 30 *People*.

All . . . failures: originally italicized. Cf. *Rev* 531.

Oligarchies . . . ochlocracies: government by the few. . . mob-rule.

the people: a significant change of Abraham Lincoln's Gettysburg Address: 'government of the people, by the people, and for the people, shall not perish from the earth' (1863).

people's thoughts: cf. Emerson in 'The American Scholar': 'In the degenerate state, when the victim of society, he tends to become a mere thinker, or, still worse, the parrot of other men's thinking' (*CWR WE I* 53).

not conform: Emerson, in SR: 'Whoso would be a man must be a nonconformist' (29 and *passim*).

passmen: those who gain a degree without honours.

14: *and a . . . crime*: originally italicized.

Vautrin: a master criminal and mentor of young Lucien de Rubempré in novels of Balzac's *La Comédie Humaine*.

penal servitude: throughout this essay Wilde voices considerable understanding of the prison experience he was to undergo in person. Faced with the reality of capital punishment, he reversed this particular stance in *BRG*.

15: *The State . . . beautiful*: originally italicized.

16: *At present . . . serve man*: originally italicized.

right there: in *The Future of Science* (1890), Renan conceives the ideal state as Greece without slavery.

Utopia: an imaginary country invented by Sir Thomas More in his *Utopia* (1516). Cf. *CA II* 279: 'England will never be civilized till she has added Utopia to her dominions.' Cf. also *Rev* 318.

17: *A work . . . they want*: originally italicized.

Art is . . . known: originally italicized.

Now Art . . . artistic: originally italicized.

18: *In England . . . interest*: originally italicized.

19: *farcical comedy*: by the nineteenth century, a burlesque parodied some current success, and could contain many music-hall elements: farce was humorous drama usually of stereotyped figures in intricate situations, with verbal humour and horseplay.

a machine: Wilde echoes the Conclusion to Pater's *Renaissance*, (1873) and the central theme of Emerson's SR, which praises Spontaneity and Intuition and opposes conformity: 'The virtue in most request is conformity. Self-reliance is its aversion' (29).

20: *The fact . . . of Art*: originally italicized.

There is . . . immorality: originally italicized.

of Letters: the French Academy of Letters was established by parliament as a tribunal to preserve and purify the language. Matthew Arnold called for a similar Academy in Britain.

Charles Kingsley: 1819–75. Best remembered now for his children's story *The Water Babies*, Kingsley was a Christian socialist. His impassioned novels *Yeast* (1848) and *Alton Locke* (1850) were extensively attacked by Church and press.

absolutely himself: cf. SR: 'To believe your own thought, to believe that what is true for you in your private heart, is true for all men,—that is genius' (27).

21: *using it*: the primary meaning of morbid is indicative of disease. In the nineteenth century it was applied to mental conditions and ideas: e.g., Ruskin in 1889 writes of 'the morbid German fancies which proved so fatal to Goethe'.

The artist . . . everything: originally italicized. Wilde added this aphorism at the last moment to his 'Preface' to *DG*.

contemptible: see the record of the journalistic furore over *DG* in S. Mason, *Oscar Wilde: Art and Morality* (1912). Wilde engaged in spirited correspondence with several papers.

22: *In fact . . . of art*: originally italicized.

23: *paving-stone*: Wilde subverts Bulwer Lytton's well-known line, 'The pen is mightier than the sword'. Paving-stones were traditionally torn up and thrown by rioting mobs. The brickbat, a piece of brick, is the typical ready missile, when stones are scarce.

the press: concealed pun: the rack and the press were both historically instruments of torture before press acquired its modern sense of newspapers and journals.

fourth estate: not Burke but Macaulay, in his *Historical Essays* (1828).

Lords Temporal . . . Lords Spiritual: peers of the realm . . . bishops in the House of Lords: together these comprise the House of Lords.

brutal extreme: Wilde himself had been a target for American journalists during his lecture tour of 1882.

24: *The fact . . . knowing*: originally italicized.

and harmful: Wilde had attended sessions of the Parnell Commission, which cleared the apologist of Irish Home Rule of inciting political murder (Nov. 1889), only to see him brought down soon after by newspapers, Church, and public obloquy, because of his involvement in a divorce case.

Radical politician Sir Charles Dilke had also at the time of Wilde's writing been driven from political life by a divorce case. Cf. *IH* 408.

Here . . . artist: originally italicized.

25: *Mr. Irving*: Henry Irving (1838–1905) established himself at the Lyceum Theatre in 1871, from 1878 in a famous partnership with Ellen Terry. He was a great actor, in Shakespeare and classical drama, but has been attacked for neglecting modern drama (see *Rev* 32). Wilde cited this praise of the actor-manager when he wrote to Irving in Feb. 1891, in an unsuccessful attempt to get him to stage *The Duchess of Padua* (*L* 285–6).

26: *Haymarket*: Irving's rival Herbert Beerbohm Tree took over the Haymarket Theatre in 1887 and worked there until he built His Majesty's Theatre in 1897. Wilde wrote WNI for Tree to stage at the Haymarket in 1893.

The work . . . of art: originally italicized. Significantly, this is the only case where Wilde opposes the doctrines of SR. Not attaching the same supreme importance to art as Wilde, Emerson has 'The picture waits for my verdict: it is not to command me, but I am to settle its claims to praise' (36).

28: *A true . . . non-existent*: originally italicized.

George Meredith: (1828–1909) English novelist, poet, and self-conscious stylist, praised also in *DL* 221. That dialogue also discusses French and Russian fiction in more detail.

Great Exhibition: the Great Exhibition of the Works of Industry of all Nations, held in London (1851), and dominated by the Crystal Palace.

29: *surroundings*: Wilde's own early lectures preached the 'aesthetic revolution' in house decoration.

The form . . . all: originally italicized.

30: *People*: cf. Chuang Tzŭ's discussion of the sword of the Son of Heaven, the sword of the Princes, and the sword of the People.

Verona: Dante (1265–1321), Italian poet. Exiled from his native Florence, he sought refuge in Verona which one now discredited account says he left because of a punishing slight from his patron Can Grande. Wilde's sonnet 'At Verona' in *Poems* (1881) begins: 'How steep the stairs within Kings' houses are/For exile-wearied feet as mine to tread'. (See also *Paradiso* xvii, 59–60.)

Tasso: Torquato Tasso (1544–95), Italian poet, was unjustly confined as insane by the Duke of Ferrara for 7 years.

humanity: 'The first lesson of history is the good of evil' (Emerson in 'Considerations by the Way').

such as he: Benvenuto Cellini (1500–71), Italian goldsmith, sculptor, and autobiographer, whom Wilde described as 'the supreme scoundrel of the Renaissance' (*CA I* 241), was pardoned for murder by Pope Paul III on the grounds Wilde indicates, but was imprisoned for embezzlement by the same Pope from 1537 until he escaped.

obscene: cf. Emerson in 'Considerations by the Way': 'Masses are rude, lame, unmade, pernicious in their demands and influence, and need not to be flattered but to be schooled', etc.

31: *Louis XIV*: (1638–1715) king of France and absolute despot who, while he presided over France's Augustan age in literature, swept away all remnants of political independence in France, and eventually almost ruined his country. Cf. *Misc* 299.

A practical . . . conditions: originally italicized.

32: *In fact . . . of man*: originally italicized.

Evolution . . . Individualism: originally italicized.

self-development: cf. Emerson in 'Considerations by the Way': 'All sensible people are selfish.'

33: *Selfishness . . . live*: originally italicized. Cf. Emerson in *Lectures and Biographical Sketches*: 'Cannot we let people be themselves, and enjoy life in their own way? You are trying to make that man another *you*.'

All sympathy . . . mode: originally italicized.

34: *Christ . . . solitude*: originally italicized.

Thebaid . . . cenobite: the territory of the one-time capital of Upper Egypt, Thebes, a favourite retreat for Christian hermits from the third century.

35: *by pain*: Wilde's admiration for Russian writers like Turgenev and Dostoevsky, and his sympathy for Russian political protest are constant: see *CA II* 282: 'The spirit of medievalism, that spirit which belongs not to time but to temperament, woke suddenly in wounded Russia, and stirred us for a moment by the terrible fascination of pain.' See also *DL* 230 and n.

36: *For what . . . Life*: originally italicized.

with himself: cf. Emerson in 'The Transcendentalist': 'Am I in harmony with myself?' (*CWRWE I* 204).

37: *fed them*: see above n. to p. 16 *right there*.

Hellenism: Matthew Arnold used this term for that form of culture, or ideal of life, of which the ancient Greek is taken as the type. Wilde's opposition of medievalism and Hellenism is his development or adaption of Arnold's opposition of Hebraism (moral impulses) and Hellenism (intellectual impulses): Wilde's emphasis on pleasure is his own.

De Profundis

De Profundis: Wilde's suggested title for the letter was *Epistola: In Carcere et Vinculis*. Ross substituted *De Profundis* at the suggestion of E. V. Lucas, perhaps because Wilfred Scawen Blunt's volume of poems written in prison is entitled *In Vinculis*.

39: *shallowness*: cf. Emerson's *Lectures and Biographical Sketches*: 'But beside the passion and interest which pervert, is the shallowness which impoverishes.'

is right: keynote of the letter, often repeated. Cf. Emerson in 'Spiritual Laws': 'What your heart thinks is great, is great. The soul's emphasis is always right.' (*CWRWE II* 84). Emerson remains an important influence on Wilde in this letter, frequently quoted and echoed. His *Essays* were on Wilde's list of desired books in July 1896, so he had them to hand as he wrote (*L* 405–6 n.).

40: *am*: Wilde originally wrote 'was' (RH-D).

Salome: the English Translation of *Salome* (1894) was dedicated 'To my friend Lord Alfred Bruce Douglas, the translator of my play', but Douglas's name does not appear directly as translator: this letter indicates how dissatisfied Wilde was with Douglas's effort: it appears that he finally accepted it with some (probably extensive) alterations and improvements.

41: *Tite Street*: the Wilde family home was at 16 Tite Street, Chelsea.

John Gray: (1866–1934) poet of the 1890s who later became a Roman Catholic priest in Edinburgh.

Pierre Louÿs: (1870–1925) French poet, writer, editor, to whom Wilde dedicated the original French version of *Salome*.

42: *Florentine Tragedy . . . La Sainte Courtisane*: a blank verse play Wilde never finished . . . and an unfinished drama the MS of which Wilde lost in 1898.

Bracknell: where Lady Queensberry had a country house, The Hut.

43: *Cromer*: Wilde rented Grove Farm, Felbrigg, Cromer in Aug./Sept. 1892 and wrote a great part of *WNI* there (RH-D).

44: *thinking*: Wordsworth, 'Sonnet written in London, September 1802' (RH-D).

dialogues: *The Decay of Lying*.

τερπνὸν χαχόν: Euripides, *Hippolytus*, 384 (RH-D).

45: *expression*: see *SL* 111.

lasts: *WNI*, Act 3 (RH-D).

46: *shambles*: butchers' slaughterhouse.

habits: in the influential Conclusion to *The Renaissance* (1873), which was later suppressed and then toned down and replaced: it appeared to license undiluted Hedonism.

Ethics: at the beginning of Book II Aristotle proclaims that 'moral virtue is the fruit of habit'.

47: *Clio*: muse of history.

Infant Samuel: the OT prophet and judge was dedicated to God by his mother even before conception, and ministered to the Lord in the temple from a very early age (1 Sam. 1–3).

Malebolge: the eighth circle of Dante's Hell: abode of a large array of fraudulent sinners, starting with sexual exploiters, and ending with imposters and deceivers suffering from foul diseases.

Gilles de Retz . . . Marquis de Sade: Gilles de Laval, Sire de Retz or Raiz (1404–40), the comrade-in-arms of Joan of Arc and a Marshal of France, turned to debauchery, devil-worship and child-murder, for which he was finally executed; the Marquis de Sade (1740–1814), author of *Justine* (1791) and other novels of cruelty which gave rise to the words sadism and sadistic, was sentenced to death for various offences but escaped the scaffold and died in a lunatic asylum (RH-D).

plays: *Agamemnon*. The words quoted occur in lines 717–28 (RH-D).

49: *Salome*: see above n. to p. 40 *Salome*.

50: *friends*: Wilde originally wrote 'Robbie' (RH-D).

family: Wilde originally wrote 'wife' (RH-D).

51: *candidissima anima* ... *Philistine*: most shining white of souls; an uncultured person.

52: *attaché*: one attached to an ambassador's suite.

53: *abroad*: when Douglas left Egypt in Mar. 1894 he was appointed Honorary Attaché to Lord Currie, the Ambassador at Constantinople, but did not take up the appointment (RH-D).

come: the seventh Marquess of Queensbury (1818–58) died in a shooting accident. His youngest son, Lord James Edward Sholto Douglas (1855–91), cut his own throat in the Euston Hotel (RH-D).

54: *on me*: *c.* 1 Apr. 1894 (RH-D).

58: *birthday*: in 1894 Wilde's birthday (16 Oct.) was a Tuesday, and Ross changed this sentence accordingly (RH-D).

60: *beside him*: Lord Drumlanrig was killed by the explosion of his gun on 18 Oct. 1894 (RH-D).

lacrimae rerum: Virgil, *Aeneid* 2. 462: 'the tears of things'.

61: *scourge us*: *King Lear*, V. iii (RH-D).

62: *conceits*: see *SL* 107.

Hylas ... *Hyacinth* ... *Jonquil* ... *Narcisse*. Hylas, Hyacinth, and Narcissus were beautiful youths from Greek mythology. Lord Alfred Douglas had written a ballad called 'Jonquil and Fleur-de-Lys': Wilde used both names as nicknames for him; see p.78. Jonquil is a species of narcissus.

the Symposium: a dialogue in praise of homosexual love, accepted by all the speakers as man's highest form of love.

either university: i.e. Oxford or Cambridge.

63: *Review*: thirty-five aphorisms of Wilde's were published as 'Phrases and Philosophies for the Use of the Young' in the first (and only) issue of the *Chameleon*, an Oxford undergraduate magazine issued in Dec. 1894. See *WOW* 572–3. Much play was made with them at Wilde's trial, and also with two other items in the magazine: a poem of Douglas's called 'Two Loves' and an anonymous story called 'The Priest and the Acolyte', which was attributed to Wilde but was in fact written by the magazine's editor, John Francis Bloxam, an undergraduate of Exeter College (RH-D).

name: The last lines of 'Two Loves' run:

'I am true Love, I fill
The hearts of boy and girl with mutual flame.'
Then sighing said the other, 'Have thy will,
I am the Love that dare not speak its name.' (RH-D.)

Friday: 1 Mar. 1895 (RH-D).

64: *£700*: this (or rather £677) was the amount of Queensberry's taxed costs in Wilde's unsuccessful action against him. The total of Wilde's debts was £6,000, but Queensberry was the petitioning creditor whose action made Wilde a bankrupt (RH-D).

65: *Egypt*: see Exod. 16: 3.

66: *Francis*: Drumlanrig (RH-D).

69: *Homburg*: in 1893 Queensberry's eldest son, Drumlanrig, who was then private secretary to Lord Rosebery (Foreign Secretary in Gladstone's last Government), was created Baron Kelhead in the Union peerage (all Queensberry's titles being Scottish). Queensberry approved this action and wrote to thank Gladstone, but within a month he was sending abusive letters to the Queen, Gladstone, Rosebery, and his own son. He followed Rosebery to Homburg, threatening to horsewhip him, and was only persuaded to desist by the Prince of Wales (RH-D). He had long been suspicious about his son's relationship with Lord Rosebery.

answer: this telegram (which was dated 2 Apr. 1894) read: 'WHAT A FUNNY LITTLE MAN YOU ARE' (RH-D).

70: *one of my plays*: *IBE*: see *SL* 128–9.

71: *scies*: boring sayings.

73: *own nature*: see Emerson SR 30: 'No law can be sacred to me but that of my nature.'

about me: see *SL* 177–8 n.

sold: the contents of 16 Tite Street, including all Wilde's books and papers, were forcibly sold on 24 Apr. 1895, at the insistence of his creditors (RH-D).

75: *Atkins was*: Frederick Atkins was at times a billiard-marker and a bookmaker's clerk. When he gave evidence for the Crown at Wilde's first trial, he perjured himself so flagrantly that the judge described him in his summing up as 'a most reckless, unreliable, unscrupulous, and untruthful witness'. Wilde, who admitted having taken Atkins with him on a trip to Paris, was acquitted of the charges brought in respect of this witness (RH-D).

77: *harness*: 1 Kgs. 22: 34 (RH-D).

world: cf. *Othello*, II. i. (RH-D).

Robert Sherard: (1861–1943) author and journalist who wrote several biographies of Wilde.

78: *Fleur-de-Lys*: see above n. to p. 62 *Hylas* . . .

80: *or gloat*: lines 6–8 of Wilde's sonnet 'On the Sale by Auction of Keats's Love Letters' (RH–D).

Lombroso: Cesare Lombroso (1836-1909), Italian pioneer of the science of criminology.

well: on 3 June 1895 Bauër published a powerful article in the *Echo de Paris*, attacking the barbarity of Wilde's sentence, the stupidity of punishing homosexuals, and the hypocrisy of the English (RH–D).

82: *Merton*: *The History of Sandford and Merton*, an improving and immensely popular book for children by Thomas Day (1748–89), was originally published 1783–9 (RH-D).

London: see *SL* 111 and n.

84: *passa*: 'Let us not speak of them, but look, and pass on.' (Dante, *Inferno*, iii. 51) (RH-D).

85: *coarse*: perhaps a reference to the Gold-Leaf Electroscope, invented in 1787 to detect charges of static electricity, though 'direction' makes no sense (RH-D). Cf. the last paragraph of Emerson, 'Spiritual Laws' (*CWR WE II*, 96 and n.).

88: *of you*: see *SL* 140-1.

absolutely: *Inferno*, xxxiii. 135–47 (RH-D).

90: *Dock*: Alfred Taylor, who ran a meeting-place for male homosexuals.

causerie intime: personal conversation.

91: *Style*: Alfred Austin (1835-1913), made Poet Laureate in 1896; George Slythe Street (1867-1936), journalist and author; poet Coventry Patmore (1823-96) had proposed that Alice Meynell be Laureate.

92: *precious*: DG 182. But SL p. 89 shows Wilde had met Douglas once at most when he first wrote this.

93: *procedure*: Constance Wilde's summons had been heard by Mr Justice Kekewich in the Chancery Division on 12 Feb. 1897. The resulting order gave Constance custody of the children, with herself and Adrian Hope as their guardians (RH-D).

moon: Hamlet, I. iv (RH-D).

94: *own hand*: cf. n. to p. 8. *except himself*.

95: *flâneur*: a lounger.

96: *my Soul*: a quotation from W. E. Henley's poem 'Invictus', which ends: 'I am the master of my fate: I am the captain of my soul.'

Infinity: *The Borderers*, Act 3; 'has' should be 'shares' (RH–D).

97: *Vita Nuova*: see p. 108; Dante's *Vita Nuova* is an account of his New (or Young) Life, and gives an account of his youthful attachment to Beatrice.

oneself: cf. n. to p. 73 *own nature*.

thorns: WNI Act 4 (RH-D).

102: *handsbreath*: WNI Act 4 (RH-D).

Renaissance: in the essay 'The Poetry of Michelangelo' (RH-D).

103: *s'allegra*: 'sad once were we, In the sweet air made gladsome by the sun.' (*Inferno*, vii. 121-2, H. F. Cary's translation) (RH-D).

God: *Purgatorio*, xxiii. 81 (RH-D).

104: *Powers*: Carlyle's translation of Goethe's *Wilhelm Meister's Apprenticeship*, ii, ch. 13, where 'midnight' is 'darksome', 'waiting' is 'watching', and 'Heavenly' is 'gloomy' (RH-D).

exile: Louisa (1776-1810), wife of King Frederick William
III. She is said to have copied these lines when she and
her husband were in flight after the Battle of Jena (1806)
(RH-D).

106: *honeycomb*: Swinburne: 'Before Parting'; 'feed' should be
'live' (RH–D).

107: *gain*: Wordsworth: *The Excursion*, iv. 139 (RH-D).

108: *Beautiful*: Acts 3: 2 (RH-D).

the world: see Gen. 2 and 3.

of wine: tradition says Cleopatra melted a real pearl in a
cup of wine and drank it, to demonstrate her love for Antony.

path: Hamlet, I. iii. 47-51.

flutes: from Pater's description of the Mona Lisa, *Renaissance*.

109: *thou art*: see CSF 183.

incarnate: a slight misquotation of the prose poem 'The
Artist', WOW 567 (RH-D).

spectator: *Marius the Epicurean* (1885) was Pater's only
completed novel, and in some ways a model for *DG*
(where Lord Henry preaches a different and inhuman kind
of 'spectating').

true aim: Wilde must have been thinking of Pater's essay
on Wordsworth in *Appreciations* (1889). After quoting
Wordsworth on 'the operations of the elements and the
appearances of the visible universe, on storm and sunshine,
on the revolutions of the seasons, on cold and heat, on loss of
friends and kindred, on injuries and resentments, on gratitude
and hope, on fear and sorrow', Pater comments: 'To witness
this spectacle with appropriate emotions is the aim of all
culture' (RH-D). Cf. *Rev* 538-45.

himself: cf. above p. 12: correctly, 'perfectly and absolutely
himself'.

110: *Jesus*: 'but there remains the question what righteousness
really is. The method and secret and sweet reasonableness
of Jesus' (*Literature and Dogma*, ch. xii) (RH-D).

Shakespeare's brain: a misquotation of an Emerson poem
printed as epigraph to 'History' (*CWRWE II* 2):

I am owner of the sphere,

> Of the seven stars and the solar year,
> Of Caesar's hand, and Plato's brain,
> Of Lord Christ's heart, and Shakespeare's strain.

111: *Sun*: the Emperor Heliogabalus (RH-D).

tombs: Mark 5: 5 and 9 (RH-D).

terror: Aristotle, *Poetics*, xiii: the emotions evoked by tragedy.

Pelops' line: Milton: *Il Penseroso*: 'and' should be 'or' (RH-D).

pain: *Poetics*, xiii (RH-D).

112: *an idyll*: cf. Renan's *Life of Jesus*, ch. ix: 'The whole history of infant Christianity has become in this manner a delightful pastoral.'

113: *lute*: Milton: *Comus*, 478 (RH-D).

call it: see above, n. to p. 1. *Renan*. In his Introduction to his *Life of Jesus*, Renan tells how the country of the Gospels was 'like a revelation to me . . . I had before my eyes a fifth Gospel, torn, but still legible, and henceforward, through the recitals of Matthew and Mark, in place of an abstract being, whose existence might have been doubted, I saw living and moving an admirable human figure'. St Thomas was the disciple who refused to believe in the Resurrection without the most tangible proof.

lifetime: in the final chapter.

or evil: summing up the lesson of Emerson's SR. Cf. n. to p. 9 *authority*.

114: *die*: Matthew Arnold, 'A Southern Night':

> 'And see all sights from pole to pole,
> And glance, and nod, and bustle by—
> And never once possess our soul
> Before we die' (RH-D).

his own: in his lecture 'The Preacher' (RH-D). Cf. Emerson's denunciation of imitation in SR, echoed by Wilde at SM 33 and n.

thistles: Matt. 7: 16.

creed: cf. the first sentence of SM, above n. to p. 1 *for others*.

115: *poor*: cf. Matt. 19: 16-24, and above pp. 10–11.

world: cf. again the poem of Emerson quoted at n. to p. 110

Shakespeare's brain above.

stairs: see *SL* 3, and above n. to p. 30 *Verona*.

dégout: last lines of 'Un Voyage à Cythère' in *Les Fleurs du Mal* (1857) (RH-D). In John Gray's *Silverpoints* (1893) these lines are translated: 'Give me, Lord God, to look upon that dung/My body and my heart, without disgust.'

116: *to be*: when Apollo beat the mortal Marsyas in a musical contest, he flayed him alive. Niobe was a proud mother who tried to rival Apollo's mother Latona: he slew her children. Arachne was beaten at weaving by Pallas, goddess of the art, and turned into a spider. Hera by her marriage to Zeus became queen of the gods, but was jealous of his many amours and vindictive in conduct, though splendid in court. Demeter was goddess of corn and mother of Proserpina, who was raped by Pluto: she was closely involved with the fertility of the earth. Dionysus or Bacchus, son of Semele, was god of the vine. In his *Greek Studies*, Pater included long and suggestive studies of Demeter and Dionysus.

117: *Enna*: at Cithaeron in Boeotia Dionysiac orgies were held; Proserpina was carried away by Pluto from Enna in Sicily.

from him: Isa. 53: 3 (RH-D).

waiting: cf. Virgil's Eclogue 4: '*Iam redit et virgo*' (RH-D).

of men: Isa. 52: 14 (RH-D).

reveals: see above, p. 105.

118: *proportion*: 'Of Beauty' (RH-D).

goeth: John 3: 8 (RH-D).

119: *compact*: *A Midsummer Night's Dream*, V. i (RH-D).

takes place: *DG* 62. An idea repeatedly stressed by Emerson. See, e.g.: 'All the marked events of our day, all the cities, all the colonizations, may be traced back to their origin in a private brain' ('Considerations by the Way'). Cf. *Rev* 405.

bilingual: Professor George Salmon, a friend of Wilde's old tutor Mahaffy, writes in *A Historical Introduction to the study of the Books of the New Testament* (1885, 221 f.): 'I believe that Greek was as generally spoken in Palestine in our Lord's time as English now is in the west of Ireland.' This view is not now generally accepted.

Charmides: the central character of Plato's dialogue

Charmides, where he appears as a beautiful young man typi-
fying the central theme of moderation (RH-D). ἐγώ εἰμι ὁ
ποιμὴν ὁ καλός: 'I am the Good Shepherd' (John 10: 11 and 14)
(RH-D).

120: οὐδὲ νήθει: 'Consider the lilies of the field, how they grow;
they toil not, neither do they spin' (Matt. 6: 28) (RH-
D).

τετέλεσται: 'It is finished' (John 19: 30) (RH-D).

let fall: Mark 7: 26–30 (RH-D).

should live: cf. 'We live by admiration, hope and love'
(Wordsworth, *The Excursion*, iv. 763) (RH-D).

121: *receive it*: in the Roman Catholic church the communicant
knelt and recited in Latin three times 'Lord I am not worthy
. . .' (Matt. 8: 8) before receiving the Communion wafer.

pargoleggia: *Purgatorio*, xvi. 86–7 (RH-D).

raiment: Matt. 6: 34 and 25 (RH-D).

said it: see above, n. to p. 12 *a saint*.

122: *knowledge*: Luke 11: 52.

wage: Luke 16: 8.

123: *sepulchres*: Matt. 23: 27.

Sabbatarianism: Mark 2: 27.

mint and rue: Luke 11: 42.

Paradise: cf. Dante's *Paradiso*, xxx–xxxii (RH-D). The story
of Ruth is in the Book of Ruth in the OT.

τοῦ κόσμου: cf. John 1: 1–14.

124: *Publican . . . Pharisee*: see the parable of the Pharisee and the
Publican, Luke 18: 10.

dangerous: cf. CA II 280, 296.

past: cf. Aristotle, *Ethics*, vi. 2 and Pindar, *Olympia*, ii. 17
(RH-D).

life: see Luke 15: 11–32.

125: *none since*: cf. Emerson: 'In Christendom where is the
Christian?' (SR 48).

Conformitatum: a massive compilation illustrating the simil-
arities in the lives of Christ and St Francis, written by
Fr. Bartholomaeus de Pisa in the fourteenth century and

first printed in 1510 (RH-D).

prose: *The Imitation of Christ*, attributed to Thomas à Kempis *c*.1418: a popular manual of spiritual devotion. Wilde claimed to have read it in his student days at Oxford: see *SL* 9.

Emmaus: see Luke 24: 13–32.

126: *oneself*: the Greek ('know thyself') was inscribed over the entrance to the temple of Apollo at Delphi (RH-D). Cf. n. to p. 9 *Be thyself* above.

a King: for the story of Saul's anointing see 1 Sam. 9 and 10.

Verlaine . . . Kropotkin: Paul Marie Verlaine (1844–96), French poet, was imprisoned for wounding Rimbaud with a revolver shot; Prince Peter Alexeievitch Kropotkin, Russian author, geographer and anarchist (1842–1921), was imprisoned for his political views and actions (RH-D). Cf. n. to p. 36 *by pain* above.

in this place: Major James Osmond Nelson, who had taken over the Governorship of Reading Gaol in July 1896 (RH-D).

127: *to try*: see below the two letters to the *Daily Chronicle* and *BRG*.

128: *membre sue*: Dante, *Paradiso,* i. 20 (RH-D).

Marsyas: see above, n. to p. 116 *to be*.

129: *little of it*: the youthful singer Callicles in Arnold's *Empedocles on Etna* sings: 'Oh, that Fate had let me see / That triumph of the sweet persuasive lyre, / That famous, final victory, / When jealous Pan with Marsyas did conspire.' But it is clear that the poet's feeling is other, and that Arnold's most famous poetry generally has the melancholy undertone that Wilde describes.

Phrygian Faun: 'Marsyas, that unhappy Faun' (*Empedocles on Etna*) (RH-D).

noble sorrow: 'Some noble grief that we think will lend the purple dignity of tragedy to our days' (*CA II* 270) (RH-D).

looker-on: Emerson, 'Essay on Experience' (RH-D). *CWRWE III* 28: 'It is said, all martyrdoms looked mean when they were suffered.'

130: *soul in pain*: cf. *BRG* l. 29.

131: *enemies*: *DG* 54.

132: *life*: Clibborn, referred to in the Queensberry trial as Cliburn, was a professional blackmailer who failed to extort any money from Wilde in respect of the letter to Lord Alfred Douglas (*SL* 107) which had been stolen from Douglas by an agent of the blackmailing gang. Clibborn was later sentenced to seven years' penal servitude for blackmailing offences. Atkins (see above, n. to p. 75) is here probably a slip for Allen, a blackmailing associate of Clibborn's (RH-D).

133: *chemins*: the last five words—which translate 'Where evil ways lead'—are the title of the third part of Balzac's *Splendeurs et Misères des Courtisanes*, in which the misguided life of Lucien de Rubempré comes to its pitiful and tragic end. O'Sullivan records Wilde saying: 'When I was a boy my two favourite characters were Lucien de Rubempré and Julien Sorel [in Stendhal's *Le Rouge et le Noir*]. Lucien hanged himself, Julien died on the scaffold, and I died in prison' (RH-D).

135: *it is*: a blackmailer who gave evidence at Wilde's trials. (RH-D).

136: *Arthur Clifton*: see the General Index to *SL* for details of these.

137: *Madame Roland*: Manon Jeanne Philipon, bluestocking and hostess (1754–93), married (1781) Jean Marie Roland (1734–93), who later held office in the Revolutionary Government. Eventually they fell foul of Marat, Madame Roland was arrested, wrote her *Mémoires* in the Conciergerie, and was guillotined, after exclaiming 'O Liberty! What crimes are committed in thy name!' Her husband killed himself two days later (RH-D).

138: *Wyndham*: the Rt. Hon. George Wyndham (1863–1913) was MP for Dover and a kinsman of Lord Alfred Douglas.

139: *to him*: Queensberry, having been divorced by his first wife in 1887, married in 1893 a Miss Ethel Weeden, who obtained a decree of nullity against him on 24 Oct. 1894 (RH-D).

for the other: this remark was part of a long speech at the beginning of Act 3 of *WNI* which Tree persuaded Wilde to omit (RH-D).

140: *by the Judge*: about whether a warrant was ever issued for Douglas: see *SL* 227 n.

141: *beautiful future*: Adrian Charles Francis Hope (1858–1904) remained the official guardian of the children after Wilde and his wife were dead. He was a connection by marriage of Constance Wilde, and was Secretary to the Hospital for Sick Children, Great Ormond Street, from 1888 (RH-D).

143: *paid for*: see below, n. to p. 152 *has to pay*.

Zeitgeist: spirit of the times.

no soul: Diogenes, the Cynic philosopher (419–324 BC), lived in a tub (RH-D).

145: *Lockwood*: the Solicitor-General, Sir Frank Lockwood (1847–97), who led for the prosecution in Wilde's second trial (RH-D).

147: *bonne-bouche*: special treat.

energy: *CA II* 274: 'The subtle law that emotional forces, like the forces of the physical sphere, are limited in extent and energy.'

148: *flame*: 'Like a pale martyr in his shirt of fire' (Alexander Smith, *A Life-Drama*, sc. ii) (RH-D).

his will: not the Brutus of Shakespeare's *Julius Caesar*, but Junius Brutus who expelled Tarquin, the last king of Rome (RH-D).

149: *appropriate emotions*: see n. to p. 109 *true aim*.

Angelo ... Tartuffe: notable hypocrites, in Shakespeare's *Measure for Measure* and Molière's *Tartuffe*.

Tusculan prose: Cicero (106–43 BC) Roman orator, statesman and man of letters. His country house was at Tusculanum, and *De Amicitia* is his dialogue on friendship.

151: *in my answer*: see *SL* 149–52.

152: *has to pay*: Wilde repeatedly echoes Emerson's 'Compensation', e.g.: 'Always pay; for, first or last, you must pay your entire debt ... You must pay at last your own debt' (*CWRWE II* 66).

154: τἀνθρώπων κακά : *Iphigenia in Tauris*, 1193 (RH-D).

155: *Linnaeus*: Carl Linnaeus (1707–78), Swedish pioneer of modern botany, visited England in 1736.

existe: Gautier's phrase is noted in the *Goncourt Journal* for 1 May 1857: Wilde uses it to describe Dorian Gray (*DG* 144).

157: *at his door*: Luke 18: 2–6.

importunity: Luke 11: 5–8 (RH-D).

coinage: Keats: 'Sonnet on the Sonnet' (RH-D).

158: *for joy*: 'A Vision of the Last Judgment'. See also Job: 38: 7 (RH-D).

Wilde's first post-prison letter to the Daily Chronicle

159: *27 May [1897]*: this letter was thus dated when it appeared in the *Daily Chronicle*, under the heading THE CASE OF WARDER MARTIN, SOME CRUELTIES OF PRISON LIFE, on 28 May, but it was presumably begun on or soon after the 24th, when the *Daily Chronicle* printed a letter from Warder Martin recounting the circumstances of his dismissal (*SL* 260 n.) and added an editorial comment: 'We are, of course, unable to verify our correspondent's statement, but we print his letter.' On the 28th Wilde's letter was backed up by two leading articles, and another letter from Martin, discussing the Home Secretary's denial (in reply to a question from Michael Davitt) that the facts were as Martin had stated them (RH-D). For more on Martin and Wilde, see *SL* 248–9, 260–1, 339 n., and *ML* 153–4.

da Romano: Ghibelline leader (1194–1259). His cruelties earned him a place in Dante's *Inferno* (RH-D).

163: *the oakum*: for 'picking oakum' see *BRG* l. 217 n.

164: *companionship*: 'Shooting Niagara: and After?' (1867), Section IX (RH-D).

168: *the prisoners*: see n. to p. 126 *in this place*; for Wilde's letter of gratitude to him see *SL* 281–2.

The Ballad of Reading Gaol

Reading Gaol: Wilde was moved from Wandsworth to Reading Gaol on 23 Nov. 1895, and served the rest of his sentence there. He was released on 18 May 1897. While he was there, a judicial hanging was carried out, the first in the prison for 18 years, and this inspired the poem. This is the only one of Wilde's works directly inspired by life, and the only work of art he created after his release from prison. But he wrote in *ML* (171):'The idea for *The Ballad* came to me while I was in the dock, waiting for my sentence to be pronounced.' See also *De Profundis*, where he talks about his feelings in the dock (above p. 145). The poem is divided into six 'cantos', but it is clear from *SL* (311) that Wilde wanted divisions indicated inside the numbered cantos: here they are marked by asterisks. There is much illuminating material about the poem and its composition in *SL*, and in *ML*, *passim*. The author's name on early editions was omitted: Wilde used his prison cell number as a pen name: 'C. 3. 3.' I am indebted for some of the notes on prison life here to H. Montgomery Hyde (ed.), *The Annotated Oscar Wilde* (1982). Yeats's version of the *Ballad* (see Introduction) consisted of thirty-eight stanzas, with the following lines: 1–24, 97–186, 193–210, 217–64, 397–420, 445–56, 469–80. Ian Fletcher's version omits only lines 313–24 and 439–44.

169: *1896*: Charles Thomas Wooldridge, who had been a trooper in the Royal Horse Guards, was sentenced to death for the premeditated murder of his wife. She had aroused his jealousy, and he lay in wait for her on the road near her house and slit her throat there three times (not in bed, as the poem says). The sentence was carried out on 7 July 1896 at Reading Gaol.

l. 1   *scarlet coat*: poetic licence: the Royal Horse Guards uniform was dark blue with red trimmings.

170: l. 37   *he loves*: see the trial scene in *The Merchant of Venice* (IV. i. 66–7):

> BASSANIO: Do all men kill the things they do not love?
> SHYLOCK: Hates any man the thing he would not kill?

l. 41   *with a kiss*: Judas.

171: l. 61   *silent men*: a prisoner in the condemned cell was kept under continuous observation.

l. 83   *leathern thongs*: the prisoner to be executed was bound at wrists, elbows, and knees.

l. 90   *hideous shed*: Wilde wrote to Ross: 'With regard to the adjectives, I admit there are far too many "dreadfuls" and "fearfuls". The difficulty is that the objects in prison have no shape or form. To take an example: the shed in which people are hanged is a little shed with a glass roof, like a photographer's studio on the sands at Margate. For eighteen months I thought it *was* the studio for photographing prisoners. There is no adjective to describe it. I call it "hideous" because it became so to me after I knew its use' (*SL* 311).

172: l. 96   *Caiaphas*: Caiaphas was high priest in the year Christ was crucified, and condemned him (Matt. 26: 65). The priests paid Judas to betray Christ with a kiss, and Caiaphas declared: 'it is expedient for us, that one man should die for the people' (John 11: 50). Wilde wrote: 'By "Caiaphas" I do not mean the present Chaplain of Reading: he is a good- natured fool, one of the silliest of God's silly sheep: a typical clergyman in fact. I mean any priest of God who assists at the unjust and cruel punishments of man' (*SL* 315; see also 318, and his letter of 23 Mar. 1898 to the *Daily Chronicle,* below).

l. 116   *peek*: usually 'peak' or pine: droop in health or spirits.

l. 120   *been wine*: cf. *DG* 63, where Dorian buries his face in lilac-blossoms, 'feverishly drinking in their perfume as if it had been wine'.

173: l. 138   *bears its fruit*: before the modern gallows, criminals were hanged from trees, usually oak or elm, from which the leaves had been shorn. Wilde's image also incorporates the tradition that if a tree's roots were bitten by an adder, this would destroy its leaves and fruit for a season.

174: l. 167   *holy night*: Wilde here recalls and overturns a famous line from Longfellow's 'The Theologian's Tale' (1874): 'Ships that pass in the night, and speak with each other in passing', etc.

l. 173   *iron gin*: trap or snare.

175: l. 217   *tarry rope*: 'picking oakum' was a traditional pastime for prisoners, unpicking old rope for caulking ships' seams. It was boring and painful, breaking nails and tearing the flesh of the fingers. Wilde picked oakum at Pentonville Prison only.

176: l. 223   *the stones*: sewing mailbags and breaking stones, more accepted tasks for prisoners.

l. 224   *the dusty drill*: a narrow iron drum on legs with a long handle which scooped up and dropped cups of sand:

known as 'the crank', it was particularly pointless work.

l. 226   *the mill*: i.e. the treadmill, often used as a punishment. The crank and the treadmill were both abolished by the Prison Act of 1898. Wilde wrote his second letter to the *Daily Chronicle* when the measure was before Parliament.

l. 237   *for blood*: cf. Gen. 4: 10.

l. 246   *numbered tomb*: prisoners were kept in solitary confinement in numbered cells: Wilde's cell at Reading was C. 3. 3., the third cell on the third floor of Block C.

177: l. 280   *a hearse*: ornaments of black feathers used at funerals.

178: l. 281   *a sponge*: shortly before his death on the cross, Jesus was offered a sponge full of vinegar.

l. 283   *cock crew*: reminiscent of Peter's denial of Christ: see Matt. 27.

l. 289–324   *glided fast*: Wilde here draws on the medieval tradition of the dance of death, or *danse macabre*, as it had been reshaped by Baudelaire and Gautier: see 'The Harlot's House', *WOW* 539 and n.

l. 291   *rigadoon*: lively dance for two persons.

l. 295   *mop and mow*: grimaces.

l. 313   *antics*: (archaic) mountebanks or clowns.

l. 315   *gyves*: shackles.

179: l. 321   *demirep*: a woman of doubtful reputation.

l. 336   *seneschal*: steward.

l. 345   *mighty wing*: Wilde here exploits a powerful metaphor from John Bright that he had frequently used in *Salome*. Speaking in the House of Commons about the Crimean War, Bright said: 'The angel of death has been abroad throughout the land; you may almost hear the beating of his wings.'

180: l. 367   *of eight*: the hour for weekday hangings.

l. 371   *running noose*: to ensure a strong jolt and a quick death as the rope tightened, the rope ran through a metal eyelet to avoid any friction.

l. 374   *the sign*: the 'sign' was the tolling of the bell of St Lawrence's Church, Reading, which began a quarter of an hour before the execution and continued for some time afterwards.

181: l. 392 *bitter cry*: see Gen. 27: 34.

l. 393 *bloody sweats*: see Luke's account of Christ's agony in the garden: 'And being in an agony he prayed more earnestly: and his sweat was as it were great drops of blood falling down to the ground' (22: 44).

183: l. 450 *quicklime*: intended to decompose a dead body quickly.

184: l. 486 *Pope's sight*: Tannhäuser, a legendary German hero, loves a medieval version of Venus, who regularly tempted Christian knights to their destruction. He confesses to the Pope his love and luxury with Venus, but is refused absolution until the Pope's staff buds. He returns to Venusberg, and then the Pope's staff *does* sprout, but Tannhäuser is not to be found. The legend forms the subject of Richard Wagner's 1845 opera.

185: l. 530 *bourne*: cf. *Hamlet*, III. i. 79–80.

186: l. 546 *evil fan*: the metaphor is from the winnowing of grain: here Wilde contrasts the Divine and the human Law. See Matt. 3: 12: 'Whose fan is in his hand, and he will thoroughly purge his floor, and gather his wheat into the garner; but he will burn up the chaff with unquenchable fire.'

187: l. 565 *frightened child*: see Wilde's letter to the *Daily Chronicle* of 27 May 1897.

l. 580 *and lime*: adulteration of bread with chalk and lime was still common. Tennyson had denounced it in *Maud* (1850): 'And chalk and alum and plaster are sold to the poor for bread' (l. 39).

188: l. 612 *costliest nard*: see Mark 14: 3, John 12: 3, where a woman breaks a box of precious ointment and anoints Jesus with it.

l. 622 *to Paradise*: see Luke 23: 43, where Jesus makes his promise to the repentant thief crucified beside him.

l. 624 *not despise*: see Psalm 51: 17: 'The sacrifices of God are a broken spirit: a broken and a contrite heart, O God, thou wilt not despise.'

189: l. 625 *the Law*: the sentencing judge.

l. 635 *of Cain*: with the death of his brother Abel, Cain

became the first murderer. But God set a mark on Cain that forbade anyone to kill him (Gen. 4: 1–16).

l. 636   *snow-white seal*: see 2 Cor. 1: 22; also Isa. 1: 18: 'though your sins be as scarlet, they shall be as white as snow; though they be red like crimson, they shall be as wool.' Basil Hallward quotes this to Dorian just before his murder: *DG* 165.

Wilde's second post-prison letter to the Daily Chronicle

190: [*1898*]: This letter appeared in the *Daily Chronicle*, under the heading DON'T READ THIS IF YOU WANT TO BE HAPPY TODAY, on 24 March, when the House of Commons began the debate on the second reading of the Prison Bill. This, which introduced some of the improvements suggested by Wilde, became law in August as the Prison Act (RH-D).

191: *or the mill*: see *BRG* ll. 224 n., 226 n.

195: *leaves a tract*: cf. *BRG* l. 96 n., ll. 191–2.

THE WORLD'S CLASSICS

A Select List

HANS ANDERSEN: Fairy Tales
Translated by L. W. Kingsland
Introduction by Naomi Lewis
Illustrated by Vilhelm Pedersen and Lorenz Frølich

ARTHUR J. ARBERRY (Transl.): The Koran

LUDOVICO ARIOSTO: Orlando Furioso
Translated by Guido Waldman

ARISTOTLE: The Nicomachean Ethics
Translated by David Ross

JANE AUSTEN: Emma
Edited by James Kinsley and David Lodge

Mansfield Park
Edited by James Kinsley and John Lucas

Persuasion
Edited by John Davie

HONORÉ DE BALZAC: Père Goriot
Translated and Edited by A. J. Krailsheimer

CHARLES BAUDELAIRE: The Flowers of Evil
Translated by James McGowan
Introduction by Jonathan Culler

WILLIAM BECKFORD: Vathek
Edited by Roger Lonsdale

R. D. BLACKMORE: Lorna Doone
Edited by Sally Shuttleworth

KEITH BOSLEY (Transl.): The Kalevala

JAMES BOSWELL: Life of Johnson
The Hill/Powell edition, revised by David Fleeman
Introduction by Pat Rogers

MARY ELIZABETH BRADDON: Lady Audley's Secret
Edited by David Skilton

ORIENTAL TALES
Edited by Robert L. Mack

OVID: Metamorphoses
Translated by A. D. Melville
Introduction and Notes by E. J. Kenney

FRANCESCO PETRARCH:
Selections from the Canzoniere and Other Works
Translated by Mark Musa

EDGAR ALLAN POE: Selected Tales
Edited by Julian Symons

JEAN RACINE: Britannicus, Phaedra, Athaliah
Translated by C. H. Sisson

ANN RADCLIFFE: The Italian
Edited by Frederick Garber

PAUL SALZMAN (Ed.):
An Anthology of Elizabethan Prose Fiction

OLIVE SCHREINER: The Story of an African Farm
Edited by Joseph Bristow

TOBIAS SMOLLETT: The Expedition of Humphry Clinker
Edited by Lewis M. Knapp
Revised by Paul-Gabriel Boucé

STENDHAL: The Red and the Black
Translated by Catherine Slater

ROBERT LOUIS STEVENSON: Kidnapped and Catriona
Edited by Emma Letley

The Strange Case of Dr. Jekyll and Mr. Hyde
and Weir of Hermiston
Edited by Emma Letley

ANTHONY TROLLOPE: The American Senator
Edited by John Halperin

The Last Chronicle of Barset
Edited by Stephen Gill

DATE DUE			
DEC 0 1 1998			